# FACES WITH VOICES

# FACES WITH VOICES

*Twentieth century lives in an English town*

*Text*
## JUNE FREEMAN

*Photography*
## JANINE WIEDEL

*Foreword*
## RONALD BLYTHE

AN IMAGES PUBLICATION

Published by Richard Castell Publishing Limited
24 Queens Road, Lipson, Plymouth PL4 7PL
Registered Offices: Bank House, Needham Market, Suffolk IP6 8DH

In association with Gainsborough's House, Sudbury, Suffolk.


First Published in Great Britain 1992


Designed & Typeset by CDP, Plymouth

Printed & Bound by The Bath Press, Lower Bristol Road, Bath BA2 3BL


ISBN 0 948134 33 X

Acknowlegements: The authors' appreciation goes first to those featured in this publication for their cooperation. We also owe a general thanks to the people of Sudbury, Suffolk. For every interview done we received help from half a dozen other people. And the interest of people in the town in the project has sustained and encouraged us throughout. We hope the result will not disappoint them. Above all we have to thank Hugh Belsey, first, for telling us we ought to do this book and, secondly, for his unwavering support once it got underway.

RICHARD CASTELL  PUBLISHING LIMITED

# FOREWORD

A face and a voice are what we notice most in a person.  Whether they corroborate one another is often our first unconscious attempt at character assessment.  Historically we possess portraits of men, women and children reaching back to antiquity, but voices - and very few of those - only for the last hundred years or so.  Our ancestors would have been intensely moved to hear the voices of the dead.  Most of us nowadays have family photographs and family taped talk in abundance, not to mention home movies, and thus a taken for granted access to the recent past, yet we still encounter each person's facial and articulated 'information' with a certain wonder.  Writers have always been keen observers of the talker and the listener, trying to make the connection between how they look and what is being said.

**Faces with Voices** asks us, the reader and viewer, to make the connection, drawing our own conclusions.  Some of the faces and names will be familiar ones to those living in or around Sudbury, but the voices far less so.  Whether reticent or candid, each in its inimitable way throws its own unusual light, or casts its own questioning shadow on the little town. The voice is far less indigenous than it was, not only because the population has almost trebled since the Fifties, but because, as with the population of Britain as a whole, the confined nature of the old life has been swept away by the car, television, multiples and all those now standardised accessories which are the commonplaces of the 1990s. These Sudbury and district people, whatever their age, talk within the context of the present.  June Freeman and Janine Wiedel see contemporary Sudbury with honesty and realism, much as any shopper or child on his way to school sees it.  A similar reality informs the choice of subjects.  Whilst a few are Sudbury through and through for generations, many are newcomers with little or no sense of local history, or of being 'Suffolk', for some still an intense feeling of identity.

Old locals and new locals alike will find much to contemplate in this book.  Some will see themselves plain, others, as E M Forster remarked of an old friend, as somewhat of an angle to the universe.  It reveals a group of country people who talk much about the economic and social facts of life, and who occasionally add a few dreams.  Pre-World War Two Sudburians remember the ancient borough of some seven thousand inhabitants in the Stour valley, and still almost surrounded with grasslands, the North Meadows, the Wents, the Target, the Water Meadows and the Spring-Waters.  And the great medieval churches, the family businesses, the poverty, the influx of farmers on Thursdays to sell stock and corn, and to eat and talk at the 'farmers' ordinaries' - the big dining-tables in the hotels.  These old natives also remind us how very much Sudbury was a factory town, employing hundreds of workers from the neighbouring villages.  Their voices - and features - are as close as we shall get to the once easily recognisable indigenous element.  Both climate and diet used to mark faces, as well as generations of inter-marriage, and of certain types of work.  Faith too left its imprint.  Old photographs preserve these regional looks.  These are far more extensive than is realised, not only the beautiful calotypes from the local 'studio', but quantities of photographs of field-work, street scenes, craftsmen, schoolchildren, clergy, fetes, outings, etc.  Amongst other things, **Faces with Voices** should make a valuable addition to the remarkable archive of photographs at the Museum of East Anglian Life, Stowmarket.  For it is in essence a picture of a place and its people glimpsed during the industrial shifts and changes of the twentieth century.  But whether we can read what some of these men and women are saying by staring into their faces  is another matter.  Text and illustration have been placed side by side to challenge our rather generalised perceptions of human nature.  The reader/viewer might even conclude that Sudbury as some kind of unifying hub is irrelevant and that the inhabitants could as well be those of Haverhill or Stamford for all they exhibit the strong loyalties which were once such a feature of the place.  But here they would be wrong.  What June Freeman has drawn from these residents is a re-thinking of their role in a particular town at a particular time.

This is a collection of talk and likenesses which creates all kinds of speculation.  So far as faces are concerned Sudbury has the rare ability to show its eighteenth  century face in a celebrated range of portraits.  Gainsborough was thirty-three when he left Suffolk for good, by which time he had painted speaking likenesses, as they called them, of many neighbours and most members of his big family.  And it could certainly show its First World War face, when, as elsewhere, the first thing a soldier did was to have his photograph taken for posterity.  Hardly a house in or around the town was without one or more of these lively sepia images of farmworkers and weavers who had simply vanished.  Similarly, World War Two produced its ritual documentation of local faces, this time informally in the shape of the exciting polyfoto.  Between the wars there was the snapshot, a casual but occasionally effective use of the Box Brownie which shows us almost another race, so much have we changed since those hard times.  June Freeman's old people recall them with a certain bemusement.  So until the tape-recorder, masses of faces but few words.  This book allows us to dwell on both, to look and listen.  It appears at a time of uncertainty on the farms and recession everywhere, and its thoughtful local language, some spoken by those whose personalities were formed by Sudbury as it was, but much of it spoken by those who know little or nothing of those days and who are now part of the Sudbury that is, tells the reader what it is like to belong to a small town which, for all that has happened to it recently, exerts its own surprisingly tough influence.  It originated as a Saxon Market and it is now a fragment of the Common Market.  Its crest is a charming dog whose master, the Archbishop of Canterbury, a Sudbury man, was killed in the Peasants' Revolt.

*Ronald Blythe*

\*     \*     \*     \*     \*     \*

# CONTENTS

PAGE

*Tom Portfleet*

# PART ONE

# Deciphering Faces:
# the Western face
# as narrative

# Introduction

# MYTHS AND TRUTHS:
## What do portraits tell us about the people who appear in them?

A hundred and fifty years ago possessing a likeness of oneself was a privilege of the few. The camera has changed that. Caught, like insects in amber, our faces now stare back at us from innumerable photographs, recording our presence at most of the life's events. Fond parents start the record in one's infancy; lovers exchange photos of each other; weddings are fully recorded. Then the cycle starts again. And new and old photographs overlap. In the crook of her arm Grandma cradles her new grandchild, while Dad crouches by a toddler putting the final pats to a sandcastle.

Most of us, indeed, collect so many likenesses of ourselves they become a nuisance. The tidy minded clear them out discarding the less flattering. Others leave them to gather in curly edged piles at the back of drawers and cupboards. But, whether we handle them casually or carefully, they are rarely completely forgotten. There is a compulsion to preserve likenesses of ourselves and those important to us. And every so often someone glances through them and has a giggle or even a private weep.

The difference between such photographs and the ones taken for this book, however, is between records of familiar faces destined for private consumption and portraits of unfamiliar faces for public display. Here we are concerned with the latter. The aim is to present the faces of a cross-section of a small English town so as to convey a sense of their quirky individuality and thereby a feeling for the richness and quality of everyday life. As we shall see this is far from being a simple or easy process.

The chapter begins by looking at some conventions or beliefs about the language, or iconography, of the face which have informed Western thinking and influenced the interpretation and understanding of the Western face. It notes how these ideas affected the practice of portraiture, and, it will be argued, have continued subtly to penetrate camera portraiture so that the production of a likeness has never been as simple as it might seem. It has also tended to lead to unknown faces being made into pastiches of the more powerful or led to an injurious, even when well-meaning, stereotyping. With one short chapter this discussion can only be introductory.

The word iconography recalls the religious icons of the Greek Orthodox church which convey their messages through a standardised symbolism. In pursuing the idea of an iconography of the face the chapter will not, however, consider only visual portraits. There are important parallels between our understanding of literary descriptions of the face and the faces painters and photographers preserve for us. Then it will turn to the tradition of documentary photography which appears to be committed to realism, and to which the portraiture in this book belongs. It will compare the messages documentary portraits have sought to convey with other kinds of portraiture. It will compare their goals with the motivation behind the taking of photographs for this book. This will include a comment on the relationship the book seeks to establish between the specially taken photographs, other photographs and the text. In doing this it will raise some general questions about photography which the book tries to explore.

## Reading the Western face

There is a long standing tradition in the West which relates particular facial attributes and body gestures to different moral traits. This is not only a visual tradition; it is equally a literary one. At its simplest and clearest it informs the fairy story. We know that the princess is good because she is beautiful. Equally we know that she is beautiful because she is good. In other words we take for granted that goodness and beauty reflect each other. Similarly the physical malformity of the witch tells us she is wicked. Today fairy stories are largely regarded as children's fare, but they were originally stories for adults. And it would be a mistake to think that parallels between the body and a person's moral makeup characterise only children's reading.

The church has for centuries exploited the idea that the body reflects the soul. Christ dies placidly on the cross. For it is hard to convey spiritual beauty in visual form except through the physical body. So Christ's agony is conventionalised into downcast eyes or an upturned glance of supplication. The body remains graceful. Mary also grieves sedately. Mother of all mothers, she is gentleness personified and her face cannot be shown, savage and distorted with pain and fury at the sight of the abominable cruelty to which her son is being subjected. Agony is reduced to pallor. Saints similarly suffer gruesome martyrdoms with detached *sang froid.*

Shakespeare's plays also constantly draw on the idea that the body reflects the inner person, as does drama generally. And novelists exploit similar assumptions. Indeed, where the standard rules about the relationship between the physical shell and the inner person are flouted, a knowledge of them may remain essential for making sense of a narrative, as when a young child is made the embodiment of evil, a frequent fancy of science fiction and horror stories.

The same iconography remains a mainstay of film and television. Thus some actors are always cast to play hero roles, while others spend most of their performing life as baddies. Luck or ingenuity might just secure Robert Redford a villain's role or Bob Hoskins a hero's. But it is not easy. Their bodies and faces are against it. Actors themselves are very conscious of how their looks affect the roles open to them. Judi Dench, offered the part of Cleopatra, needed considerable persuasion that she was suitable. Vanessa Redgrave did not. Tallness is regal.

From childhood on, then, we absorb assumptions about the relationship between the body and moral character. Close set eyes are shifty, a high forehead denotes intelligence, a receding chin marks a weak determination. And so on. As we get older, we recognise and respond to clues in novels, plays and pictures which posit a more elaborate relationship between the inner and outer person. But the basic rules of the fairy story remain remarkably tenacious and continue to pervade our response to works of art and the imagination despite our knowing that in the reality the connection between physical features and spiritual attributes is random.

### Realistic portraiture
Portraiture has to be considered against this background.

In their early, mediaeval forms, Western painted portraits were concerned above all to render the subject's social position. They sought to tell people that here was a king or a bishop or a rich merchant. Producing a realistic likeness came second. In time, however, people became interested in leaving a true likeness of themselves behind. Yet the idea of the existence of a patterned relationship between a person's physical and moral attributes did not die. As a general concept the idea continued to infuse otherwise potentially vacuous human figures and faces with meaning. This encouraged portrait painters and their sitters to devise ways of relating realistic likenesses to its schematisations though different periods produced variations and modifications to the pattern. At a simple level clothing and the inclusion of different material possessions could be used to indicate social position and interests. More significantly, however, in terms of the relationship between a realistic likeness and a schematised iconography the subject's posture could be, and was, manipulated. The positioning of arms and hands, the angling of the head, the direction of a glance could all be made to imply attributes of character and temperament. And frequently these postures are clearly not habitual. Finally, less flattering features could be gently massaged into a greater compatibility with the dominant iconography if necessary.

It is true that some of this arose because portrait painters were under pressure to satisfy their clients' vanity. Most human beings like to feel they are beautiful and good! But from our point of view it is more important that implicit references to an iconography of the face and body right into the 19th century offered people important clues as to what they were supposed to see in, and how they were to understand a portrait.[2]

### The camera and the portrait
It might be thought that the advent of the camera put an end to these practices. A mechanical instrument, it would record just what was there. But the tradition did not die. On the contrary portrait photographers have continued to exploit it.

The early camera led to the rise of the commercial high street photographers. For a modest fee they offered to record ordinary people and their children for posterity. Public response was enthusiastic and the new photographer needed a method. The nearest one to hand was that of the painted portrait, and a study is now detailing the way these studios picked up on and continued the old conventions of portraiture.[3] More expensive studio photographers also appeared, to whom the better off had recourse. They spent more time with their clients, but for the most part worked in an essentially similar mode.

In time, however, the tables, chairs, arbors and palm trees, all the now comical looking props the early studios used to reflect the dignity of the comfortably off and inflate that of the less well off, disappear, but by no means to be replaced by greater realism. The dominant form of photographic portraiture gradually comes to be typified by the film star portraits of the 1930s and 40s.[4] Photographers throw their energies into lighting and angling the subject's head and shoulders. Their exploitation of the fall of light and shadow in these mid-twentieth century portraits creates effects which resurrect the old mythologies. The camera which can apparently only record what is there creates a fantasy world of pure types. Bold, masculine men consort with beautiful, flawless women. No wonder such pictures were widely enjoyed as pin-ups in the workplace or bedroom. They were invitations to dream and fantasise. Not to be outdone, however, local photographers began to press the faces of their ordinary clients into the same moulds. However much their clients may have been flattered by the results, today they seem almost wholly vacuous, embodying no sense of a real person.

## The documentary portrait

The so-called documentary photography tradition grew up parallel, but in contrast, to this kind of portraiture. Though the term was initially applied almost casually it stuck.[5] In the hands of different photographers the approach varies in spirit and technique. But photographers in this tradition have seen themselves as sharing a commitment to conveying a sense of the world as it really is. Their work  is the antithesis of the film star portrait. It is also the photographic genre dedicated to the celebration of the uncelebrated.

*Documentary... dignifies the usual and levels the extraordinary. Its subject is the common man, and when it is not, the subject, however exhalted he be, is looked at from the common man's [sic] point of view. So documentary showed the rich, the powerful, the renowned as just regular guys...And vice versa.*[6]

Yet although documentary photography seems to proceed from radically different premisses to general camera portraiture, it too has continued to operate within the same tradition. One might argue, indeed, that one of its most notable achievements has been to exploit and refine some key assumptions in the old iconography. Basic to the success of much documentary work has been the photographer's capacity to construct faces as types. It is this which has repeatedly given images of the uncelebrated meaning and infused them with the power to touch, amuse or disturb us.

This partly derives from the selection of images. Unlike the portrait painter the photographer captures only a passing moment. But contemporary cameras can capture thousands of such moments providing a vast choice of image. Documentary photographers have also become highly skilled at creating the illusion of informality while actually structuring their shots closely.[7] Practice has also made them adept at recognising moments we can read as human pain, pleasure, surprise or hatred. So there is now a large and impressive body of documentary photography, including work which seeks to alert us to the plight of the humble or deprived, looks ironically or critically at the materially well off, or curiously at the bizarre. Its impact depends on our ability to generalise from the images offered. For we rarely have more than the vaguest idea of who the people are.

Yet portraiture is central to this tradition.[8] Both individual and group portraits have proved a most effective medium for offering a commentary on society generally.[9] But though portraits have proved both moving and forceful, most have done so at a cost to the people portrayed. There are exceptions but the images of individual people in the documentary tradition have worked their power by dint of denying our sense of their individuality.[10] Documentary portraits commonly work as icons. The people they show have become symbols of a social condition such as poverty or injustice. And we know that some of the most celebrated documentary photographers waited and manoeuvred to capture the expression they wanted on their subjects' faces.[11] One does not find, in 1930s American documentary photography, for example, poor people grinning broadly or even, indeed, smiling. Photographers preferred expressions the public could read as tiredness, weariness or suffering. These conveyed the photographer's message more clearly. On a day to day basis, of course, endurance and survival require aggression and a capacity for laughter. But documentary portraits which are part of a campaign to bring a social problem to the public's attention find it hard to deal in rounded people.

Newspapers continue to present us with photographs in this mode. All wars produce their quietly brave or suffering madonnas, their innocent children, their decent soldiers, tired in defeat or compassionate in victory: individual faces, presented in close-up, neatly transformed into types, these images are profoundly anonymous.

## Faces with Voices
Yet having argued that the realism of the documentary tradition has by and large denied its subjects a distinguishing individuality, that its most moving images often derive their force precisely by severing any sense of the idiosyncratic individual this is the tradition to which this book, with its proclaimed commitment to seek to depict quirky individuality, belongs. The book's democratic approach made it the only available choice.

## Classification: constraint and liberation
The issue the book faced was how to make the photographs reveal individuality rather than reflect a type, while recognising that faces of unfamiliar people had to be endowed with a communicable meaning for the general public.

The answer has been to build the book round a paradox. The chapters are a system of classification, a form of stereotyping, into which people are slotted. Implicit here is an acknowledgement that in searching for the stranger's individuality we have to start with categorisation. Only in this way can we impose coherence on the bewildering complexity of human life. Classification offers us, like the pioneering botanists, a system which, by noting similarities, was enabled to discern differences.

It is not the intent here to ennumerate all the visual stratagems we have used to try to elicit for the reader a sense of the unique personalities of the people who appear within its broad categories. We simply offer some examples.

Sometimes we have used photographs which flout in some respect the stereotyped image of particular occupations. The rector appears in an open-necked shirt, the journalist in cricket togs. Sometimes we have offered more than one

image. The Salvationist appears both in uniform and stripped to the waist. The dark formality of the one seems to write out the flesh; the bare torso of the other draws it forcibly to one's attention. Neither image leads one to expect the other, and our response to the two images is very different. They help to challenge the idea that there is a correct image for a person. Something as simple as the use of two photos of the same person in different moods also hinders stereotyping.

Juxtaposing Janine Wiedel's photographs with earlier ones, both amateur and professional, further helps to highlight the way the same person will at different times in their lives appear in a different light and rounds out our perception of them. The auctioneer is a case in point. In addition, everyone plays several roles in their lives. The most obvious are roles such as father and husband and mother and daughter. We are so practiced in them that most of us move from the one to the other effortlessly. But to draw attention to these roles through old photographs can be telling. It becomes hard to engage with the policeman simply as a policeman when you also see him as a slender young husband, then, his jaw now broadened, as the father of three. And both inform one's response to his portrait taken for the book.

The inclusion of old photographs, because almost invariably taken in a different photographic mode, also helps to highlight the documentary technique and enhance the viewer's awareness of the content of the special pictures. In themselves none of these visual devices is particularly innovatory. Together they significantly enlarge the photographic viewpoint, thereby enriching our response to the specially taken photographs.

## The word and the image
The most obvious device employed for enriching the main images, of course, is the words which accompany them. *Faces with Voices* is far from unique in using photos and words to complement each other.[12] Where it differs from nearly all earlier matchings of pictures to words however is, first, in the weight it places on the voices of the actual people themselves, and, second, in its unqualified rejection of the idea of establishing any hierarchical relation between words and pictures in the book.[13]

On the one hand the book sees the visual image as adding an important dimension to our understanding for which no written text could ever act as substitute. Yet at the same time the book is premissed on the belief that visual images are frequently impenetrable and ambiguous on their own and that when they are not it is often because, consciously or not, we bring to the image information which is not contained within it but which is necessary to its understanding. In the case of portraiture, for example, there is a vast difference in our ability to interpret the face of a celebrated person and that of a generally unknown person.

The voices in this book are seen as essential to our appreciation of the images. Their loss would diminish the photography. But the fact that the photographs benefit from a verbal accompaniment is not seen as a failure on their part. And at no juncture are the photographs seen as illustrations. In helping to light up the images and sensitise us to all kinds of little niceties and nuances in them, the voices help to draw out the photographs' accomplishment. And as they do this the pictures in turn enrich the text.

## The artifice

In summary, an integral part of the human condition for most of us is the possession of both verbal and visual faculties. And there seems no *a priori* reason why we should not use them concurrently to enlarge our understanding of the world. What the following pages offer, therefore, is a partnership between a writer and a photographer. By working together we believed we could generate a sharper awareness of some of the sensibilities and experiences which characterise English life today in a way neither of us could do separately.

Our view makes no claim to be objective. It is interpretive. In selecting from the lengthy accounts people supplied of themselves the writer constantly made decisions about what would best reveal the temperament and character of those spoken to. Similarly, every time the photographer pressed the camera shutter its click marked a decision to preserve one image, one action, one angle rather than others. Consistently, however, our concern during this cooperation was not the production of photographs as art or words as literature, but the people of the book. Photographs and text act in their service, in the attempt to reveal to the public what deserves to be continually celebrated, the rich variety and vitality of everyday life in a small English town.

FOOTNOTES:

1 Aries, P. (1962) *Centuries of Childhood,* Jonathon Cape.

2 20th Century portraiture is somewhat different. See Strong, R. (1991) *The British Portrait 1660-1960,* Antique Collectors' Club, p29, but arguably nothing like as much as Strong at this point seems to suggest.

3 Linkman, Audrey (1990) *Commercial Camera: the portrait photographer and the family album.* Unpublished manuscript.

4 Few things in the visual arts are ever entirely new and examples of this kind of approach can of course be found in chiaroscuro painting and 19th century photography, eg Nadar's Sarah Bernhardt. What concerns us here is its massive proliferation in photography.

5 See Stott, W. (1973) *Documentary Expression and Thirties America,* University of Chicago, on Grierson and the genesis of the term, and how 'historical', 'factual' and 'realistic' failed to catch on.

6 Stott, 1973, p49.

7 As also their cousins the 'straight' photographers, the photojournalists and the news photographers.

8 Lewis Hine, Margaret Bourke-White, Walker Evans, Dorothea Lange, Bill Brandt are only a few of those who have exploited it.

9 There is a parallel here with the written word. For many people the diary of one young girl, Anne Frank, has brought home the horrors of the holocaust more vividly than all the figures on the literally millions of deaths which took place ever did for them.

10 The most notable exception has been Walker Evans in conjunction with James Agee. But it is true even of images like Dorothea Lange's powerful *Migrant Mother.* Indeed, the alliterative, generalised title reflects this.

11 There are vivid accounts of Margaret Bourke-White doing this. See Stott, 1973.

12 Hareven, T. and Langenbach, R. (1978) *Amoskeag: Life and work in an American factory city,* Pantheon Books, is the closest and a distinguished precursor.

13 Agee's humility in the face of Evan's photographs in *Let Us Now Praise Famous Men,* (1965) Peter Owen [first publication 1941] has no parallel here.

**PART TWO**

# The Place

# Chapter One
# SUDBURY'S HISTORY AND SUDBURY TODAY

We now turn to the people who appear in the book; a random selection would not be of much interest to anyone other than themselves. In addition they are social creatures who live in groups and express their individuality within the framework of communal activity. So in selecting people to talk to and photograph there are good reasons for starting with a place, as a likely influence on behaviour and feelings. To learn, indeed, about a person is commonly to learn more about the place in which they live. To learn about a town, on the other hand, usually involves learning about those who inhabit or inhabited it.

The people we present here are all part of the same community, in that they depend on the various services the town provides. Many also provide services in return, so we start with the town.

Sudbury is old, listed in 1086 in the Domesday Book. But even prior to 1066 it is known to have had a regular market. By 1397 it had acquired the right to have a mayor and in 1554 it received a charter which gave it the full privileges of a corporate town. Full recognition of its status as a community came in the early sixteenth century when it began returning a parliamentary representative.

Like most towns it has had its economic ups and downs. The fifteenth and sixteenth centuries were a boom period. An enormously successful wool weaving trade produced profits which made East Anglia a manufacturing area of major national importance. Though less weaving was done here than in the smaller neighbouring towns and villages Sudbury thrived by acting as a collecting centre and market for the trade.

At the end of the seventeenth century and the advent of industrialisation, however, wool slumped. East Anglia lacked the new conditions required and the trade moved north. Like the rest of the region the town suffered a recession. Many parts of the area never recovered but Sudbury had the advantage of having been less specialised in its commercial practices than many of the communities around it.

Not only were there fewer weavers in the town but they found a way of re-deploying their skills. By accepting lower rates than the Spitalfields silk workers they were able to move into silk weaving. At first silk weaving was pursued as a cottage industry, and though factories were set up later home work did not finally die out until the 1920s. Today the town is still an important silk weaving centre, with three nationally renowned firms in operation. They avoid competition as each specialises in a different kind of silk manufacture.

Towards the end of the last war an important new form of employment appeared in the town when a large diesel engineering company moved one of its factories down from London. In the booming Sixties this firm was greedy for labour, and with the help of the GLC a mass of new housing mushroomed just outside the town. With this came an influx of strange new people with different accents who would work at the factory. There was considerable suspicion of this London 'overspill'. Many of these people had an urban sharpness which the townspeople found discordant and disturbing. Not that newcomers to the area were a new phenomenon. A look at the census returns over the course of this century show a steady trickle of foreigners of various origins into the area. And there were always people moving between the town and other parts of the country. But the numbers involved on this occasion were unprecedented and the locals' sense of controlling their world was threatened. Twenty-five years on, the dust has begun to settle. The 1990s recession has also destroyed the diesel company's dominance over employment; and the appearance of the town is again beginning to change in response to fresh social and economic forces.

While this covers the main lines of the town's historical development, the backdrop to the book is incomplete without a visual perspective of the town.

Sudbury bears the marks of its long history. During its early period of prosperity money was invested in houses and churches. There is no building from this time which is obviously outstanding; nothing to knock the breath out of you, as in some of the villages round about. But the town still has a liberal sprinkling of pleasant stud and timber framed houses. They add variety to the streetscapes and generate a comforting assurance of the lasting nature of human activity.

In time, and with changes in architectural fashions, people began - just as they do now - to re-furbish older houses, and some of the Neo-classical brick facades are only fronts on earlier timber structures. New building, of course, also continued. Architectural discordance was not an issue at that time, and the new red brick of some 18th century building must originally have looked quite raw and aggressive. Time has softened it, however. And it too has now suffered alteration to meet new needs. Today Georgian drawing rooms have become customer service areas for the high street banks.

Rows of weavers' houses from the cottage industry period are also dotted around the town, readily distinguishable by their narrow three-storey fronts, the middle storey once housing the loom. Building has continued steadily in the town, in answer to the new needs each decade has brought, though the economic boom of the 1960s is long over.

For this is still a living town with sufficient manufacturing vibrancy to avoid getting caught in the well-meaning but often dessicating grip of the contemporary passion for conservation, a grip which has some of the town's neighbouring communities in a stranglehold. Conservation is what is done to something that basically has no inherent vitality of its own. A living town, by contrast, will always tend to want to destroy any older parts of itself which seem to stand in the way of its present development. In this town the new constantly jostles the old. But the time when economic expansion could unquestioningly take precedent over any other consideration is over. Present economic interests, though still driven by the same aggressive energy as ever, are increasingly forced to negotiate their relationship with the past; they can no longer just ride roughshod over it.

The town clusters round the Market Square and St Peter's, an old square-towered flint church, set towards one end of the Square. God, particularly in His polite Anglican form, continues to lose His draw for the townspeople, however, and the church now stands empty. Periodically it hosts some musical or charitable event and it seems unthinkable that the Square should be without it. But though it is still a compelling reminder of the town's past, for the moment it lacks a firm anchorage in its current culture.

For safety reasons the church tower is not open to the public. However, a series of enquiries and a trip to the Council offices can sometimes result in the loan of two enormous iron keys, eight to ten inches in length. With these you may unlock the tower, mount its narrow ladder, and squeeze through a couple of trap doors to join the pigeons and their droppings on the roof. There, standing by the now featureless stone men who guard its corners, the climber can survey the town laid out against the surrounding countryside.

In the Square immediately below, the market still gathers twice a week. The stall-holders arrive, some to set up trestles and polythene awnings and unpack crates of fruit and veg while others wheel out hangers of skirts and blouses, or lay out sheets of foam for mattresses, chairs and other household purposes. By mid-morning the aisle between the stalls is noisy and crowded. An infant starts to squall and a shopping trolley painfully scrapes a heel. After lunch selling begins to drop off and by three o'clock stallholders begin to think about packing up and try to shift the last of their fruit and veg. For a while the loud hoarse voices of the tattooed boys from London exhort house-wives to treat themselves to 'two lovely caulies for the price of one'. By five-thirty the vans have gone, leaving behind a desert of discarded boxes, blue fruit paper, bruised leaves, and a scattering of potatoes and tomatoes. By the following morning the Square is again a tidy little car park for the rest of the week.

Around the Square is a jumble of old and new buildings, so seeing it from above gives a new perspective on their relationship. Behind Lloyd's Bank a solitary garden with a bright green lawn and a single huge tree has escaped the onslaught of twentieth century commerce. All the other gardens have gone. In their place one can pick out the long flat-roofed concrete boxes which house modern shopping chains like Boots and Dorothy Perkins. Or, concreted over, one-time gardens are now covered with storage sheds and garages. But the rows of older windows above the ubiquitous plate glass, perspex and company logos of modern retailing are now more apparent than at street level, and one notices how many of the old peg-tiled roofs are still intact.

Looking further afield one can distinguish little groups of odd, unkempt buildings which linger in the nooks and crannies of the town. Most seem to have been unoccupied for several years. At street level they look increasingly bedraggled with each season. One supposes that someone somewhere must be keeping an eye on them and their appearance of imminent collapse is misleading. One gaggle of old three-storey weavers' cottages, which had become a well-known slum, was cleared some time ago, however, and one can see the trim new fire station which was erected on the site.

Beyond the fire station one can see the Meadows, the townspeople's name for the old Common Lands. These still embrace the town on three sides and appear scarcely to have changed in centuries. One use they have had as long as anyone can remember may be passing, however. Mothers are increasingly unwilling to let their children cross the road which circles the town just where the houses meet the Meadows, for now it thunders with traffic all day. So fewer children scamper across to the Meadows in the care of an older child to play-out after school or till bedtime. The insistent high-pitched chatter of children is heard there now only when the schools take groups down. Then little boys still devise ways of crashing into one another or failing this, simply tumble over anyway. And little girls turn cartwheels or, heads together, swear each other to secrecy before passing on the latest gossip.

Cattle still graze here. This increasingly lends the Mead-ows an air of the past. For the farmers in this part of East Anglia have shifted almost wholely over to cereals and fruit in the last two decades, and cows have become a rare species.

The Meadows' main use today is for Sunday strolls and exercising the dog. And as the train from London now finishes at the town, the embankment which used to carry the railway across the corner of the Meadows on its way to the villages and towns beyond, has been made into a public footpath, increasing the variety of pleasant, easy walks available. These flat, placid acres, bisected by the

river dotted with little bridges, and rich in bird life, meet a variety of needs for today's townspeople. No feature of the town is more widely or deeply appreciated.

In another direction the latest outcrop of new building in the town becomes visible, a rapidly expanding Business Estate cutting its way into previously unbuilt countryside. Its great warehouses full of carpets, bathrooms, kitchens and a mass of DIY aids prove a magnet for those who spend their weekends improving and extending their homes.

Cutting through the business estate is the latest stretch of raw, new by-pass where the earth on the verges has still to fully green over, and the trees, which in fifty years' time may be casting welcome shadows across the hot summer tarmac, are still wearing their little protective stockings.

This description is not offered with any nostalgic regret for what the town has lost. Talk to the townspeople and too many remember 'the good old days' with distaste, if not bitterness, to make one cautious about mourning what has gone. From time to time insensitive demolition and re-building plans have been proposed in the town. Some have been stopped; others have gone through. But increasingly the refurbishment of buildings which have lost their original rationale, but are capable of taking on a new role, seems underway. So from the tower you can now pick out

the Corn Exchange which houses the library, the renovated granary, now the theatre, and the hotel which has taken over the old Mill.

As in other parts of the country, battles and arguments - sometimes decidedly acrid in tone - will undoubtedly re-occur from time to time as the town has to confront the need for new buildings and facilities to cope with contemporary life. One is already underway regarding the siting of the new hospital. Whatever is finally decided on these occasions will always displease some people. This is part of the town's civic vitality. In the end, time, as it has so often in the past, will mellow today's contentious innovations so that when the time comes for their demise some group will set up a public outcry.

Descending from the tower which the people of the town put up five hundred years ago during Henry V11's reign, you rejoin their twentieth century counterparts in the streets in time for lunch. In a town where a generation ago most foreign foods were labelled 'muck' the options now available include Tandoori, Chinese, Cypriot, French and vegetarian.

This then, briefly, is the town which the people in this book regard as their town by dint of currently living, working or shopping regularly in it.

# PART THREE

# The People

# Chapter Two

# THE PEOPLE - AN INTRODUCTION

We would be able to talk to and photograph only a few people. Yet more than twenty thousand people live in or on the fringes of Sudbury and a recent survey calculated that as many as forty thousand people shop there. We would want the people we approached primarily to tell us about themselves, and a major thrust of the project was, of course, to photograph them as individuals. At the same time all those we approached would be living in and helping to form a community. So, in being seen and heard as themselves they would simultaneously offer impressions of life in a small town today. Their personal stories would also have a general relevance.

Selecting people for this purpose would not be easy. Alongside their established inhabitants most towns have their newcomers and the last chapter noted some to Sudbury. For people have always moved around more than is supposed, pulled by economic necessity, drawn by the lure of the strange, through marriage or even fortuitously. Others stay put. By temperament they thrive on the familiar, and under the sense of belonging which the familiar gives them, grow expansive.

Both kinds of people contribute to the vitality of any town. A town which never got injections of new blood would soon become claustrophobic and fossilised, while a town without a core of people who loved it and felt they were rooted there would find it hard to maintain that nebulous but important quality we call a sense of community. In Sudbury both newcomers and those whose families have lived in the town for generations have held civic office: the one bringing a determination to see that the town keeps abreast of the population's needs today, the other a sense of the need for each generation to ensure the town remains a pleasant place in which to live. The idea of talking only to people who were born and bred in the town therefore was too limiting. In addressing the issue of photographic portraiture it was also important to look at a cross-section of people.

Selection called for a plan. Part One noted the way art has frequently typed people. It also noted the role classification has played in human understanding generally, as a means of imposing sense on a complicated world in order to be able to cope with it. Less benignly our habit of typing can, as Part One also recognised, become a closure on our ability to see others for themselves so that it has often encouraged an insidious denigration of the ordinary and uncelebrated. And, at its worst, typing lies at the roots of racial, religious and sexual prejudice. Used appropriately however, classification can ultimately help to refine understanding.

A common way of classifying people is by their work, and this is where we started. Work after all often imprints itself on our appearance. So we frequently have to guess the kind of work a person does from their dress. Many people, it is true, go further and it is not uncommon for people to make all kinds of assumptions about another person's lifestyle and interests on the basis of their appearance and manner.

Certainly the relationship between people's dress and manner, and their social and cultural interests is not random. But repeatedly assumptions made about this relationship break down as we come to know someone. We wanted the portraits shown here implicitly to address this. Related to this we wanted to explore a possible alternative or supplement to the visual imagery which relies on predetermined body and facial features and mannerisms for indicating different qualities of character, and thereby inhibits the recognition of individuality. This would not involve jettisoning the visual traditions of the past indiscriminately. Some kind of social categorisation would remain a useful starting point. But it meant selecting and using these categories with a more refined discrimination than is often practised.

Even if desirable, to draw a representative occupational sample was impractical. The occupational structure of even a modestly sized modern town is far too complicated. And paid work is also only one form of important social activity. A great deal of political, charitable, sporting, cultural and religious activity is unpaid. We therefore opted for an impressionistic approach, devising a series of headings to cover some of the most important occupational and social groups as well as cultural activities in the town. Because they were impressionistic, we often had to make an arbitrary choice about which category to put someone in. There was the builder who was a keen churchgoer, the journalist who loved cricket, a teacher who played a leading role in the amateur dramatic society, and so on. Like people, the categories are therefore not cut and dried.

They allow, nevertheless, for a broad review of activity in the town. They display no preference for certain kinds of occupations over others, such as professional over manual, service over retailing. They include equal numbers of men and women. And there is a wide age range, though the young are under-represented.[1] Ideally they should have had a category to themselves,but because the number we could interview and photograph was extremely limited we succumbed to favouring those who were well settled into occupations and lifestyles.[2] In addition, as a society we privilege youth. Not only do the media give young people considerable coverage, but as a high profile group they have challenged, more successfully than some groups, the stereotypes people have tried to impose on them. Despite this limitation our categories will enable readers to see parallels between the interests and occupations of the people of Sudbury and people in other similarly sized towns in the country.

These categories also provide a useful framework for addressing the specifically photographic issues of interpretation raised in Part One. They help to alert us to the kinds of props documentary photographers employ to give their work meaning and to show how, far from being simple records of their times, documentary photographs are always part of a process of interpretation and commentary and ultimately must be judged accordingly.

In this instance it should be clear by the end of the book that the photography here stands or falls on the success with which the portraits leave the reader with a feeling of shared humanity and, simultaneously a sense of the idiosyncratic and inimitable features of character which distinguish each of us from everyone else in the world. The only question will be whether it has done this with conviction.

---

1      Age distribution  (n=45)

| Born before 1911 ie in their 80s | 16% |
|---|---|
| Born 1912 - 1921 | 70s 13% |
| 1922 - 1931 | 60s 20% |
| 1932 - 1941 | 50s 16% |
| 1942 - 1951 | 40s 24% |
| 1952 - 1961 | 30s 11% |

In actual fact one person was 29 and one over 90 at the time of interviewing.

2      It was a matter of doing the best we could or not undertaking the project. Finance was inadequate and time short. From contacting the first interviewee to the appearance of the book there was a year and a half.

# Chapter Three

# BY MACHINE AND HAND

**M**anufacturing is a fundamental part of the modern town. For manufacturing companies not only provide employment, but create further work to serve the needs of their employees. While it seems appropriate to start with some people who have spent their working lives in factories, an interview with a blacksmith is also included. For the huge nineteenth century surge from handwork to mechanisation has continued throughout this century, more quietly but relentlessly eroding once commonplace, centuries-old skills.

**Tom Portfleet,** born 1895, is the oldest person we talked to and photographed. He spent most of his long working life weaving coconut matting in one of the town's oldest factories, his one break being the First World War, when he found himself transported to the Dardanelles. His frame has shrunk, his sight is badly impaired, and his long-fingered hands have grown slender and soft, but Tom Portfleet is still spry and alert, his voice clear and animated. Sitting in the comfort of the little terraced house his daughter and her husband have caringly modernised, listening to him recall the course of his life one begins to feel again the presence of the straight-backed man he once was and acquires a sense of the quality of this man's everyday life, its odd jumble of hardship and tragedy, pleasure and fun. Though work features in Tom Portfleet's account, for him there are other more memorable events. The challenge for the photographer was to capture a sense of Tom Portfleet's feeling for life.

By contrast **John Sayers'** interests and sense of personal identity intermesh so intimately with the silk mill he manages that he starts his own life history with the story of another man and the history of the firm. This makes the inclusion of some historic photos of the workplace and its founder seem a useful aid to our appreciation of his character. They offer us a sense of the world to which he feels himself heir, recording for example a world where work involved mastering a craft.

Set up as a business venture the firm's commercial viability still carries priority for John Sayers, but his impulse to maximise efficiency so as to maximise profits is less clear. What animates his features and speech more is the idea of producing a quality product and an interest in the craft skills this demands. John Sayers is not obsessive however. Alongside his enthusiasm for managing The Gainsborough Silk Weaving Company is an interest in realising his social concerns in the arena of local politics.

Employed in two of the other silk mills in the town **Winnie Eady** was a weaver virtually all her working life, but she did not identify particularly strongly with her work; the church engrossed her more. The main point she wished to record in her interview was that she started work the day before her thirteenth birthday. She still has the Certificate allowing her to do this, which states that *This Labour Certificate entitles the holder to exemption from attendance at School between the ages of thirteen and fourteen on condition that such child is beneficially employed...* Seventy years on the loss of that year of education continues to rankle with her and she still feels she is owed a year of education. She has in fact tried, unsuccessfully, to obtain financial assistance to study for some A levels. Her bookcase, which she jokingly calls 'My University', shows evidence of her continued interest in learning. *The Oxford Library of English Poetry*, Kenneth Clark's, *Landscape into Art*, C S Lewis', *Mere Christianity*, *The Pelican History of the World...* sit side by side among other volumes.

Winnie Eady's nagging sense of unfulfilment, bound up as it is with memories of childhood poverty, has killed all nostalgia for the past. This does not mean she spent a joyless youth. Early snapshots show her both having fun and looking very elegant. Nevertheless, in her opinion, these are the best years of her life. For physically and mentally still sprightly she is now living in light, airy, council-built sheltered accommodation. She has treated herself to a 'nice' carpet and though she misses a garden her window-sill houses a collection of African violets and geraniums.

You press the tin against the nozzle. This releases a blob of glue. Securing the lid with this you dispatch the tin along the little carriage-way to the next stage of the process. From time to time **Pat Cecil** is put on other work. But for the most part this is her job. She has been doing it for many years, perched at her machine, as the portrait shows her, on a plinth above the factory floor, effectively cut off from her fellows. Many people would consider such work intolerable. Mary Barlow, who appears later in the book, remembers that when she left the factory she vowed never to return. But Pat Cecil likes her work; she feels she is good at it and finds the job satisfying. To attribute Pat Cecil's equanimity simply to mental dullness or a sluggish imagination would be wrong. She has an open, engaging manner, and her story gives the impression of a considerable capacity for enjoyment. She is also a woman of deep emotions. No-one who speaks to her would doubt the strength of her feeling for her late husband.

**Frank Nice**'s story describes a life which maintains a delicate see-saw between old and new and to see him as the old fashioned village blacksmith is a mistake. The way someone reconstructs a meaningful life when the need for their traditional skills has disappeared, presents the photographic portraitist with the challenge of recording change.

In the photograph on page 44 Frank Nice and his brother stand side by side in their garden. They confront the camera with none of the self-conscious poise most urban dwellers would adopt in such a situation and seem deeply rural. At first sight, the photo of the forge too, appears to record an anachronism, the kind of relic museums now conscientiously reconstruct. But there is a difference. However good the museum reconstructions, they never wholly convince. By contrast Frank Nice's 'shop' doesn't have to. It is organised like a modern office, round its user's personal work habits and, like a modern office, seems haphazard and inconvenient to other people.

Most significantly, what Frank Nice makes, and the sensibilities he displays when speaking about his work, reveal him as very much a man who has adjusted to a changing world. The head and shoulders portrait of him, where the turn of the head suggests an enquiring cast of mind, seems to capture the modern slant to his intelligence which exists alongside his traditional outlook.

# Tom Portfleet
Coconut mat maker, born 1895, King's Lynn,
Norfolk

*'I heard her say, "Who is that swanky fool?"'*

I'm the last of the family. I've got two sons, two daughters, eight grandchildren, eighteen great-grandchildren. I ain't got no great-great-grandchildren - not yet anyway - though there's some old enough.

My dad was a Dutchman. He used to come over to bring tulip and daffodil bulbs. He married a King's Lynn girl, and got a job with Armes. When Armes left King's Lynn and came to Sudbury, he came too. I had six brothers, three sisters, and three sisters who died. My dad, my older brother, the brother next to me, and my middle sister was at Armes. I left school when I was thirteen on Friday, May the 17th, 1908, and I started up Armes six o'clock on Monday morning, the 20th. I went six in the morning till six at night, including Saturday morning till eleven, for two and six a week.

The first day I was there I nearly got the sack. We started at six, and had eight till half past, breakfast. Then at half-past ten, we had ten minutes' break. We'd sit in a ring on the factory floor all the boys, talking together, and all round the factory there was big display cards about saving the slaves in South Africa. Well, I said, they want to put bills up about the slaves of the schoolboys and schoolgirls in England, working for two shillings and six pence for fifty-four hours a week. And the boss stood behind me!

Of course he sent for me after lunch, up to the office. He started laying the law down about causing unrest. "You'd better go and get on with your job and don't have so much to say for yourself". Of course I had to pack up talking about it then because I had to look after my job. There was no other work about. I shouldn't have got that if it hadn't have been for my dad working up there, and my brother. I left Armes on the 30th of September, 1960. So that'll let you know how long I worked there.

When I left school I was a regular sports boy. I was a footballer and I played for Sudbury Town. Then I had a trial match with West Ham and another with Sheffield Wednesday. I was going to sign on as a professional for West Ham. Then, of course, I was called up and that put the tin hat on my football.

We left England in May and we was passing through the Bay of Biscay on my twentieth birthday. We went up to Lemnos, about eight miles off the Dardanelles, and then we had to get on small boats and make a landing and run up the beach. The Turks all laid along the top and were bringing us down like ninepins. There was 45,000 killed there in seven months and we only drove the Turks out of one line of trenches. I went on with the same shirt I come off with, and it'd only been washed once. My brother older than me, he was in the same state, and when we left there he come up to me and he had his kit bag with him. So I said, 'Have you got clothes in there Alf?' Well he got me a pair of socks out, and I sat down in my dug-out and took my puttees and my boots off. That's the first time my boots had been off for three months. I slept in my boots and my socks.

Anyway, I took my sock off and flung it on the bottom of the trench to put the other one on. My brother sat over the other side of the dug-out. Then he shouted, 'Look at your sock, Tom, it's a-moving along!' And it was, just like a caterpillar, up and down. You couldn't prick a pin in for lice. It was terrible! And yet I never felt it. I suppose I got so used to it I didn't notice. Another thing, from the time we landed on the 3rd of June till the 17th of December 1915, I never seen a piece of bread or a cup of tea, only four-inch square dog biscuits and corned beef, breakfast dinner and tea.

Well, we went to Egypt and had a fortnight's delousing. While we was there, the Turks started marching in Palestine, and they got to Suez, and we had to rush to fight them off the Canal. Then we captured Damascus and Jerusalem. The day the Armistice was signed I was on the Mount of Olives, and I was taken bad with diphtheria, me and another chap. I don't know how the other fellow got on, I think he died. But I got in a big hospital just outside of Cairo, on the way to the Pyramids, and I got recovered.

That meant I had to go back to my regiment, but just the night before, a sergeant come running in the hut and asked could anybody play football. Not thinking I said, 'Yes, I can', just like that. I hadn't kicked a ball for years. 'Well, get ready for a game', he said. Well, I played for Cleopatra Signals and I played a smashing game. I surprised myself. And the Monday morning I was on parade and again a sergeant come running across the parade ground. 'He's not going back to the regiment, he's got to come with me.' Well I played for them, and we won the All Egyptian Sultan Challenge Cup. I've got a rare big medal for that, 'Alexandria United Services Challenge Cup, 1919. Winner, T W Portfleet' it's got on it on one side, with the entrance to Luxor Temple. On the other side

there's a big head of Alexander the Great. So it wasn't till July 1919 I got back to Sudbury.

All my brothers came home except the youngest. He got killed a week before the Armistice. He was two months off eighteen. The silly young fool, he went and volunteered to go abroad and he wasn't over there about a week. He was killed before my mother knew he was out there. I got home just time enough to have a big feed at the drill hall, what Sudbury Council was giving the return soldiers. I had a lovely feed there. And I hadn't been at home a fortnight before I was Captain of the Sudbury Town Football Club. And I was captain for four years - 1919 till 1924.

I was also back at Armes, making mats. We used to make these ordinary floor mats what you wipe your feet on. That was very rough. I finished up by making hand-woven matting, which was a plastic matting with squares and different stripes in it.

I met my wife when I was fourteen, and I'll tell you how. My dad, he had an allotment, and I used to go down to Clovers Mill, which is now the big hotel, directly I came home from school, because the horses that brought the wagon-loads of wheat used to stand there, four horses in some wagons and two in others. I used to go down there with a barrow and a spade and get a load of manure and then take it up to this allotment. So I used to come down this alley into Girling Street.

The girls and boys they all used to play in the street there. All the girls would be playing 'follow the leader' or a circle with 'kiss in a ring'. And then about fifteen, twenty yards further down it would be the boys, and they'd all be playing marbles, or buttons, or 'kit-kat'. And I used to sit on the end of the barrow and watch. One night the girls was playing 'kiss in the ring', and my wife what was, she came up and said, 'You've been sitting there watching us every night. Would you like a game?' So I first met my wife like that. But I never went out walking with her or nothing.

That was the war what done that. I was away five years and then I'd forgotten all about her and so she had me. But when I came home in 1919, the next day I went up to Armes to see about my job, and the manager says, 'Yes, your job is waiting for you and would you like to have a walk round now you're up here and see some of your old friends?' Well, my father was working there still, and I went and had a few words with him. And there were several girls there and I stood talking to one that lived next door and the next one behind her was this young woman what was to be my wife. That's the first time I'd seen her for about six years and our eyes met, and I thought to

myself, God, lummey, I know you. But I couldn't bring her to mind. And she flunked down on the seat, and I spoke to her, asked her how she was, and had a little chat about the war and walked off. I was still in my Army clothes and I don't reckon she recognized me because I heard her say, 'Who is that swanky fool?'

Then the Sunday night I was walking up the Market Hill. There used to be a little shop by the side of the Town Hall with a low window-sill and there was a row of these here girls what worked up at Armes, sitting on that, all laughing and talking to each other. And they all got up and come round me. And then they say, 'Well, which one are you going to take for a walk tonight?' So I said, 'I don't know. Sit down and I'll tell you.' So they all sat on the window-sill, and got up one at a time. The wife, she was the last and she didn't get up, she still sat there. And I said to her, I said, 'Well, would you like to show me round Sudbury? I should like to see the changes in it.' She said, 'Yes, I should be pleased to.' And I started courting like that. Eighteen months we was a-courting. And I married her at the Registry Office in Prior Street on Christmas Day, 1920, and that was a lovely sunshiny day.

We went and lived in Gregory Street, two doors from my mother. They were silk-weaving houses with a middle floor sixteen yards by nine yards for a big silk weaving loom. When the wife first had it covered with linoleum I know she said she had twenty-two yards to cover it. When they pulled the houses down for the fire station I had to go into these flats.

I've spent a lot of time on the Meadows in my life. My mother used to take our shoes and stockings off when we had holidays from school and we never used to see them no more till we went back to school! We used to be on the Meadows all day long, from early morning till long as nine. And later I used to take the children on during their summer holiday when I had my fortnight's holiday. Because for the first three years or so, when the Government brought the holidays in, we never got paid a ha'penny for them. So that's how we used to go out and spend our holidays. One day they used to go swimming, all day long, splashing in and out the water, racing about the meadow. We used to take food and water with us. Then the next day I'd take them up to Brundon Woods, about a couple of mile away, and there used to be primroses and violets and bluebells. We used to take a barrow with water and a kettle and teapot, and food, and stop up there all day.

Then when the time come that I got a bit hard up during my holiday, I went pea-picking. The lorry used to come. A fellow from London used to go round the farms and buy the fields up as they stood. And then his two or three lorry drivers used to come round the roads, and ring their bells shouting 'pea-pickers', and them what was going all used to rush and get in the lorries, ready to go wherever they went. I went five o'clock Monday morning, and I never come back no more till Friday night. I made this here little shelter to crawl in and I slept in the field.

You had to bend down and snatch the pods off and drop them in the bags. We got a shilling a bag for forty-two pound, and I picked a bag in three-quarters of an hour. The chap lived next door to me in Gregory Street, he lost an arm during the war, he used to come as well, only he used to put them underneath his elbow and snatch them off. And he used to come home every night to Sudbury, and the next morning he used to bring me my food and my bottles of tea.

I earned about eight pounds fifteen shillings. That was a lot of money that time of day. And I took the wife and the three children we had then to Clacton and had a week's holiday, with the eight pounds what I'd earned. That was the only holiday me and the wife had together in our married life. We used to have a day off, mind you, now and again, to go to Clacton. We never used to have a lot of money to fling away, but what we did have, we used to make use of.

Then in 1944 the wife fell downstairs when they was bombing on Sudbury. She was unconscious five weeks and the shock gave her diabetes, and she hit the stairs with her head, and that caused a tumour on the brain. When she had that taken off it left her paralysed and blind and she couldn't hardly walk unless you held her up. I used get up of a morning and wash her, give her a hot cup of tea, and innoculate her with the syringe. Then while she was having her breakfast I used to have a wash and she used to comb my hair, because she had one hand she could use. Then I used to have a snack myself, and go to work at eight. At dinner time I'd come home and get her up, dress her and sit her in the chair, and help her all I could... I had nineteen years with her like that, altogether. She died a week before our golden wedding.

The best week of the year that was, was 'Sudbury Gala Week'. That used to be a lovely place for carnivals. On the Monday there used to be all water races, boat races, water polo, and stalls all the way along the river bank. It started at ten and never used to finish till about seven at night. Crews used to come from Norwich, King's Lynn, Ipswich, all over the place, to compete down Sudbury here. The Tuesday that'd be the children's day and the trip to Clacton. Wednesday would be a dancing day. The

Territorial band used to get on the Market Hill in the afternoon, playing, and at seven o'clock the Sudbury Town Band used to get on and play till half-past nine. They'd break about eight o'clock, go and have a glass of beer in the Black Boy, and then they'd come back and play for another hour. And the police used to stop all the traffic and send it out of the town. And there was dancing all round the Market Hill, and crowds of people all lined up each side on the pavement.

And then Thursday, let's see, what used to be on Thursday? Oh, the children's Sunday School outing to a farm at the top of Ballingdon Hill. The children were took up there by horse and cart, and brought home at night. And they used to have racing all day long. The Friday there used to be what they called the annual thanksgiving service for the week. Well, that used to be all parades. The Territorial Army had a lovely brass band of about forty and two big drums and four side drums. Then there used to be about forty or fifty troops follow that, and then there'd be the Sudbury Town Band. Behind them would be the Salvation Army Band, and behind the Salvation Army Band there'd be the Church Lads' Brigade Band. That used to be bugles and drums. Then there used to be the cadets. They had little blue tunics with yellow bands and little pillbox hats with yellow bands. After them used to come the Life Brigade Band. And they used to have red tunics. And their band was a drum and fife band, all piccolos and flutes with the drums. There used to be lovely carnivals there did, that time of day.

A fortnight or three weeks afterwards, they had the nurses' parade. That was at night time. All the business people had motor cars and bicycles and horses and carts, all dressed up with coloured papers and ribbons. Armes would have somebody mat weaving. Another lorry would be a silk-weaver's lorry, the next would be the corset factory girls all with sewing machines. And they used to give all the young men about seventeen or eighteen, a torch on a stick. They used to give dozens, hundreds away and they used to be alight all the time. And people took boxes round for money for St Leonard's Hospital. Oh, but we used to have lovely parades then.

\*   \*   \*   \*

# John Sayers

Managing Director, silk weaving company, Town
Councillor, District Councillor, born 1935, Sudbury.

*'It's unique, it's exciting and it intrigues people.'*

I'd like to tell you about the founder of our business, Reginald Warner, who was born into a Quaker family, and lived in Highgate, London. Once when he was a very young boy out with his nanny, he was attracted to a shining object in a pawnbroker's shop and nagged his nanny to obtain it. When he was about ten he rediscovered this coin and on one side there was a weaver at his loom. He immediately said, 'I want to be a weaver.' His mother thought no more of it. But when the time came to leave school, he went to his father and uncle and asked if they could help him get an apprenticeship with a weaving firm. He did some designing, and learnt the business with a silk weaving firm in Ipswich. Unfortunately the firm didn't prosper and eventually failed. But Reginald found the trade absolutely fascinating. It was a marvellous way of expressing his artistic skills especially on the design side. So he went yet again to father and uncle. He knew that all the old hand looms and Jacquards and ancilliary equipment were going into the sale yard in Ipswich. And so father and uncle lent Reginald some money with which to purchase the items.

Next he looked towards Sudbury. There was weaving and winding and processing of yarn going on there at that time and already skilled labour in this area. So he started his business in Sudbury in 1902. And it was successful. He concentrated on making figured velvets, elaborate silk brocades and damask, plain velvets, and a lot of tapestry weaving.

It was in those early days Reginald found himself in need of an apprentice on the design side of the business. So he went along to the art teachers in the local schools to make enquiries as to whether there were any up and coming young artists in the classroom. I think my father at that time would have been about thirteen, and Father, being keen on art, and loving the countryside, had done a lot of paintings of trees and flowers. I think they attracted Reginald's attention because obviously nature-forms present themselves in textile designs. He asked the teacher if he could have a word with my father, and Father expressed a keen interest to be an apprentice and join Reginald. But my grandfather said an emphatic no; he

wanted my father to go into their business, which was coach and horses. But Father was persistent, and eventually his mother persuaded his father to let him come up with Reginald. And he worked in this factory all his life, and managed the business when Reginald retired, though the family still are the major shareholders and control it.

I got involved prior to going away to boarding school. Father used to bring me up here to this very office, at weekends, and I used to play on the roof. At home, many important designs had to be to be done in the evening, when Father would spend time with his paintbox at the dining-room table. I used to sit alongside him and have my own paints and some paper, and Father taught me how to draw and paint, and I used to do little drawings.

My brother, who is older than me, didn't come into the business. He felt he would like an outdoor life and he went down to Kent to learn about butterflies and moths, and their breeding habits. But there wasn't a lot of money to be earned in that so he went into the wine and spirits retail trade.

I have three children and my youngest son, when he left school, came to the factory, but it wasn't just the thing he wanted to do. There wasn't a lot of scope for him to express his bit of artistic flair, so he's with a local sign-writer, quite a skilled man, and he's learning from him. But I was always fascinated by the place, and when I left school I came here.

Of course we worked from much earlier in the morning than we do now. Most of us were in here by half-past seven, and we had a long day till six. And I think Saturday morning it was more or less compulsory. In fact you needed to work Saturday morning to get a reasonable living wage in those days. I've got a little tin in the office, with three ivory dice in it. And at lunchtime we'd sit round the benches - that's the men (the men were segregated from the women then) - and we used to throw the dice for pokey-die. The first prize used to be ten Woodbines, the second prize was a tanner, the third was a threepenny bit.

Some of us have been here a long time. Rita Cresswell, she's been a warper here for, I'd say, forty-two years. In fact she taught me the art and skill of making warps; I used to sit alongside her on the warping on many, many occasions when I was doing my apprenticeship, passing the threads to her when she was entering the reed. Steven has been here, I think, a couple of years longer than I have, about forty. These days we rely on Steven a great deal to look after quality control.

We've about forty-four employees and a good mix of males and females. But over the years we've lost a lot of skilled women workers, who have left us to have families. And there's times when we would wish these people to come back but they haven't been able to place the children. So we've built a nursery. We called it 'Bobbins', which we thought was rather appropriate! And it's taken off very well. It's available to the whole estate. I understand the fees that we are charging compare favourably with ordinary childminders.

The family realize that there could be a problem of continuity in the management. A member of the family chairs the Board but we've got a management team with people from the design department, accounts and marketing. They've got ideas, and a real enthusiasm for the firm to succeed. I think we will do well in the future.

We're considered to be a noisy industry. Years ago they used to measure the level of deafness by getting an employee to walk away from a senior member of staff who would have a bell he would ring continuously; when the employee couldn't hear it any more, they would measure in yards the distance from the two people, and they would say that the person has so many yards of deafness. Of course today they come round with very sophisticated equipment and ear muffs are a statutory requirement by law. Likewise with smoking. There is no smoking in the factory these days; there used to be, but things are not so relaxed now.

There's a relationship builds up between yourself and the business. I think it's to do with having a love of beautiful fabrics, and we do make some exceptional materials here. And a sense of belonging to a community of work people,

*Reginald Warner, founder of The Gainsborough Silk Weaving Co.Ltd.  1902*

*Factory premises  1904*

who have that same feeling... you could say it's an intense feeling of satisfaction at producing something which is rather exceptional in the market. For me it's liking traditional things. Our fabrics are modelled on original documents, a famous walling fabric that we may have to reproduce. It inspires one to try and maintain standards. There's that challenge to get it right. We went to great pains to do trials and colour selection for a walling fabric for the National Gallery in Trafalgar Square. And that looks absolutely magnificent. In fact it was required for the Gainsborough and Constable paintings room, so it was rather appropriate. It picks up the colours in the actual paintings, so you get this lovely harmony. When you visit the galleries, the fabric shouldn't be dominating at all; it should not distract from the paintings. They're now applying this thinking up in the Norwich Castle Museum, where our fabrics are being used in most of the rooms displaying paintings.

Mr. Reginald Warner must have been a compulsive hoarder. We moved from hand loom weaving in 1926, but Mr. Warner didn't cast all the old hand looms out; he put them in some old Army huts near the factory, and gradually we're having them renovated. We also have a wonderful archive of fabric. Since Reginald Warner's day we must have accumulated at least a thousand designs, and we have some lovely examples of the early tapestries. We're having those sent away for conservation with a view to possibly putting them on display. And we have a unique collection of the first generation of power looms in the country. Many of them are our own creation, direct descendants of the hand looms, and a lot of them are peculiar to us, because Reginald Warner and my father developed an attachment to the standard Jacquard machine. One of its effects is what we call the Medici. It's much admired and we're the envy of a lot of other weaving concerns because they're rather mystified as to how we achieve it.

I want to talk to you about having maintained the factory as it was originally. A lot of the machines are really well made, good cast iron, and they've proved themselves to be effective. The preparatory machinery is virtually as it was when it was put in here in 1924. Our policy is that if something works and produces profits, leave it alone. Obviously one has to progress. Most of the old, original looms have now had bits of electrical gadgetry attached to them to make them easier to operate. So the weavers really don't have to be involved with the day-to-day running of a loom as they used to. It's looked after by the engineer, whereas in the old days, if a man's loom stopped he usually knew why, and fixed it as he went along. We buy in a lot of the parts now.

We are aware of modern weaving technology and we now have one or two faster weaving machines. The trouble is getting a machine which will do what we want it to do. Steven was also saying that he finds working on the two German-made high speed looms extremely efficient, but there's not the job satisfaction. He's explained to me many, many times, that they are so easy to operate, that boredom sets in. That really is unfortunate. I think a lot of people, when they go to work, don't derive a great deal of pleasure or satisfaction from what they do. Here, there still is that loom-weaver interest, which is all-important, because the job then becomes more stimulating. And I think the fact that one's got a series of looms, and they're all different, and the weavers move around the factory, makes their working life more interesting and pleasant. They've always got that challenge. They aren't just operating a battery of looms.

But more modern machinery will open up the scope for new fabrics and new designs and composition, which we're not doing at the moment. So those that are more involved in the business will do specialist work, and the more run-of-the-mill fabrics we'll produce on the modern machines. But we're trying, through Steven - who's training officer - to take youngsters coming from school through the whole process, though we don't have apprenticeship schemes now. But for those who take to it and find it's something they really want to do, then we'll go to great pains to teach them all the loom parts and their association with one another, so we don't lose the skill and expertise which is in the factory.

Perhaps this factory should be made available to the general public. It's unique, it's exciting, and it intrigues people. We could invite people on a conducted tour and possibly we could capitalise a bit on it. We don't have a museum in Sudbury, so perhaps we could have a working silk museum and then put some of the new machinery into a modern weaving section.

I've nearly done my four-year introductory period as a councillor, and hopefully I'll be re-elected in May. We try to make it a pleasant town to visit, so there's a display of hanging baskets and troughs and planters in the town, and a great deal of emphasis recently on approach round-abouts. I've felt, though, that the local Town Council doesn't have the say in local affairs it used to have in the old borough days. Unfortunately there's politics in the Town Hall these days, but I'm putting up for District Councillor now as well. The District Council gets involved with planning on a bigger scale. They really have a lot of the say in local planning and development, which is interesting.

# Winnie Eady

Silk-weaver, born 1908, Sudbury.

*'The choice was the factory or service.'*

We used to call Saturday 'ha'penny day' because that was our pocket money, two farthings. There was a little baker's shop, and the lady also sold sweets. Every Friday night she emptied all her sweet jars and with bits of newspaper she made up little bags of sweets, and sold them for a farthing each on Saturday morning. And with my ha'penny I could buy one of those little packets of sweets and a strip of liquorice or something of that sort.

In those days, if you had bread and butter you didn't have jam. You had bread and butter or bread and jam, or bread and dripping. And my mother used to make us soup with a shin bone, and for breakfast we always managed to have an egg. In my cousins' family there were ten; when they had an egg it was cut in half. It was cut on one person's plate one day, and on another's the next, so they had the little bits that fell off. That was how poor people were.

I used to go to see my aunt and uncle and grandma at Middleton, and I used to really hope that my uncle would cut the cheese because he would cut me a big bit. My grandma cut me a tiny bit and, mind, you had no butter on your bread with your cheese. And she'd say you must eat your bread and smell your cheese, so I used to keep that tiny bit of cheese until the last, just to enjoy it.

We had a clothing club. We took sixpence on a Monday morning and in October the church put a penny to every shilling you'd saved, and the shop where you bought your things, they put in their penny to every shilling. Well, I mean, two pence in every shilling was a lot those days. My mother used .o buy me woollen stockings, and long-cloth to make our clothes. She made chemises - when I got big enough I had to do the blessed things myself - and petti-coats. And we knitted our vests. When I was small we not only wore a vest, a chemise and a liberty bodice, and knickers made from long-cloth - which were buttoned on to the liberty bodice - and a white long-cloth petticoat, but in winter we had a flannel petticoat under the long-cloth one! And we never left a vest off - only to wash it. We wore the vest day and night, summer and winter. You had three of everything, unless you were very poor. Everything was clean Sunday morning and washday was Monday, and you had one garment on, one ready and one in the wash.

The roads weren't like they are now. There was only horse-drawn traffic, so in the streets we could play spin-ning tops, bowly-hoops, hopscotch, and we could have a skipping rope, with one girl one side of the street and one the other, turning, and you all skipping in the middle of the road. And the horses left their trademark, as did the cows. There was no end of cow sheds where the dairyman would have just a few cows and supply milk to the immediate streets around them. And of course the cows would be walked down to the meadows, so you would get the cow muck as well as the other. You can still see shoe scrapers let into the wall by the front door of some houses.

Of course, cars were coming in. Then you had to be more careful, but mostly it was still horse-drawn traffic. And when I was at school we were allowed, if you can believe this, to go out into the playground and watch when a plane went over, it was so unusual.

I lived in Gregory Street, where the fire station is now, in a four-room, two-up two-down, and a loo up the top of the garden. We had no water indoors and no sink, and although the loo was a water closet it didn't have a flush. So every time you went up the garden you had to get your bucket of water from the tap outside - there was two taps to serve six houses - and up the garden you went, carrying your bucket of water.

And this cottage, the rain kept coming through the roof. You put a bucket to catch it, but with two beds in each bedroom, sometimes you couldn't. And if it was coming on your bed you'd have to have old coats and macs on your bed. Now I'm not saying that was always happening; it possibly only happened two or three times in a year.

Washing was practically a day's work. You put the things in to soak on Sunday night, and Monday morning you washed them. The dirtier ones you had to scrub on the scrubbing board. Then you rinsed them. And we had a copper in our living-room which you filled from the tap outside. So then you'd boil them. Then they had to be rinsed again before they were put out on the line. And my mother wrung them by hand. She had a mangle, but there was no room for it in the living-room; it had to be in the front room. Of course we could have lived in the front room, but my mother liked to keep one room nice to go in on Sundays and birthdays. So she wasn't taking wet things through in the front room, and she wrung them by hand. She did mangling for her neighbours, though, who hadn't got a mangle, to spare all the ironing. Sheets and big things they'd bring her in a basket, and she would do them. I think she charged a penny.

*Winnie Eady (on left) about 18 years old*

*About 25 years old*

She did this because after my father came home from the First World War his job went. You see his trade was horses. He could harness four in hand. He could drive a brake. That was a big thing. I don't know how many horses they had to pull it. And at election times, he would drive the candidates. He had to wear a yellow tie when he drove the Liberal one out, and a blue tie for the Conservatives. But that all went. Then he took every job he was sent to. He did beet pulling. Oh, his hands when he came home, pulling beet in cold weather. And they put him on the dust carts and all different jobs he did. Then he collapsed, and was unable to work for twelve years.

The doctor said he must keep his allotment going to have something to do. So to pay the rent for his allotments, and to buy seeds, my mother made big sacrifices. She hardly had anything to wear. Then after twelve years he started a job in gardening. And that was much better. But of course every day it rained: no work, no money. And it could rain for a week. But one or two people he worked for would give him jobs in the kitchen. And when he got old he did

go to some people as a charwoman doing housework. He wasn't lazy.

But we survived. My mother was wonderful, she really was. How she kept us out of debt I do not know. Some of the children at school, if they had terrible shoes, they were given shoes. But we were never in that humiliating position of having to have any shoes given us though we were given some cast-off clothes. But I ran errands, and for one old lady I ran all the way for a sixpence, and another lady who was a dressmaker, I think I had about one shilling and six pence a week off her, which was good money. And odd errands you'd get a penny. An auntie and uncle were caretakers at North Street School. I used to go up there every Saturday morning and dust every desk and I got ... was it ninepence, I forget exactly. But those monies I saved up, and we had one new dress a year, and the next year it was let down for school. We also got a summer dress as well as a serge one for the winter.

When people talk about the good old days, they weren't,

they were hard. I remember how worried my mother used to be because if you fell in debt there was the workhouse. There were no family allowances. You could get a little parish relief, but believe me that was a little. And my father's insurance ran out and he had no pension. And they said my brother and I had to keep the home going. So at thirteen I was in the factory.

Well, I thought if I got out to work I would be a big help to my parents. I had very little pocket money, and quite a lot of my friends were leaving. The choice was the factory or service. They had even less free time at service than what you had in a factory. My sister went into service and she had one afternoon and an evening a week off. Anyway, I didn't want to wear caps and aprons. But you got your living; you didn't get much money but you got your living at service.

My birthday was January 1st, so my education ended at Christmas. It really ended at twelve didn't it? I was at work the day before I was thirteen.

We did a forty-nine and a half hour week, Monday till Friday, eight until six with one hour mid-day break when we ran home and had a dinner. And Saturday mornings, eight until half-past twelve. We had a week's paid holiday. The forewoman wrote to the boss thanking him for giving us a week's holiday with pay. But you lost your holiday pay if you got twelve black marks. A black mark was for being late; or if you went to the dentist that was a black mark. And for the other holidays you weren't paid, not Easter, nor Whitsun.

I started on eleven shillings a week, and I gave my mother the ten, and she clothed me at that point. But out of my shilling I had to buy things like hair ribbons that we wore then - wide hair ribbons at the top of your pig-tail and the bottom - and gloves, and small items; they all had to come out of that shilling.

I was a weaver when I was sixteen. I was a weaver right through. During the war they put me on weaving man-bearing parachutes. You had to take the bad with the good. Sometimes when the average wage for those who were on time was twenty-three shillings a week, you could earn, if you were lucky, thirty shillings a week on piece rate. But sometimes you couldn't earn more than nine shillings a week. Life was tough all round, really.

And I've gone through life begrudging not stopping at school till I was fourteen. And you see my university in there in my bookcase. I still love learning. And I took a couple of O-levels - did I tell you? - when I was fifty-nine and sixty. Much earlier I took a correspondence course in Sunday School teaching and at nineteen I started teaching infants; at twenty-one I was teaching ten-year-old boys. I loved teaching Sunday School. I think I could have made a teacher.

\*    \*    \*    \*    \*

# Pat Cecil

Glue-to-tin worker, fuel injector factory, born 1930, Chelmsford, Essex.

*'If you work quick and take an interest in it, it won't be boring.'*

Well, life has been good and bad for me; we all have ups and downs, don't we?

I went to school at the Convent. Late - you got the cane. Didn't behave - you got a knock on the head. I got a few knocks on the head. I even got the cane for falling down a tree I shouldn't have been up after conkers! On a Sunday we had to go Mass in the morning. That was about ten o'clock for an hour. Then Sunday School in the afternoon, and we had to put our penny in the plate. If we kept it the priest would tell our parents. And then we had Benediction in the evening, about six o'clock. I didn't mind it. You grow up and get used to these things.

I was a bit of a tomboy I'll admit. Used to go out every evening playing on the Meadows. I suppose there are things I shouldn't tell you. A bunch of us we broke into a house. It was empty, but it had a caretaker! And he was hollering his head off, and running up the stairs. We all just flew out the window - two floors up! And ran for our lives. Once I got into trouble for playing on the snow outside the Convent. We used to have mountains of snow. Or it seemed a lot, perhaps, because we were small. But we used to love playing on it. And we got into trouble. I know the cane was used, but I can't remember whether I had it or not. We used to go scrumping. One of us used to go up the tree to pick the apples and throw them down. I was up the tree one day when someone come along with a dog, everyone else ran and left me up there. I stayed as quiet as a mouse, and I wasn't caught. And I remember once we were friendly with the girl next door and we bored a hole through the bedroom wall! And hung a picture over each side. Till her mother took the picture off to dust, and nearly had a fit!

In those days children did things like that. You didn't have videos and television sets. We didn't have a radio! As we got a little older the neighbour had a radio and she used to turn it up and we all used to listen. Be as quiet as anything so we wouldn't miss anything. I loved my childhood.

I left school at fourteen. Left school and left the church. But I always say my prayers at night. And someone in trouble I always mention. My husband, he used to laugh at me, and say, "Ask Him if He can hurry up and see I win the pools!"

After school I worked in a shop for 10s 6d a week. Out of that I had half-a-crown, the rest was for my keep. I went to live with an aunt in Chelmsford then for a while, to see a bit of life  Anyway, young and stupid, I got married and went and lived in London, near Heathrow. I didn't like that. It was noisy, planes all the time. Then I moved to Northern Ireland, because I married a soldier. I enjoyed it there because it was in the country and we used to go for long hikes. Then I had a baby and came back to Sudbury.

I worked at the hospital for six or seven years, and got divorced. Then I got a job here and after two or three years I met my second husband. He worked here too. We were married for twenty-two years when he died; we had a really happy life. He was a really humorous sort of person you know. Everybody who knew him said he was a character.

When he died that was a terrible shock. He was on night shift and he came home just after seven, bright and cheerful as usual. I asked him what he wanted for his dinner because we go down the town Wednesday lunchtime and do a bit of shopping. And he said, "I'll have a nice big pork chop with the kidney". And I got back and walked in, bag of shopping in my hand, and there he was just laid on the floor. It was a shock. It took me ages to try and get the doctor, I couldn't dial properly, I couldn't see properly. And he was ready to go for a month's holiday in the Far East.

We'd been planning it for over a year. I don't travel much. Oh, no, I couldn't. All those hours in an aeroplane! Never! But we planned it together. His brother died out there in the war, on the Burma railway. And we was just talking one evening and he said, "There's something I've always wanted to do. I'd like to see where George was buried". I said, "Well, why don't you?" He said, "It's in Thailand. I could never afford to go there!" I said, "It's only because you spend your money. If you really want to go, you'll go." So I helped him to start saving twenty pence pieces, and told him to get a jar and seal it down, and put a little hole in the lid. It took him two years to save enough, and he went with the FEPOW, the Far Eastern Prisoner of War Organisation. He just took hundreds of photographs so I could see everything and I've got a video of Kampachooy cemetery, or some name like that. It was a long word beginning with a K. [*Kanchanaburi*] And I've got pictures of where he's standing with the name on his brother's grave. They actually found it. So this was going to be his last big holiday, to visit the people that he'd made friends with.

When he died everybody here was really great. I had lots of people come up and see me and that was good, better than sitting on your own. I had company practically all the time.

I've worked here thirty-one years. I've four years to go, so I might as well stay. There are different shifts. thirty-nine hours a week, seven-thirty to four-thirty on the day shift. I hate to rush so I get up about half-past five, have a shower and breakfast. I always have a breakfast. Tidy up and make the bed. I enjoy coming out to work.

We used to be in another factory. They sold it and carted everything up here, including us! None of us wanted to come; we all loved it down there, because that was a really happy place. It's definitely lighter, definitely cleaner here, but I didn't like it the first few months, I'll admit. In fact, I thought it was depressing, even though it was light and clean. When we first came up there was problems with things that just weren't properly put right. Just little things, niggly things. And you had to keep stopping. Some really hated it up

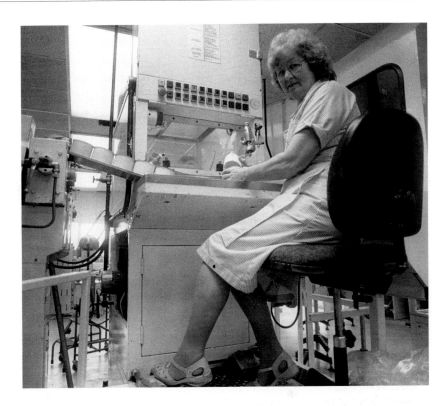

here and left. I've got used to it now and I quite like it.

When I started here we used to pack the coils. Then I progressed and went winding. And I was good at it. I did that for quite a long while, about fifteen years I think. And then they wanted somebody on glue-to-can. I seemed to be quite good at that, and I enjoyed it more, because I was on my own, and I didn't have to rely on other people to keep me working. The machines then were real huge and hideous and it was really dark down at the other factory.

If you work quick and you take an interest in it, it won't be boring. It depends on the individual. Some people will do the job I'm doing and really hate it and think it's boring. But if you work quick, and you concentrate on what you're doing, the time flies. In fact I've never known the time to go so quick as it does! It just flies by.

There is a canteen here, but I don't have my lunch here. I bring a sandwich and a couple of apples, because I enjoy cooking, so when I go home I always cook a dinner. I like fish. And I like chicken, it's so versatile, though this weekend I had a pork joint, because my son and his wife and the children come over on Sunday to dinner.

I usually spend Sunday morning making cakes. I make one for my brother-in-law and sister, and one for my son

to take back with him because he's in the army, and buns for the children to take to school for lunch. My son's coming out of the army in the New Year so he's looking for a four-bedroom house. The idea is I would live with them.

We do get on great together: I enjoy their company. But I'm one of these people who don't like change. That's why it's took me a while to get used to the new factory, I think, and I'm worried about putting the house on the market. I've been living there for thirty-seven years. It's a long time. Still, it's really too big for me on my own, and an enormous garden. It's an awful lot to cope with when you're working full-time. And there's a lot of things I'd like to do, and I might get round to them if I move.

CAV is a good place to work. They look after you well. If you come here and you don't get on with the job you're doing, they'll put you on another. You don't have to sit and do something you don't like doing. Things are different now to what they used to be. If you've got any worries or anything there's always someone you can talk to. Most people who come here stay. It's just the odd one or two, usually younger people, who leave. They want a posh job. They don't want jobs working on machinery. But, I mean, everybody can't do well-paid jobs; somebody's got to do all the others, haven't they?

# Frank Nice
Blacksmith, born 1927, Gestingthorpe, Essex.

*'There's no substitute really for forge-made work.'*

I've just lived here, in the house I was born in, all the time. I'm not married. Rhona, my sister-in-law who lives next door, looks after me, so I'm lucky. I have my breakfast and my supper in here but I go in there and have my tea, and my dinner.

My father was a blacksmith and a farrier, and my grandfather was a blacksmith and a farrier, and I think my great grandfather was too, and they all done it here. That was all farm work of course, in that day. Shoeing horses, repairing harrows and binders, putting handles on forks. After the war, in the Fifties, the tractors came in and the horses went out and the work that my father knew began to decline.

My father struggled a lot of the time; people owed him money and wouldn't pay. You get the odd bad payer now, but... there was a lot of them about in his day, I'm afraid. He didn't have much money - well, he earned it, but he didn't get it.

When I first went to work, I went down to the old Whitlock engineering firm. I worked in a forge down there for some time, and then I went on to other things, like welding, repair work, fitting, and jig-and-pull making. But though I was doing that during the day, I was always doing a bit here at night.

Then I was called up when I was eighteen, and went in the Air Force for about three years. I went to Egypt, then to India, and then to Singapore and then Malaya. That was somewhere where I wouldn't have gone otherwise, isn't it. I left just about the right time because afterwards it got a bit nasty.

I went back to the old firm again, when I come out of the RAF until I was made redundant. Then I worked here full-time. I was doing farm repair work. But as time went on, the farmers, they either bought a new part or repaired their own machines. And the wrought iron work, I was doing that more and more, and the other work I didn't do hardly any really, just a little bit now and again. There's two farmers in the village that I do work for, but that's about all now.

I was always interested in ornamental ironwork. I don't mean the cold bent stuff. That doesn't mean anything to me at all; it's just bent bits of iron. Hand-made ornamental ironwork, the forge work, is what I like doing. It's much more interesting than a lot of the other work that I used to do. I don't advertise at all, but I'm still busy.

When I go over to Cambridge, I always wander round where they've got these lovely gates. There's some wonderful work in Cambridge that the old smiths made. It's nice to see it. There's some good blacksmiths still scattered about the country, though. The British Artists Blacksmiths Association, I belong to that. They send a magazine out every quarter. There's some quite interesting stuff gets in there. Some of the smiths, they do more abstract type things. It's very nice and quite clever some of it. They're good smiths. But it doesn't do anything for me, I'm afraid, although it must do for some people, because they make it and sell it. But I like the traditional stuff really.

A lot of the stuff I do are one-off, so it's something you've got to work out every time, and perhaps even design, because people don't always know what they want. You have to give them a bit of a hand. I do scale drawings and show them, and go from there.

Some things I do I develop my own way of making. That cage handle I showed you, I probably make that different to another smith, although the result is often the same. The chain handle? That's a newer sort of thing. I can't remember where I first saw it. It's not as difficult as it looks. But it's different, and people like different things, I think.

If you make cold work, it's got to be very light and flimsy, because without heat, you can't make a heavy scroll, and you can't form different ends; you've just to cut off straight. Often at the end of the scroll, it should be a continuous curve but it's not. Where they put their jig it's flat on the end. Those scrolls are not like the ones I make. They're not shaped on the end. You can get very complicated ends and ordinary ends. But even an ordinary straightforward end should be tapered and thinned down. It makes it look much better.

There's no substitute really for forge-made work, if it's done properly, no substitute at all. I know it takes longer, and it costs more money, but it's much better to look at. It depends what people want, I suppose. The trouble is a lot of people don't know the difference, that's the rather sad part about it. Not until you've got the two together; then you know. I talked to a lady some little time ago who didn't know anything about ornamental ironwork. Now she tells me that everywhere she goes she looks at the gate and says, 'that's not a proper one, and that one is'. She's got the idea now and she weighs them all up!

I enjoy making decorative stuff, especially if I haven't made it before. And if, when I've done it, the people like it, that's also enjoyable. It took me about three or four months to make one pair of gates. There's a lot of work in them, and you began to wonder if you was going to see the end of it. But when I got them done, I was glad I did them. They went quite well in the end.

If I'm here, I'm usually working in the workshop. I'll go out on a Sunday afternoon maybe, to a book fair. I've got lots of books on ironwork, which are nice to look at, about how they used to do it years ago. But most of the better quality books are out of print. You've got a job to find them.

The shop hasn't changed very much. It's more or less like it was when my father was there. I've got an electric welder that he didn't have, and I've got a power hacksaw. But everything else was there when he was there. I'm using some of the tools he used. In the roof of the shop there's a beam drill, which they used to use to drill holes with. I've never ever seen it used. I could show you that before you go. There's not many of them about, I wouldn't

think. We had the shop done up a bit, because the roof leaked and it was in a right old muddle. The builder wanted to put a window in so that we would have lost the beam drill. But we didn't have that...we kept it there and had a different window. I'm glad we kept it because that's part of the character of the place.

Oh I have other interests. I used to do a bit of photography. The Camera Club used to meet at Gainsborough's House. I don't do as much as I used to, but I've got my little darkroom out there. And then, as I say, I go to book fairs. And I started making a model traction engine. It's a lot of work, isn't it, making a traction engine.

Then I go and have a bit of folk dancing sometimes, at Bulmer. I used to go ballroom dancing at Ipswich; I used

to do a lot at one time, ballroom dancing. Had some wonderful times over at Ipswich. I used to go over every Saturday night, and sometimes on a Tuesday. It's a fair little way from here, Ipswich, but it's nice when you get there. And I used to go down and watch the ballroom dancing competitions at Clacton. I didn't go in for any

thing like that. I just used to go and enjoy it, you know.

I used to play cricket as well down at the village. I'm a member of the Parish Council and have been for some years now. I don't like to see all this building going on in the countryside, ruining our villages. That's one thing I don't like. But there's not much you can do about it, unfortunately. I like to see the footpaths remain and not close down. I've lived in the country all my life you see, so I'm a real country person.

I occasionally go to Colchester or Ipswich, but I do my shopping in Sudbury. I go up to the market on the Thursday. I like looking there. So Sudbury really is my town,

although I'm in Essex and Sudbury is in Suffolk.

A dangerous job? No, I think the worse thing I've had is the odd burn now and again. Sparks fall on your hand, or you pick up the wrong end of a bit of iron.

I don't know what will happen to the shop when I don't use it any more. Still there's not much that I can do about that. I've got no family or anybody interested in it. One nephew is in engineering, but not blacksmith's work. The other one is into horticulture. So, I don't think they will take it up. It'd be a shame, wouldn't it, but it will probably turn into a little antique shop or something. They quite often do, don't they.

# Chapter Four

## SERVICE WITH A SMILE

I f it seemed appropriate to start with people working in the manufacturing sector, it seems equally appropriate to look next at some people working in retail, though it is impossible to represent the variety of retailing which goes on in any even moderately sized town today, from the great barns selling household goods, the supermarkets supplying groceries, the different chain stores offering clothing, shoes, stationery and books, car and bicycle parts, chemists' supplies, to the last of the old departmental stores; while the abundance of new little shops sell almost everything you can think of.

There was no way of surveying people involved in such a variety of retailing, and this chapter limits itself to looking at just three people running small businesses.

Like many grocers, the Kisbys' way of life has been radically affected by the advent of the brilliant new marketing techniques which gave rise to the supermarket. Many small businesses working with limited capital could not compete with these new sales methods and have literally shut shop over the last twenty years. **Maggie and Derek Kisby**, however, have pooled their initiative, imagination and energy to revitalise their family grocery business. The achievement has brought them pleasure and the photo of Derek Kisby surveying the world from the doorway of the shop captures a quiet complaisance. At the same time the continuing hard work involved has left the Kisbys ambivalent about the idea of their children taking over from them.

**Michael Hills** has a watchmaker's and jeweller's business. He is also the town's Archivist and a man with an exceptionally strong attachment to the place of his birth. The shop has been in his family for generations and he lovingly cherishes a collection of memorabilia from the past, including a pile of old ledgers listing all the shop sales and repairs, and a family bible literally salvaged from a neighbour's dustbin. His vivid sense of family makes it seem appropriate to include, as part of his sense of himself, a reproduction of an early daguerrotype depicting some of his forebears. But Michael Hills is not a backward looking conservative. He notes without acrimony - indeed, with some admiration - the advances in technology which have ensured that he will be the last member of his family to run the shop. Yet not everything will disappear. In his sons' jobs one senses a continuation of their father's interests. One son displays his interest in the mechanical, though on a larger scale, maintaining the engines of Boeing aircraft; the other works at Sotheby's and is interested in memorabilia and the past.

What strikes one immediately about **Rafi Fernandez** is how tiny she is. Not simply in terms of height. She has a delicate bone structure very different from a European one. The other thing one feels, without knowing anything of her story, is a sense of competence and energy. She seems a far cry from the classic stereotype of the shy Asian flower, obediently submitting to the dictates of her family. In fact Rafi Fernandez' story reveals an intrepid adventurer. Fortunately, she possesses an intelligence to match her boldness and has established a place for herself in the community with a small business which appeals cleverly to the English fascination with the exotic. For her portrait we selected a picture of her sampling her cooking. By freezing a moment of obvious movement, we are made conscious of time arrested and of there being action to follow. Indirectly this helps to suggest something of her sprightliness and energy.

# Maggie Kisby

Family Grocer, born 1949, Sudbury.

# Derek Kisby

Family Grocer, born 1946, Sudbury.

*'All the time you've got to be trying to find the gaps'.*

DEREK: I never intended going in the shop when I left school. I wanted to go in the Merchant Navy and see the world. But somebody had left and they were in a bit of a muddle, and Dad said, 'Can you help us out?' I've been there ever since! Still temporary! I'm still going to leave and join the Merchant Navy!

I drifted into it: two months became three months, became six months, became a year... But I've been lucky, I've travelled quite a bit, which is what I've always liked to do. I've been to Italy several times and Malta. Then I've been lucky enough to go to South Africa three times. I did a wilderness trail there walking with a game ranger, and we camped out. We got chased by rhinos - seven of them. We climbed up this thorn tree just in time. I can remember looking down. You could touch them, they were that close. I was so frightened! But I always think the game ranger knew they were there and it would be a tale to tell when we got home, because he stood his ground and just side-stepped them like a matador.

MAGGIE: Your dad was very good; he always pushed us to go on holidays, 'Go on boy, you go off.' I think he knew the shop was going to be more of a tie for Derek and me than it was for him, because in his day he had several full-time men.

DEREK: Seven. It was a traditional grocery shop. There were two men, a warehouseman, two if not three ladies, and a clerk for the book-work, because in those days there were a lot of monthly accounts. They had this big ledger, and there was a Day Book, so everything that people bought went into the Day Book, and then it was transferred into the ledger, and at the end of the month it was made up into monthly accounts. But it was also harder than now in that they had to weigh everything up. Sugar was weighed up, tea was weighed up.

We've actually got a machine - I think it has 1914 on it - for taking the stones out of raisins. It's got a sort of funnel on the top where they put the raisins. And they used to turn this handle, and there was a thing which used to push the stones out. In theory the raisins shot out one side and the stones the other.

We still roast some coffee, but when I first left school it was all done by hand in a room out the back. There was this huge drum and you had to sit there, turning the wheel. You get a terrific lot of smoke from coffee, and there was no extractor fan, not even a chimney. And when you were doing the continental one, the really black one, the smoke used to build up and get lower and lower. You could just about manage to do it before it choked you to death. I can remember, on my hands and knees, sort of gasping out the door for air. Eventually I said to Dad, 'I'm not going to do that any more. You can either get a machine to do it or...well I'm not going to do it any more!' And so we bought this second-hand coffee roaster.

A person couldn't start up a shop like ours now, and we wouldn't be here now if we didn't own the property. If you look in Sudbury, the family-owned businesses are all freehold properties.

MAGGIE: I think it's very difficult now for a small independent business to come in and rent premises. Mind you, it's more difficult for us now. All the time you've got to be trying to find the gaps. You think, well, we'll concentrate on the personal side and the specialist side. Now the latest supermarket is trying to offer this personal service. And they get more specialised. They never seem to want to let you have anything!

DEREK: So we're always on the lookout for new things we think we can sell. We'll spend two days up in London next month, at the International Food Exhibition. You can't stand still in the shop. People say to you, 'Do you hope your son comes in the shop?' I wouldn't like to see the business go, but I don't know if I'd wish it on him. There must be easier ways of making a living. Not that I worry about working hard, and I'm sure he wouldn't, but...

MAGGIE: You wonder where it's all going to end though, don't you, with the business. You can never sit back. With your Dad...the shop always closed at one o'clock, and he had lunch, whereas we might get a five minute break. I started doing the hampers in his time, and I'd be down there perhaps in the evenings working, and he'd come downstairs and say, 'That's enough, go home to your bed!' Now I've come home two o'clock in the morning. I work till I've finished what I've got to do.

DEREK: The supermarkets started the change in what we stocked. Also, the shop was quite small until about eight years ago?

MAGGIE: The cellar was in the middle of the shop, so the area where the customers came in, at busy times, just wasn't big enough. Some of the regulars would wander out to the warehouse and get their own cereal, or jam.

They knew where it was kept.

DEREK: There was no real refrigeration.

MAGGIE: And you wanted a serve-over cheese counter. We'd been to look at one, and the big question was: where do we put it? We went home that night and we stood in the shop, didn't we...

DEREK: We mulled over it for ages.

MAGGIE: And I said, 'It's this damned cellar that's the bugbear.' We decided to close it over and open up the back of the shop for the new counter. The builders shifted stuff up to the front end of the shop, so that we could carry the business on. Dust crept through everything!

DEREK: Even though they put double dust sheets up. One of our customers came in and dusted, she felt so sorry for us!

MAGGIE: It was Dr. McLauchan's wife. She came in with a duster and her rubber gloves, and she went round the shelves.

DEREK: We were very conscious of keeping the old image. You've seen that long teak counter we've got with glass shelves. In some ways it would be nice to take that out and have a long cold counter there. But that would spoil the shop.

MAGGIE: I'd always wanted to do the brasswork up on the shop front. Years ago I said, 'Oh, why don't you uncover that?' But you and your dad said, 'Who's going to polish the bugger then?' I've got my way on that now and we've had it lacquered.

I used to have an awful lot of people saying, 'I don't like to go in...' So we always have the doors open now, even in cold weather. People come in and say, 'Oh, do you want the door open?' We say, 'Oh, we never have that shut.'

DEREK: We've got a lot of regulars, but we get strangers, a terrific number of tourists and foreigners. And we're getting a lot of young people coming in, and people from the surrounding villages. Because now we've opened the shop up people can browse.

MAGGIE: There's still certain regulars, though, that only Derek serves - certain ladies - and there's this banter that goes on. You might have a stranger in and you see them stand there and they're quite amused.

DEREK: We still do a few orders, but not many. It's just a throw-back from people who have been customers for years and years and you don't like to let them down.

MAGGIE: Peggy Scrivener now. She never leaves her house. Derek's been going to her for years, and I think if he said, 'I'm not delivering to you', I think it would have a bad effect on her really.

DEREK: Yes, and I wouldn't not deliver.

MAGGIE: At Christmas time she'll want to do some presents and she'll say, 'Can you bring me some things over?' Derek has to take a big box with a selection of what we do.

DEREK: I leave it there, then pick it up the next day.

I'm lucky that I've got Maggie. We wouldn't be where we are now if I hadn't married Maggie.

MAGGIE: Well it's very much a team effort really. People ask me what it's like working for your husband. On the whole we get on well.

DEREK: As long as I do what I'm told, I'm all right.

MAGGIE: I'm irritating! If I'm in the shop too long I start saying, 'Why isn't this done, and why isn't that done?' you see. They send me out the back.

DEREK: Yes, she can be irritating. But what woman can't!

MAGGIE: I do all the book-keeping.

DEREK: Thank goodness!

But I think Maggie worries about things more than I do; I say, well it's only money... I get uptight at Christmas though. People wish you a happy Christmas and you think, if anybody else says that I'll tell them where to stick it. It's trying to keep up with the ordering and you're busy in the shop. You've got all your regular lines you've got to stock, plus all the extra Christmas ones you've got to show as well, because they won't sell in a box out the back; you've got to stick them under people's noses, and there's a shop full, and you see a lorry turn up: 'I've got fifty cases for you'. You put them in the side passage, and you've got to come back at night, check them off, and mark them up, and get them on the shelf. It's quite a headache to keep up with.

Then I collect our Stilton from a farm about eight miles north of Melton Mowbray. I do it all year but always at Christmas. They're the last independent Stilton maker in the country. People say, 'Oh, your Stilton's really good'.

MAGGIE: That's because you go and pick it up! He always goes the last Wednesday in November. I like being in the shop at Christmas. It's a lovely feeling... and always to me, it's Christmas when the Stilton arrives. It comes in and goes down the cellar. Then there's always that little anxious moment...

DEREK: Are they going to be OK? The secret is getting them to peak just at the Christmas period, you see. You don't want them too ripe when you get them. The worst thing you can do, though, is gouge a Stilton out and put port in the middle. Everybody thinks that's the thing to do. Have a glass of port with it, yes. But I mean you've got a beautiful Stilton cheese, you don't want to dig it and put port in it, do you?

But Christmas is a long hard slog. Finally the last customer goes. Father always used to have this little ceremony. He'd put the shutters up and say, 'Right, that's it for another Christmas.' Stick his two fingers up and say, 'Bff everybody!'

MAGGIE: Now Derek does it. We all stand round while he does it! But you're a lot different to your dad in your relationship to your staff.

DEREK: He was more old school. It was always Mr. so-and-so, and they all called him Mr. Kisby. The girls all call me Derek. Most of the customers call me Derek. I can remember, when I first left school, there used to be a Group Captain Green, and he was very much a Group Captain. He always used to call everybody by their surname. With Dad it was always 'Kisby'. And he'd always call me 'boy'. I'd left school and it used to really annoy me. 'Morning Kisby, morning boy!' And I used to say 'Good morning Mr. Green' you see. And Dad said, 'You can't call him Mr. Green, you've got to call him Group Captain'. I said, 'If he calls me boy I shall call him Mr. Green!'! And so I always did.

We still don't open Saturday afternoons. It started as an experiment in the summer, which got extended to the winter because I started to play hockey.

MAGGIE: October to December we open Saturday afternoons. That's worth doing. But we've got a young family and it's more important I think we have that time with them, going off down the coast with your children..you don't get that time back, do you?..

DEREK: My father was very friendly with Michael Hill's father. They went to Rotary and what's the other? Round Table, that's it. But I was never interested. My greatest love has been hockey, I still play for the Veterans' Eleven, so I've been playing hockey; for Sudbury for twenty-eight years now!

MAGGIE: Well, it's important he has time off outside the shop. I joined the Dramatic Society when I worked for Edward and Michael Hill. There was a play coming up... it was *The Crucible*, Arthur Miller, you know, and they wanted a young girl in the bed that was bewitched. And I went along for the reading and got involved.

DEREK: I do some lighting for the plays. I can always remember one of the pantomimes I did. I was doing the spotlight, and there were three girls doing a belly dance. One I really fancied, one I half fancied, and one I didn't fancy at all. Well I never did go out with the one I did fancy, I went out with the one I half fancied, and I've finished up marrying the one I didn't fancy at all!

MAGGIE: I was the skinny one!

DEREK: Yes, that's right. Yes, I remember you had to do a sort of belly dance. She was a bean pole! Fattened her up a bit!

MAGGIE: When I first started going out with you, you always used to smell of cheese.

DEREK: Did I? Well you've got used to it now!

MAGGIE: I'd met Derek in the January at the Mayor's Ball. But prior to this, every time I walked down each night, Derek would be out the front, sweeping the pavement. Old Dingwall who worked in the shop said, 'We couldn't make out why he'd suddenly taken to sweeping the pavement at 5.30! Never happened before!'

DEREK: But going back to the shop. There's always something to do. You could be there twenty-four hours a day. Every Sunday morning this time of the year I go down. Weekdays I'm always down by seven. Then most Monday nights I go to a wholesaler either to Ipswich or Bury, depending on which is more pressing. I'll have been in the shop since seven when I get everything down and perhaps have a cup of tea with Mother upstairs for quarter-of-an-hour. Anyway, I'm in the shop all day. Then come half-past five, it's into the car and straight over to Ipswich. Usually it's nine o'clock before I get home, because you've got to unload when you get back. Maggie's dad quite often comes, which is a help, but you're pretty shattered. You don't feel like doing anything when you get home. But tell her about that funny dream.

MAGGIE: It was after we'd altered the shop, and I woke up the next morning and I said, 'I had a most peculiar dream last night. I dreamt I was down in the shop working late' - which I often do, go down at night, - and in this dream I was working on the window. And I turned, and at the back of the shop stood old E W King. It was so vivid! And I was aghast to see him. Then he said, 'I've just come to see what you're doing'. And it was as if he put the seal of approval on it.

# Michael Hills
Watchmaker, born 1933, Sudbury.

*'I can visualise that alarm clock now.'*

We came to the shop when my grandfather died, in 1938. So I was five years old. I had a little single bed in what is now my workroom. In the other corner my brother had a cot.

I remember going to the shop before we lived there. I must have been four, sitting up at the table and being told to make sure I behaved correctly. And my short, stout grandfather coming in and carving the meat. He was very fond of the condiments, and thrived on hot peppers and sauces and chillies. He was also a snuff-taker. And I can remember him being rather a naughty grandpa, sitting me on his lap and saying, 'Have a pinch of snuff boy', much to my mother's disgust.

Then the war arrived. Daddy put the old Standard car into the garage behind the shop, up on brick blocks, and had a store of petrol ready in case we had to escape. But the car wasn't used right through the war and my brother and I used to play in it and pretend we were driving to exotic places.

Although we were never blitzed, the town was right on the route for the German planes and we almost got used to the moaning of German aircraft, and seeing them high in the sky. At the beginning of the war, mostly in panic, the air-raid siren went at the slightest opportunity. We had a maid and I can remember her taking me to school, and almost getting to the school when the air-raid siren sounded, and the maid, who I suppose was about seventeen, panicked, and we ran top speed all the way back to the shop rather than take shelter in the school.

Because of the danger of bombing, Father unearthed from the cellar all the sorts of things that families have in cellars, including many of our ancient record books which were in the coal hole. And the cellar was converted into an air-raid shelter.

We also knocked a hole through into the cellar next door as an escape route. And in there lived at night a very old lady who looked rather like a witch, the mother of the next-door tobacconist; and I can remember looking through and seeing her in her cellar, which hadn't been converted as my father had done ours, sitting in the darkness with one candle.

We were not regularly bombed by any means. I think most of the bombs that fell were those dropped to get rid of them on the return journey, although late in the war we did have a danger of doodle-bug attacks.

We had become more bold by that stage of the war, and we slept in the room which is now the office on the first floor. If we heard a doodle-bug coming, Father would wake us up and we all ran down two flights of stairs to the cellar. I can vividly remember waking one night and seeing the doodle-bug coming, and hearing the engine stop before we got to the cellar, and then an almighty thump over the meadow somewhere.

The Americans arrived early on. 1942? Waldingfield Aerodrome is very close. The excitement of these foreign men coming! And jeeps and chewing gum. The town was a lively place because of it. But we had danger then of Liberators and Flying Fortresses, sometimes not taking off very well and crashing, or returning and failing to reach the aerodrome. But it was really exciting for us as children; we hardly recognized the danger.

I progressed from North Street school to the grammar school, and met the history master. It was a terribly dry and boring subject, but I knew I had a great sense of history. It's a wonderful thing to have. I feel that I've lived back, certainly into the nineteenth century, into the history of my family. Now I don't go to the shop in the evenings. Our insurers prefer me not to, for security reasons. But I often used to go up to the workshop in the evenings to pursue my work, which is also my hobby, and there, alone in the evenings, I felt a presence of my ancestors.

The business was founded in 1818. That's the date that has always been painted on to the front of the shop. My great-great-grandfather, Benjamin, acquired it in 1830 and bought his first vellum-bound cash book, till book and ledger, and got going.

My father was a lovely father, but he didn't have the sort of appreciation of history that I have. He wasn't anti-history, but he didn't have a particular sense of history. In fact the old Daguerrotype photographs had been on the wall for donkey's years, and I can remember asking him who they were, and he didn't know. 'Just an old family photograph', he said, 'filthy dirty, don't get it down boy, you'll make your fingers dirty.'

But he knew that I loved history. Now and again he would say, 'Oh, by the way, you'd better look after that', and give me some wonderful thing. For example, one day he said, 'You'd better look after that', and it was my great-great-grandfather Benjamin's apprenticeship certificate, the

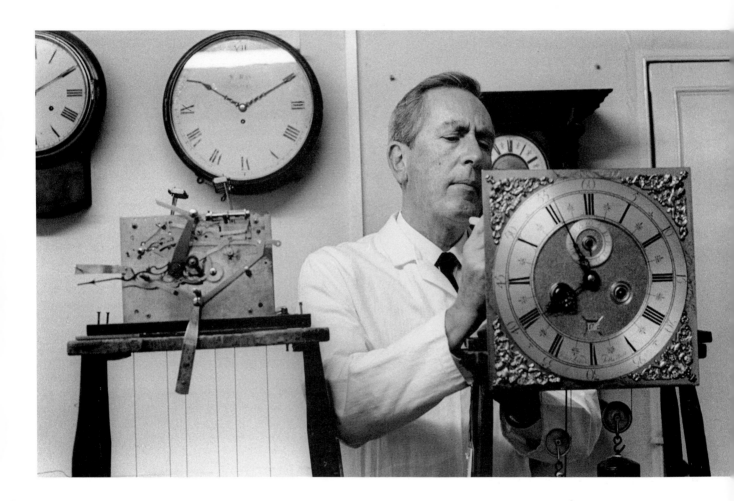

first person in my family to become a watchmaker. It starts in 1821 when he was fourteen years old, and he served a seven-year term until 1828.

Well school days and the war were coming to an end, and I suppose I was beginning to wonder what I was going to do for the rest of my life, without a thought that I would ever enter the business. I took School Certificate, but I wasn't very academic. I went to see my headmaster and he said, 'What are you going to do when you leave school, Hills, because I think it's about time you left? And I always recommend my boys, when I know they come from solid family backgrounds, to think very hard about joining their family business.' So, for the first time in my life I thought, 'Well, I wonder what the business is like?' I didn't think anything about the jewellery side or the dealing with customers. I made a bee-line for the workshop, which then was in some medieval building, which I loved, behind the shop. There were two rooms and a long old bench and the old workmen there. Whenever we had asked 'Can we go and watch in the workshop?' Father had always said 'No, you'll get in the way.' He didn't encourage us to go into the business, either my brother or me. In fact I could say that he discouraged us.

*Christmas display 1920s*

So I went into the workshop and asked if I could take an alarm clock to pieces. I can visualize that alarm clock now. With some assistance I got it together again and wound it up. And it ticked! It was amazing! And I realized that this was going to be rather an exciting thing to do. So my father said that if I wanted to be a watchmaker I couldn't just leave school and go to work for him, I would have to go and study properly.

And that was a great bombshell, because I loved my home and family, and the thought of leaving, although I was coming up for seventeen, was rather horrendous. Where would I go in London? Where would I live? And how would I manage? But I set off on the train in September 1950, took digs in north London, and took the trolley bus into Clerkenwell for eight pence every morning to the National College of Horology and Instrument Technology, housed in the Northampton Polytechnic. And my goodness, it was lovely when Friday came and I could get on the train and come back. Because...I didn't enjoy the experience.

I soon made friends. I've never had difficulty in making friends. But the standard of education was quite high, and I found it difficult to begin with, and I had to realize I'd got to work really hard. I didn't much enjoy the smell and the hurry and rush of London, so it was a joy to get on the little train at Marks Tey. It was a wonderful little train, just with four wheels and a very tall funnel. And Friday night, the 4.57 from Liverpool Street platform nine was the one! To catch it, I had to leave college a quarter of an hour early. If ever I have a nightmare it's usually about missing the train during my first or second year, because it meant I couldn't get home until seven o'clock.

Ultimately I enjoyed college. The study was very wide-ranging. The purpose, strictly speaking, was to encourage students to go into instrument manufacturing, the Government having found that during the war there were hardly any people capable of fine instrumentation for submarines, aeroplanes and ships. But of course I wasn't interested in going into a factory. I knew from day one that when I had completed my five years I should come back into the family business.

The idea was that we went from a post-graduate training course into industry, such as Smiths, the big watch and clock manufacturers, or one of the various other firms. Most of the students went into such places. I searched round and discovered that the Royal watchmakers, Charles Frodsham & Co. in Brompton Road were willing to take a student. I went along hoping against hope that I might be asked to go. And I was. And I spent two

*Benjamin Hills and family, 1852*

wonderful years seeing some of the finest clocks and watches that there are ever to be seen. Not that I was allowed to work on them. But we also manufactured little reproduction clocks in very small quantities. It was all hand work, down in the basement of that shop. We also did some secret government work, making special camera equipment, prototype work which was quite interesting. And then that was five years completed.

I will hopefully get through my working life as one of the last of the small family businesses. I think there is considerable danger in being ambitious. Those who fly high have the furthest to fall. I like to tread an even, carefree path. I don't like worry, and I think probably, to be truthful, I avoid it. I plod along so I can always sleep easy. And I do.

Well, I tried to recall the excitement I felt the very first time I wound up a clock which hadn't been going, and found that I had made it spring to life. That experience is enhanced with every watch or clock that I make to go. I talk more about watches because watchmaking is a progression of clockmaking, and although every apprentice starts with clocks, if he has the ability and the feeling, and develops sufficient lightness of touch and accuracy, then

it's a natural progression to move on to watches.

I love to take to pieces old watches, some of which I know the history of, because the little numbers scratched inside refer to our books and I know who it belonged to. And also from previous numbers I can tell whether my great-grandfather had repaired it at some time, or my grandfather, or other workmen.

Very few people ever see inside the mechanism of a watch. And in old watches, the watchmakers went to considerable pains to beautify them. It was lovely workmanship. Many little works of art are revealed inside a watch which nobody other than another watchmaker would ever expect to see. Certainly not the owner of the watch, unless he was rash enough to take it to pieces himself. I think they just loved creating a piece of artistry out of metal. I love to do it. I always try, if I am restoring an old watch and there is a piece broken, to make the piece identical. There's no need to make it identical, to make it look pretty, but it's a lovely thing to be able to do. Nothing gives me more satisfaction. I suppose every artist or artisan, having developed the skill, reaps the enjoyment of being able to practice that skill.

And so having taken this old watch to pieces, and seeing things which probably nobody else will ever see, and putting a watch together which my great-grandfather perhaps put together the last time, and wondering if I shall ever take it to pieces again in my lifetime, or whether anyone else will ever take it to pieces, comes the moment I apply the key, or the winding knob, and wind up the mainspring, and it springs into life. Now, that watch or clock has been dead. Only I, I fondly think, can bring it life again! And especially if I've had to make a part for it.

Of course I have to say I'm talking about antique watches, because since the war the mass production techniques and interchangeability of watches is absolutely marvellous. We can order specific parts for specific watches, and when they come they will just drop in, made to a hundredth of a millimetre.

But most of my working life has been in working on mechanical watches. The mechanical watch reached perfection. There was really nothing to do other than to apply fiddly gimmicks to it. Then the era of the quartz watch came in and revolutionised timekeeping at a stroke because it is accurate beyond belief. Very few people can possibly need that perfection. In fact, I notice that people don't bother to set their watches to the second. So here we've got this tiny miracle of engineering, being applied cheaply, on everybody's wrist, but we don't need time to that accuracy.

My watch is right to the second. Yes, it's a quartz watch.

People say, 'Why don't you wear an old one?' But when I put a battery into someone's watch I always set it right to the second. You might imagine that I would be obsessed by time! But I'm not, because I realize that time is man-made. If we didn't have clocks or watches we would scarcely bother; we would see the sun come up in the morning. I often think it must have been lovely when you didn't have to make sure you were out of the house at a certain hour in the morning, and to clock on at work at a certain time and to stop at a certain time. I don't think I do watch the clock. And time doesn't worry me; nor does the passage of time. I think my own philosophy is that it's important not to consider the passage of time too seriously, because you cannot stop, or reverse, or do any-thing about it.

I love Sudbury, and I love the Suffolk countryside. These are my roots. I go away on holiday, yes, but I return with more pleasure. I go in search of history! We had one holiday in Crete which was very enjoyable, but I was completely out of my depth. That is another civilisation and I couldn't accommodate that in my mind. I saw it, I marvelled at it, but I couldn't get it into context of what I recognise as history. Julian, our son, went to Egypt and thought it was absolutely marvellous. I don't think I have a great yearning to go to Egypt, because it's not my civilisation, and I feel out of my depth, I can't relate another civilisation to our own.

When I was a young boy, most of the shops in Sudbury were family businesses, and the families lived at the shop; you didn't have to go to work, and it was a completely different world. I think the twenty-first century is the end of family businesses. I'm just at the very end. It's sad. But oh, I'm sure I would rather Jonathan and Julian, our sons, do what they want to do in life. They've both got good jobs, and I'm happy for them. Julian works at Stanstead doing overhauls on the large Boeings for an independent company. Jonathon works in London at Sotheby's.

# Rafi Fernandez

Spice Shopkeeper and Cook, born 1944, Hyderabad, India.

*'The English are very reserved and everything is formal.'*

How to start? I arrived December 1965, snowing, no coat, three pounds in my pocket, because that was the allowance. No job. No accommodation. Nothing. I just made getting into the UK in the secretarial batch before they started reducing the professions that could enter. Now, as you know, you have to be in the top professions to come.

I came to the UK so I could marry a Malaysian Catholic. I was an Indian Muslim, and it would have been very difficult to get married in India, because of our different religions, and because he was a foreigner. Mum accepted it. So did Dad. But when you live in an extended family, it's not just Mum and Dad that matter.

I had to depend on friends in the UK, bedding in one room, then transferring to another, not to be obliged to everybody too much. I had to take whatever job came by so I worked in a betting office. I knew nothing about betting. After a couple of years I stumbled into a travel agency job, which was fantastic. Then in 1970 I realised I was expecting my first son. I wasn't sure if I could cope with a job plus a baby, because I had no family here. The year previous, however, my father-in-law died, and left us severe debts, plus responsibility for the five of his ten children who were still at school. We couldn't any more go into even a fish and chip takeaway. The family grew very fast too, because we brought those five children over here, one by one. This meant I knew that if I did stop work it would have to be for a very short time. It also became necessary that I learn to cook so I used a book.

Anyway I resigned, had my baby, and after three months went back to work. Then I got the job at Air India, which was absolutely brilliant. I became their public relations officer. That's where I gained all my knowledge of the East. But having done that for nearly ten years, and had a second son, I really couldn't take London any more. My sons were being neglected. So I moved into the cottage down here.

Then, I started wondering how I could keep myself occupied after the hectic pace I had led, and on an off-chance I asked my local pub, the Eight Bells, if they would consider a once-a-month event, 'West Meets East Through Food'. So I made cooking into a profession purely to keep myself busy when I resigned from London. It was a nice way of meeting new people once a month. I wanted to be a participant in the community, and this was my way of doing it.

I did all the cooking at home, carried it to the pub and served a banquet. I did Malaysian, Chinese, Indian, Thai, Indonesian food. And for about ten minutes I would talk about the country from where the cuisine came, to make people see the connection between the food and the country. It became so popular I needed a larger venue.

I found another pub and ended up cooking for a hundred. I am still doing all the cooking at home, carrying it in with my own little gas cookers plus my hot plates, and then carrying back the dirty dishes of the hundred people, in big laundry baskets, to wash up the next day. One night this car was following me all the way, and I was wondering why he is not overtaking me, because this was three o'clock in the morning. He was only my local PC Smith, wasn't he, wondering if I'd had a few too many! I had all this crockery, you see, rolling about.

One table used to book for the next month on the day they ate. I knew their names, but I didn't know they were from a publishing house, Faber & Faber, until the lady approached me and said, 'We've had about eleven meals here. Why don't you write a book about the menus?' I wasn't sure if I could write. 'Still,' she said, 'put forward a proposal'. And I put it forward exactly the way I'm speaking at the moment. And they loved it. So my first book came out. Then I got the vegetarian one, and before I finished that Sainsbury's approached me for the third. Now I'm doing 'The Little Classical Cookbook of India'. And that's the story of the books.

By now I was also teaching evening classes, taking my pupils from basics right up to a banquet. They didn't need to learn the recipes, they needed to learn the techniques, just like I needed to master English equipment, to combine with my cuisine. So I went to Robert Carrier. It was amazing how much I didn't know, like about food processors and oven timings.

Then I developed the idea of the shop, and insisted with the bank manager that it should be Sudbury, because I may look a foreigner here, but to me this is my home. When he said, 'But Sudbury is very small', I said, 'Don't worry, I'll make it work'. Initially it was only a shop though I sold my own frozen dishes. Now I call it my little theatre. Once

a month it becomes a school, and once a month it becomes a restaurant. But the restaurant is not like normal restaurants where you sit quietly at your table, the waiter bringing your food and that's it. My guests become friends, and by the time the evening is over, everyone's got new subjects they've found out about. Plus again I tell them about the menu. We have no facilities in the back, so I am still cooking at home, and take everything back home.

My to-be husband has now expanded our family kitchen because cooking in it had become impossible. We are sometimes doing seven, eight curries, and I'm talking about fifty pounds of meat in each pan. Though he is in building, I find Dan has patience with my cooking. I give him a job to do, and he will master it, like cutting up vegetables in quantities of twenty-five kilos. And he won't mind being told. Likewise, when I am helping him on the building I'm the same; I'm a good pupil you know!

I didn't cook in India. I was a pampered child from a fairly rich family. In fact I was spoilt. I used to demand of the chef, and if the food wasn't to my choice I could get into tempers. Now that I'm doing it I appreciate what is involved.

Although I am cooking with all the mod cons here, I still use some of the lovely old-fashioned methods that survive in India. Each time I go back, the first morning the grinding stones wake me up. My mother lives in a flat so you can appreciate every floor's servants, sitting there grinding, so there's a lovely, musical rhythm from the stones that wakes me. Then there are the vendors. Even though you are starting to get supermarkets, a lot of housewives still prefer this old-fashioned method. My mother lives on a seventh floor and all she has to do is pass her basket through the window on a rope, and then pull it back up with her vegetables.

I do miss India, I miss it a lot. Through my teaching I'm hanging on to memories of it. India is a country with so much to give. If modern technology and education tells us that the old is wrong, it will be a great pity. To become modernised is one thing, but to lose your traditions is another, you know. One can combine the two very harmoniously. That is what I keep telling my audience. Don't cheat in your cooking. Jars and all are fine, but there is nothing like combining the ingredients. That's one of the reasons why my food is popular. It's home cooking so no two batches of curries in that freezer will be identical. I may have used a little more chillies, or a little less. That's housewife's cooking.

My final dream is to move to Devon. I'm quite happy to return to Sudbury every month to do the demonstration

*Mother & Father, 1948*

and check stock. But I went for the Easter break to Devon and saw a hotel: fourteen rooms with dining-room facilities. I could have my shop, my school, my restaurant, plus accommodation!

My mother has been here on holiday. She saw me first in London, grabbing the babies and their nappy bags, getting them to the nursery, then rushing off to work, and then back home again. Then she saw me the first winter we moved into Suffolk. We had the worst snow, and I had no experience of it so I hadn't prepared myself. I forgot to order the fuel, and nobody would come out. I used to have to go into the fields and just pick up wood to get the fire going to keep the children warm. I had never had to do any of these things in India. She was fascinated with the way I coped.

I remain Indian when I am in my four walls; I'll never change. My children, sadly, are very English. I have accepted this but my mother couldn't. But they have been raised with Indian etiquette, so when I take them to India they know how to behave in front of their grandmother which I don't see a lot of in the UK. My children can change back to UK style when they return here. When I go to India myself, I know that there are many times I am right and she is wrong, but out of respect I swallow my pride and say, 'OK mum', because I don't want to create any wars. She's only going to have me for six weeks, and then I won't see her again for five years maybe. I haven't seen her now since '88; it's a long time.

The only racialism I have noticed was in the late Sixties, when we needed accommodation. Then people could say openly to your face, 'Sorry, no coloureds.' The flat I was living in, the landlady said, 'Rafi, no children,' and unfortunately, I didn't know I was pregnant already. When it dawned on me I went to her and I said, 'I'm very sorry Sheila, but I'm pregnant. And I really didn't do it on purpose.' And she said, 'Don't worry Rafi, you must stay here . I can't let you go now.' She was an absolutely marvellous little Jewish person.

In London we've also got the odd tease in the street but not in the country. We ignore it. In London when you live amongst the Indians so much, if you carry a chip on your shoulder you notice racism more. I had a lot of English friends. But a lot of Indians stick to Indians, and that's where the mistake lies. If you can blend in, people then will come to learn that you also have etiquette and manners, and an education. When I first moved into Suffolk, they thought, 'Here comes India!' And nobody would talk to us. It was I who made all the approaches. Through that I did make friends. But it took them quite some time.

The English are so reserved and everything is formal. You are expected to arrive only if you have been invited, whereas in India houses are open houses. Nobody needs a paper invitation. You pop in when you want. I grew up with that lifestyle, but because I am here, I have to accept the lifestyle here. Sometimes you miss the other style; sometimes you are glad of the English one. Indian hospitality can be very imposing and you can't get out of it. Like if you come to my house, you may be stuffed with food, but I will insist you eat!

Indian hospitality can become too much at times. When my cousin's sister got married in India, for example, the first day we had seven hundred guests, all ladies, to bless the bride, and we did a simple dinner. The second day was four thousand guests, and a posh buffet, where we served cutely made sandwiches and things. The third day was the actual banquet. There we had two thousand people. All the cooking was done by the family, along with the servants, of course. We had twenty-one courses because it was a happy event, and twenty-one is a very respected number because we have twenty-one imams, or head priests. We would start always with a sweet - then eight or nine courses of fried things, cutlets, kebabs, soups. Then the

*Home in Secunderabad*

rice course with all the different curries. It doesn't matter in which order, but the total should be twenty-one.

The twenty-one dishes are often chosen to show how much money you have got. Both the jewellery the bride was given, and her trousseau, are put out on display; I don't like all that. I mean if I had to get married in India that's one thing I would definitely not do, put anything of mine on show. I used to tell my father, if I have to get married, just give me the money, don't go buying me all the things. Because in India it's very hard for the poor people. Each time the wife gets pregnant the man is desperately frightened. A daughter means another headache. And although dowries are supposed not to exist any more, the rich are maintaining the custom and so the poor are finding it difficult to break away from it. Anyway, that's India!

Those five in-laws I talked about bringing over to finish their education: two became solicitors , two became matrons, one became a manager for a travel agency. So I think I've done quite well! Now I must see what my children will do. My older son is travelling round the world at the moment with his girlfriend. Then he'll go to university. The younger starts A-levels after the summer. Having made my junior in-laws successful I hope I'll achieve the same with my two sons. They see me work so hard, so it's got to rub off a bit, even though they don't show signs of it! Especially the younger one. Oh Jesus, he's lazy.

And now I've got to go to London. I've three warehouses to visit to collect stock.

# Chapter Five

# SOME PROFESSIONAL SERVICES

A solicitor's clerk, an auctioneer and a journalist comprise the mixed bag of people in this chapter. They represent those well-established occupations now called white collar jobs. The most recent goes back to the eighteenth century. All continue to be found in every British town because they meet some fundamental needs of any modern urban community.

**Roly Oliver**, the auctioneer, also farmed a substantial acreage for many years and has been mayor of the town. A Sixties newspaper photograph shows him just on the right side of stout, standing confidently above the pig-pens in the auction yard. We photographed him on the same site, though the pens have now gone, in conversation with a buyer today. Though not full figure the angle of his head and shoulders suggest a less upright stance than in the past and the image is a gentler one. Yet there is no reason to suppose he has changed radically, so we see how ambiguous the clues we use for reading faces often are. Roly Oliver's own account of himself is valuable in helping us decipher his face.

Though included here by virtue of his job as a journalist **Alan Cocksedge** is as much a cricketer, and in fact we show him in his cricket gear taken on a summer afternoon when Sudbury was playing host to a team from Sheffield. By including a photo of an early cricket team alongside his portrait, we draw attention to the continuing tradition of cricket playing in the town to which Alan Cocksedge is deeply conscious of belonging. The juxtaposition, however, of the photographs gives the contemporary image a touch of the caricature. Alan Cocksedge's posture and expression suggest he is not unaware of how he might appear to someone who was not a cricket enthusiast.

Finally **Leonard Cadge.** At first sight his portrait must meet many people's expectations of what a solicitor's clerk might look like. In his story he recalls his own first visit as a boy to the office where he eventually worked, and remembers thinking what 'a miserable looking lot' they were. Yet though his own expression is not miserable, the way Nature has shaped Leonard Cadge encourages us to see him as solemn. Even seated you can sense that he is a tall man, and with the passage of time his long face has acquired vertical creases. Reading his story thus helps to enrich the image. For he comes across as an unassuming man, pursuing an extraordinarily long, working life in the employment of one firm. Remarkably, he has also suffered widowhood twice.

# Leonard Cadge

Solicitor's Clerk. Born 1906, Sudbury.

### 'No-one laughed much in a solicitor's office'

Fortunately I wasn't at school with girls. There was a high brick wall, so we couldn't have too much contact with the girls, and they went out by a separate gate. And I think that's how it should be today, and I think that's the cause of a lot of the trouble. I think we used to have more respect for them.

Later in my school time, I don't know what they'd think now, but our teacher had just come back from the Army; he was a sergeant and we used to go on parade in the playground, and form fours and dress, and turn left, turn right. We used to hand in our books, and then we used to march in step - we used to get in trouble if we were not in step - into the schoolroom.

The next thing of course there was half an hour or an hour of religious instruction, which used to consist mainly of bawling out all the psalms of the day. The subjects taught were reading, writing and arithmetic, history, geography. And the ex-sergeant he was the master of the local evening school. He was keen to get pupils for that, so at about ten we used to start Pitman's shorthand.

When I was eleven I used to go to this evening school to do Pitman's shorthand. Because my father was called up in the First War lots of his friends promised that they would keep me in order. So one way of keeping me in order was to go to the evening school. It kept me busy. And then as regards the weekends, I had three maiden aunts. We all attended at the Trinity Congregational Church. One aunt went to the morning service, or assisted at the morning Sunday School, and the other aunt assisted in the afternoon school. So on a Sunday I had to attend the morning school, the morning service, and the Sunday School in the afternoon you see. And I couldn't dodge any of it, because one or other of the aunts would be there and I should get in awful trouble if I didn't turn up. So they kept me busy and in order over the weekend.

When my time came for leaving school, I don't know how it was, but I was picked to go and see the firm of Bates, Wells & Braithwaite. I knew something about the office because Braithwaite was the correspondent of the school, and he'd give me notes to drop in at the office on my way home. I used to go in and think, 'Oh no, they look a

miserable lot in there, I should hate to work here!' And I finished up working there sixty-eight years!

And any rate, I went to see Mr. Braithwaite with my school books. He had a look at them. And he eventually said that yes, he would be prepared to take me on. And I could start I think it was next week. I had to sign a little agreement, saying that I would do my best, and that I would not speak to anybody about the business of the firm. And I had...I'm not sure whether it was five shillings or seven and six a week. And that was that.

Well I wasn't all that excited. As I said, I thought they were rather miserable. But of course that's how solicitors' offices were run you know. No-one laughed much in a solicitor's office because that wasn't intended to be a laughable thing; it was supposed to be very serious, and it was part of the trade to look serious.

You weren't exactly taught in the office. You were just told to get on. You had to keep your eyes open and hope for the best. My first duty in the morning I used to knock at the door next to the office. Braithwaite was a bachelor and he lived there with a housekeeper and one maid. I was scared of the housekeeper. She used to say, 'Wipe your shoes before you come in'. And I used to have to get up three buckets of coal for the three coal fires. I had to open a trap door, go into the cellar and get this coal. The fire was already laid by the caretaker, but I used to have to put the coal on and light the fires, which used to worry me sometimes, because they used to go out. I wasn't very expert at lighting a fire.

There was one book we had to keep. Every day the partners and the senior staff they used to write down on a sheet of paper everything they'd done the day before. Those sheets used to be given to me, and I used to have to copy it all in this Day Book, we called it the Day Book. I was only fourteen and I had an awful job to read their scribble. It was always behind, very often up to three months. We used to get in awful trouble, me and this other chap. We were both responsible for writing up the entries. It was a monotonous job. I used to take the book home and work on it at nights, because in the spring time, when the holidays were starting, we knew that if the book wasn't up to date we had no holiday, so we had to make a special effort. And sometimes we did get it more or less up to date.

There are all these mechanical aids now. In those days Wills...well, they didn't favour them being typed at that time for some reason, they all had to be done by hand. And it was a laborious job. The point is you couldn't erase. If

*c1916*

you made a little mistake you couldn't erase it, and you very often had to start again. I can remember on one occasion, there was a very long Will. And of course I was doing it in the front office, and you'd write about two lines and somebody would come in and say, 'Oh, I would like to see Mr....'. That would take your mind off it, and when you went back you'd start at the wrong line. I'd got nearly to the end of it, and the managing clerk came in and said, 'You're getting on very well. I can arrange for the client to come in'. Well it was just after that I made a most horrible mistake, and I had to start again. And about two hours afterwards he came in and said, 'I expect you're finished now. Oh, you haven't got as far as you had when I was here before'. No, you couldn't erase or alter a Will, because that would be queried when the Will was proved you see.

At that time we also used to write all conveyances. But luckily, after a few years, the legal profession took to typing conveyances. But it was some time before they started to type Wills.

They never called you by your Christian name, you were always given a surname. And you called the boss 'Sir'. Of course the office now is full of girls, but I can never remember the Christian names. Now if they told me the surnames I should remember. But you get two Dorothys and you don't know who they're referring to.

We used to carry on like a police station. The discipline was almost the same. Which was a great help to me really, because when I joined the RAF in 1941, I didn't notice the discipline at all. I thought it was slacker than the office! It's funny how these things help, isn't it? I mean that sergeant who told us how to form fours and march in step, well, when I went into the RAF, I could march in step, and turn and form fours - well we formed threes, they changed it. But you know, I had no difficulty at all.

I often used to have to go out on the old bike to serve writs for the larger debts, you know. They had to be served personally. The farmers then were in a very poor way you know; they could hardly make a living. And they were in debt, and they weren't very good tempered about that. You'd go with this writ, and of course they were always at the other end of the farm, down some muddy field, and you'd have to trudge down the fields to find him. Of course you hadn't got any wellingtons or anything, and you used to get in an awful state finding him. Eventually you did, and served the writ. Some of the farmers threatened to shoot you. I had all sorts of threats!

In time I got married and we moved into Friars Street. The children were coming along and it was an old double fronted house standing alone, in about half an acre. There was a big lawn for the children to play on. It was five hundred pounds. My father said, "You must be mad". It was so much.

I left Friars Street in 1954, because my first wife became ill. I was looking after her, and I couldn't do the garden as well. She died a few months after. My second wife was eighteen years younger than me. She was only sixty-two when she died. So I haven't been very fortunate in that direction. Yes, they say lightning doesn't strike twice in the same place, but it does doesn't it.

When I married the second time we moved after a while out of town and Alma, she was always very fond of animals, started breeding golden retrievers. I liked them, they're marvellous. I had one. He didn't die till August, last year. He was fourteen. I miss him. Used to take me out you see! I don't feel like going on my own.

I was working for Bates, Wells & Braithwaite's till two years ago. I was eighty-two then. I've retired now, except I go in on a Thursday to have a chat with them about things.

# Roly Oliver

Chartered Surveyor, Auctioneer, Farmer, born 1910, Great Cornard, Suffolk.

*'...we were like general practitioners; we had to know about everything.'*

Our connections with the town go back to 1650, when Stefan Oliver was an upholsterer. About 1766, the family added auctioneering, and the selling of property to the business, because upholsterers in those days were also weavers but the wool trade was deteriorating. My grandfather and his brother built Sudbury Brewery, in about 1845. They had about a hundred houses in this district until in 1922 they amalgamated with Greene King. The family have also been wine merchants and grocers. My father revived the auctioneering business and farmed. When I joined him we were the only auctioneers who had offices in Sudbury. There must be about fifteen auctioneers and estate agents today.

I started school in Sudbury and then went to the Glebe House, Hunstanton. I remember it used to take my mother a day to take me there in a Model T Ford. From there I went to Aldenham, a school whose governors came from the Brewer's Society, and then returned to Sudbury to take my exams as a chartered surveyor. As my son didn't want to go into the business I sold out when I retired. But I continued farming at Newton Hall, where my parents lived, which had about eight hundred and fifty acres, and at the same time I lived and farmed at White Hall, Great Waldingfield, another three hundred and fifty acres, which I bought in 1938. My son now lives at White Hall and farms both farms, and I've returned to Newton Hall.

It's not unusual for agricultural auctioneers to farm. To be a good agricultural valuer you want experience of farming. But because our main business was auctioneering and general estate work during my father's time the farm had to be run by a manager. But I always took an interest in it, and it was interesting to see how farmers coped with the bad times up to the last war. A lot just went broke. From about 1928 onwards my father laid the whole farm down to grass and we kept about ten thousand free-range hens, a hundred cows, and four hundred breeding ewes.

Going back to auctioneering, we were like general practitioners; we had to know about everything. As country auctioneers not only did you have farms and estates to deal with, we dealt with many of the houses,

shops and factories in the area including cottage property. I did all the selling of the cattle and livestock but we also had a junk sale of furniture every week. And during the year we might have about ten or twenty good furniture sales. And you had to know your furniture values just like you would anything else. You picked it up by experience. Then you had many probate valuations of furniture and effects. That might be a cottage, it might be a mansion. You come across some very interesting things when you are doing probates. We came across the original logbook of the Earl St. Vincent, who was one of Nelson's admirals. It showed he'd bought a five hundred-piece dress and dinner service. If I remember rightly, it cost about ten pounds a piece in those days. If we were lucky enough we got the opportunity to sell such things.

You generally expected to sell between sixty and a hundred lots an hour, depending on the importance of your item. If you had a junk sale you sold quicker. It was the same with the farming stock sale. Of course in the Thirties, the horses were the most important thing on the farm, and the farmers expected you to take a lot of trouble over selling their horses, because they took a great pride in them. Since the war if you have a farming stock sale you're selling tractors in the place of horses, and combines in the place of binders. On the property side whether you were selling a house, a cottage or a mansion by auction, you had to treat them as the same.

I must say I always enjoyed the sale. I remember selling some calves. We'd come to the last lot, and the bidder was the other side of the pen from me, and I was taking bids and then he said to me, 'Who's bidding against me?' So I looked round. I said, 'Someone's been hitting my leg.' When he'd winked at me for bids his dog wagged its tail! It was the dog's tail... he was bidding against himself!

In those days you were used to pitching your voice. If the crowd got too noisy, you just dropped it so they couldn't hear you. But I can remember a furniture sale at Chelsworth Hall we had in conjunction with Hampton's who had all the modern gadgets. We actually sold the furniture in the the house itself, and they had a microphone. In those days we were not accustomed to using microphones, in fact I've never used one for a sale. And it was the first time my father'd used one. Of course he got up and started selling in his usual voice. It was deafening. And the next thing we hear,'How do you switch this bloody thing off?'

When you're selling you know where your bids are going to come from. I don't know how you know. I think it's just

*1965*

experience. I was most likely selling by auction twice a week, farming stock, furniture, houses. You're in training. You can get the feeling of a sale, and know if you're going to have a good sale or not.

It was always nice to have a good quality sale of antique furniture. Again, you knew what you should ask your customers to start the bidding at. That's experience; you can't teach it. And the same with valuations. You're taught in a professional way how a valuation should be worked out. But the question is, what will something make? Again, it's experience.

I've seen many changes in Sudbury. At one time you practically knew everybody in the town. The big change came when we had the London overspill. It changed Sudbury tremendously. And the Town Council has changed. Before the overspill it was principally Independent members, and some members of the Labour Party. But it was not run on political lines. The councillors were interested in Sudbury. Also there's been a big change in the shops. Nearly all the businesses in Sudbury were family businesses. Now of course multiples have taken over.

Our family has taken an active part in the Borough of Sudbury. When I was Mayor in 1958 it was the twenty-fifth time an Oliver had been Mayor of Sudbury in one hundred and fifty years. Once when father was Mayor,

and he'd just had a big sale, instead of taking the Minutes in numbers, he called them out in lots until the Clerk said, 'Mr. Mayor, perhaps you'd better stop selling the Council!'

Gainsborough's House came up for sale during my time on the Council. And at that time Sudbury was not very interested. The feeling was we'd done Thomas Gainsborough proud by giving him a statue. It was outsiders that took the interest in it, and tried to persuade the Town Council to buy it. Now, I must say, it's a great success. But I certainly didn't see it. Personally I'm not a great admirer of portraits, no, I much prefer a Constable to a Gainsborough. And I like a Rembrandt.

I haven't, I think, told you a lot about the district, but I've thoroughly enjoyed my eighty years of life. I've hunted, shot, played most ball games, and still potter round a golf course. I've enjoyed my years as an auctioneer and an estate agent. I always told my father I preferred White Hall to Newton Hall, but my son wanted a bigger house, so we did a move-around. I have always preached to my friends and clients with big houses, you should move before you have to. I did not take my own advice. So here we are, in Newton Hall, too old to make a move to a smaller house.

# Alan Cocksedge

Journalist and cricket enthusiast, born 1942,
Cockfield, Suffolk.

*'No doubt my days in the fourth team are just round the corner'*

My mother and father separated soon after the war, and in 1948 I moved to Sudbury with my grandfather, grandmother and mother. Our house overlooked an area of meadow called People's Park, which is now the site of the town's new hospital. Most of my spare time I spent sitting on the front gate-post, overlooking People's Park, which was only grazed by cows but I whiled away the hours, sometimes going over there and playing football and cricket in the evenings, and watching the Barkers Fair coming and going two or three times every year, which as a youngster I found fascinating. The first one of the year always followed on the Whitsun fair at Long Melford, so you would always know when it was going to be. All week long they set it up. Every day I would rush home from school and see how many tractors and trailers and caravans had arrived, and watch with delight as the roundabouts went up. And the excitement of the music on the Thursday, Friday and Saturday night! And occasionally I would go skipping over to go on the dodgems. The dodgems are always my favourite, a little bit of fun without too much danger. The fair now goes down Priory Stadium.

I also got my first glimpse of Sudbury Town Football Club when they came and played right opposite my bedroom in about 1953, because their ground was flooded. It was my first experience of witnessing any organised sport in Sudbury.

I then succeeded in failing the eleven-plus, which didn't really disappoint me too much. Football and cricket and generally enjoying life was still my major priority. Then when I was fifteen I had the option of staying on at school for a year and taking a couple of O-levels, or doing a shorthand and typing course, mainly used by girls. That wasn't the reason why I decided to enter it, but it wasn't a bad reason! I did the shorthand and typing, and managed to get reasonably proficient and I saw an advert in the 'Suffolk Free Press' for a cub reporter. I went for an interview one Saturday morning saw the editor, and he said, 'OK boy, you do shorthand and typing, you start here in August.' I stayed eight years. Then I applied for the job of the senior district reporter on 'The East Anglian Daily Times' I've now been a journalist thirty-two years in Sudbury.

I am not a great writer as such, but I know how to interpret facts and put them down in a presentable manner. And if you can reflect what's going on locally, you're doing your part in community life. Sometimes there are stories that people don't want you to write. But if afterwards they will look you in the eye and respect you for what you've written, I think that's one of the most rewarding things, that you don't have to lose friends by having to do what a man's got to do basically! Obviously I have made enemies, but generally I think I've made more friends.

The man who taught me shorthand and typing was also the captain of the cricket club, and a qualified MCC coach. He taught me all I know probably about cricket, and put a lot of time in with me. I managed to play for Suffolk schoolboys. Suffolk has never been interested in me since, but...I did enjoy that and I started playing for the town cricket club when I was in my mid teens. I played Saturday and Sunday for many many years. My wife and my two girls tolerate me. They know I live most of the summer down the cricket ground. My wife has been a cricket tea maker for many years, but she certainly doesn't bother to follow my cricket exploits. I have given up playing on Sundays, but still most days in the week I can be found at the cricket ground at some time or other.

I have been captain of various teams. We've got four teams and I now manage to be a regular in the third, though no doubt my days in the fourth are round the corner. My most important job at the moment is keeper of the balls. They all have to be polished up, you know, and looked after. It's a small ground and we have to look after our balls because they get hit out and disappear, so it's a quite important job and no-one else is interested in doing it apart from me.

The cricket club is the longest established sporting club in the town, being well over two hundred years old. It's woven into the history of the town. I must confess that history has never been a subject I took the slightest interest in at school. But somehow the history of the cricket club has caught my imagination. From the people who have been the captains, the medical officer of health, the grammar school headmaster, the local doctor, or the bank manager, you build a picture of town life. And as you know there are a hundred acres of common lands, and they are a marvellous facility for Sudbury, but they are grazing meadows and the public have footpath rights across them but no rights to any recreation on them, and once, early on, I believe the men of Belchamp and the men of Sudbury were playing a game on there one day, and one of the freemen came down and laid down on the pitch, and exercised his rights, and the game had to be abandoned.

*Sudbury Cricket Team 1896*

We've got about sixty playing members, a part-time groundsman and barman. We also have a qualified coach, which has been a great asset and built up the strength of the club considerably. We're quite well organised. We've spent eighty thousand pounds extending the club house and rebuilding the changing rooms, so we've got excellent facilities.

I'm a bit of a dying breed as a local journalist. Journalists tend not to hang around on provincial papers these days. It was tradition for the district man to be born and bred in a town. That doesn't happen now because many trainee journalists are graduates, and they see their first newspaper as purely a stepping stone to radio or television or something. Not many people like myself are prepared to hang around in one place all their lives. But in fact that has a tremendous benefit inasmuch as you know so many local people.

The basic lessons of writing for a local newspaper haven't altered. The technology has altered a great deal though, with word processors, and being able to transmit direct into our computers at Ipswich. We don't have to telephone stories over to copy takers or send stories on vans and buses. Also we can take portable computers into council meetings and courts, and while there's a lull in the proceedings we can write so we can come out of a meeting virtually having written the story which enables you to do something else when you get back to the office rather than slave over a hot typewriter! We also do a lot more on the telephone. When I first started it was not unusual to spend Saturday afternoon cycling out to a flower show. Many people weren't on the telephone so if you wanted to find anything out you had to go and see them. I regret that to some degree. I'd get to know people; it is a retrograde step from a social point of view.

But I feel privileged to have been a journalist in Sudbury. I might have been a carpenter or something had I not done that shorthand and typing, and I wouldn't have known the people I do now. It's broadened my education. I would probably not have put my foot inside Gainsborough's House had I not been a journalist. Now I'm always most welcome there, and I get first-hand news of any exciting purchases, and I find it a very interesting and rewarding place to visit and to know the people who run it. The same with the Quay Theatre, the local councillors, and policemen. I know them all and many of them are personal friends. I wouldn't have been able to mix with these people had I done something different.

I live, eat and drink the job really. I'm never off duty. I live in the town centre and I can cock an ear for everything. If I'm gardening, I can hear the fire engine go out. So I find it difficult to relax when I'm not on call. You have to think, 'I'm not indispensable. Just let them get on with it.' But once you get involved in a community it's difficult to turn your back on it.

I think we're here to reflect the community we live in. But by showing that we're prepared to report the community properly, to look after the interests of everyone in the community, probably makes the community behave itself. So whenever I see anything that's got 'Confidential' written on it, it always gets my hackles up and I think, this is something I ought to know about. I was involved in a major dust-up with Babergh when they began marking a lot of their papers 'Secret'. I've a liberal selection of moles in various councils and quite a selection of confidential Council Minutes in my office. I think the Council know from chief executives downwards that if I want to know I'll find out. And that probably is not a bad thing for them to be aware of, though I do appreciate that certain things have to be kept below the line and I hope what I have used so far I have used responsibly.

I like walking in the Lake District and my wife is equally enthusiastic. I've been once already this year and I'll be going again in October. It can be quite gruelling, some of the long walks over the high fells, but it's lovely when you get to the top of a peak and see the superb views. And even if it's not a very good day and you might come back wet, it's a challenge. We went with friends to the Lake District a few weeks ago and we had the Wainwright for the actual hills we were on. We were able to sit down and have a Wainwright reading at the appropriate place! We made quite a ceremonial play of this. It was good fun.

I hope to be walking in the Himalayas in a year's time. That's to celebrate our silver wedding actually. Then I will definitely forget about Sudbury for three weeks!

# Chapter Six

## FARMING AND THE LAND

The town is still sufficiently compact for many of the townspeople's routine journeys to work and shops, friends and relatives, to take them through open land. In the past many of the older people walked through it daily, into the town to work in the morning and back home again each evening. Others bicycled into the town or to their local station for the train across the corner of the Meadows. That has now all gone. For a long time it has been a countryside most people see from a bus or, increasingly, a car window. But people still cannot help but be aware of the changing appearance of the land over the last twenty-five years: the disappearance of the animals, the depletion of the hedges, the increasingly small and identical looking fruit trees in the orchards and most recently, the blazing yellow of the rape for the margarine companies and the hazy blue of the linseed destined for the motor and aircraft industries.

A number of people who use the town have always had a more intimate relationship with the land, however. Here we listen to and look at three of them.

In traditional East Anglian fashion Arthur Butcher is never called by his real name. Most people could not tell you what it was. Everyone knows him as Chub, and he is a bachelor. For a boy with his background growing up in the first quarter of the century, there was the land and some people appeared ordained to work it. This is not to say **Chub Butcher** is a man who bore everything passively. If he felt he was used unfairly he could get angry. But in his way of talking about the land, of the burdens it imposed, and of the demands his horses made there is a distinctive traditionalist acceptance. Chub Butcher is a conservative. The strident, forward thinking tone of much modern conservatism, however, is quite alien to him. One feels this in his photograph, as well as in his words.

The contrast between Chub Butcher's experience of farming and **Ashley Cooper**'s is marked. Ashley Cooper grew up in a farming world where mechanisation had largely driven out men like Chub Butcher. Ashley Cooper is still there because he owns the land he works. He is self-aware, verbally articulate and passionate about the meaning the land gives his life. Also a bachelor, he cherishes his farm as another man might a wife. When it suffers, he suffers too. One expression of his respect for the land is his habit of always wearing a tie for work, whether ploughing, top dressing or combining. In the course of explaining and displaying some of his farm equipment to us an opportunity arose for photographing him from the roof of his tractor, typically dressed and waist high in long-eared barley.

**Michael Raymond**'s relationship with the land is different again. He is a man with a mission and the land is a means more than an end. After twenty years as a Lloyds underwriter, he returned to the area to continue his father's work of restoring the family home after years of neglect. To do this he has had to force the land to give him an income. Gathering together what acreage he could, he has learnt how to farm. But his acreage is limited, and he is always glad of opportunities to supplement the income he gets from farming. His efforts are showing dividends, however. The rich orange-red bricks of the house's graceful facade today emanate a sense of well-being. His portrait had to include the house.

# Chub Butcher

Farmworker and Horseman, born 1907,
Little Waldingfield, Suffolk.

*'Messed things up completely when they mechanised.'*

I never had a father to bring me up. Because I wasn't no more than six months old when he died. He was gardener down at Holbrook Hall and he happened of an accident. They used to have to raise gravel, because the paths down to the Hall used to be all gravel. One morning when that was frosty, they sent him down the gravel pit. When that's frosty anything can happen and it caved in and he got squashed.

I was just thirteen when I started work. I had to look after the chickens, clean the knives, pump the water, get the coal and wood in, light my fire every morning for the cowmen, so they could wash the churns. We were a busy boy! About two or three year I was doing that. Then I have to get out on the farm, and I don't think it's anything you can say on the farm that I haven't done. I done ditching, I done hedging, I done everything, I tell you. I done milking, I was with the sheep, I used to have to look after the fowls and the pigs, I was a horseman. And I used to look after the skivvies!

You know what a skivvy is, don't you? She's a servant! They used to come up after the milk and I made sure I was down there pumping the water so I'd see 'em and have a little chat.

If you took to being on a farm it was all right. I took to it so I was happy enough. But we was the worst paid that ever was, on a farm.

I tell you what I did try to do once, though. I tried to get in the police force. But they asked about my legs. Well I got varicose veins. They didn't want to know then, because they used to do a lot of biking and walking. Today they just sit on their bottoms in cars; they don't do no biking hardly. If I'd have got in there, I don't know where I might have been now!

Horses used to do the lot on a farm. I was horseman for about thirty year, and I used to break two young'uns in every year. I was interested in horses more than anything. Real heavy horses. They weren't these little ponies.

I used to get up there at five in the morning, all the year round. I used to call the gov'nor at about a quarter past five

and we used to have a breakfast at ten, and a dinner at three o'clock, and go back at four o'clock, to bate and groom all the horses down, and rack 'em up for the evening. You got some were pretty awkward. Like people, you get some of them awkward too! Yes, I've had them up in the air, and had to shoot under them out the way several times.

I didn't get a week's holiday or anything. Tell you the truth, I reckon most of my working days was a seven-day week because when you had horses to look after you'd got to go in an hour in the morning, and an hour in the afternoon. We did knock off at twelve o'clock on a Saturday, but I'd still got to go up to the stable to see to the horses about three o'clock time. And Christmas, they'd got to be fed twice a day, morning and afternoon.

When they bought the colts for breaking in they didn't give a lot for 'em. You could do a fair bit with a colt in three weeks, but that would take a year before you could say it was a good horse. After I broke the young'uns in and got them nicely for work so they'd do everything, the boss he used to send them to Ipswich, what they call a society sale. And then they made a good price.

The first thing you do with a colt, you put a head stoop on it so you can get it in the stable. Then you put a piece in the mouth for a bridle, and you put a pad on the back so you can tie that bridle back. Those that didn't like the piece, the mouths used to bleed. Made 'em sore you see, because they weren't used to it.

That's how we started them off. Then we put trace on them, so they could go on the plough. We used to have a big whole log of wood, and let 'em pull that about. I seen them kick and kick. But I used to like horses so much, I took it as no trouble really, and you got some good ones and you got some bad ones.

They didn't have any tractors then. Oh, I drove a tractor. I had a week on a course at Ipswich on ploughing, drilling, and all jobs, what you do with them. But messed things up completely when they mechanised, between 1950 and '60. I mean, one bloke do what they used to have twenty to do! There was four for the horses, two milkmen, cowman, and about seven or eight daymen, what done the hoeing, the brushing and the fences.

These years they they got hedge cutters and things for cleaning the ditch out. They don't know how to use a spade and fork in the bottom of the ditch now. And we used to plough an acre a day with the horses. Today they have a five-furrow plough, and they can plough fifteen

acres in about five hours. And we used to drill ten acres a day. Today, they can drill pretty well a hundred! It don't take no time and you don't want the blokes do you? Plenty of them plough over thirty acres a day now. That'd have took we four weeks to have done. But we was fitter then than they are today, I bet.

Thrashing was the worst job. You didn't have things to put over your nose and mouth then and you got all that dust that wasn't very nice. But we never took notice of it. Nowadays, they just sneeze once and 'Oh, I've got a terrible throat!' No, we used to have to rough it then. Now you've got everything. Even in the house they don't know how to work, do they? They don't get on their knees! No, they got all electric things to do it, even polishers. Of course I ain't. I still got my own broom and brush. That's what I use.

Sacked up, barley used to weigh sixteen stone a sack,

wheat weighed eighteen stone, beans weighed twenty. That's two hundredweight. Oats were the lightest, they only weighed twelve stone. You used to have to heave them, the sacks, across your shoulder. Some days you had a hundred and twenty of them, or a hundred and thirty. You'd got to lift them into the tumbrel first, and cart them, eight sack at a time, up to the barn. And then you'd got to get them on your back and run up this little old board and empty them out. Then you got to go back and begin again and take more of them. And you used to have to go up the granary with some of it, and then you had to carry it up the stairs. Now they won't let a bloke carry a hundredweight, much more two.

Cold. Oh, God blimey, we had to go out in the cold. You'd got to go to do the ploughing. There's some soil lighter than another, so it'll plough easier, and then you get some that's heavy. It would want a lot of pulling then. The horses was warm enough at work though and that was

better than hot weather for them because they didn't have the flies worrying.

I couldn't get the sack. I tried, that's the truth. I had a row with the gov'nor. What done it, he found fault with me, through his foreman. And that was a lie and I told him. I say 'I know that's untruth, and you've got him indoors. Fetch him out will you, to here, to me. He had this horse pond. It was a big'un that stood in the middle of the yard. I say, "I'm going to fling him in there, that's what I'm going to do with him.' And I said, 'I've had enough of you. If I don't suit you, I'm off.' But he wouldn't give me my cards so I couldn't leave. Of course if I'd have left, I'd have lost a week's money, and I couldn't afford that.

I used to like a bit of toast with plenty of butter and some sugar on for breakfast. Or I had a boiled egg. For dinner, a few 'tatas, bit of swede or turnip. We didn't have anything too high up. If you was lucky and you caught a rabbit, perhaps you'd have a dumpling and some soup. Meat during the week? No fear. And when I was a youngster, it wouldn't do to say, 'I don't want that,' because you wouldn't get nothing else. Today they say, 'Dear, can't you eat that?' and go and get them something else, don't they? They don't bring 'em up today. They let they bring the parents up.

I semi-retired when I was sixty-five but kept going about half a week till I was seventy. After I stopped that game I used to go and pull walnuts and chop the sugar beet. So I reckon I worked till I was over seventy-four. As long as you feel half tidy you're better doing a little than you are sitting about.

In the War they never took we what worked on the land. So the longest I'd been away from my home, I went up to London one Friday, and I spent a Saturday and come home on a Sunday. Then, five years ago come September, I had an operation in Bury St Edmunds, and I was there about five weeks. I liked being in that hospital. I had a woman doctor, a young 'un too. She's lovely! And so was the nurses. They was all nice. Yes, nice lot of gels there.

I reckon I was six foot one or two when I was right up. But I don't reckon I am six foot now, because I'm growing down!

I was born in this house, 84 years ago come August. So I do hold one record in Little Waldingfield. There's nobody else that's lived so long in one house. I should know my way up and down them stairs. They're the same old stairs as when I was a nipper. I had the Raeburn put in and electricity. I didn't want three bedrooms and one made a

lovely bathroom and I've got a nice little airing cupboard in there.

I'm pretty regular at having a pint. And I smoked ever since I was thirteen. And still do! But not so much, because they're so dear now. We don't get the money like ones that work; this country has the lowest paid pensioners there is. And yet we won all the wars. So what do you make of that? I can't make nothing of it.

We used to play cricket summer nights. And we had a parish room we used to go down for two to three hours, in the evening, to do a bit of boxing. Make one another's nose bleed! We didn't have pools to go bathing. We used to have to get in the pond. I couldn't swim. I was built like a brick! Go to the bottom! We used to have dart matches. And crib matches. I like crib. That's a sitting down job. And nowadays I don't want to keep running about with darts.

Yes, they was the good old days I say! Well, they was as far as we was concerned. But these modern ones wouldn't think so, would they? They wouldn't think they be good days. God blimey, we thought more of a penny then, and what they do with a fiver today.

We used to have a decent Christmas. We had a rabbit pie. We thought that was wonderful for a Christmas dinner. I don't know what they'd think of it today, because a turkey ain't enough for them, they want a leg of lamb or pork as well. And we had Christmas stockings, but we just got an orange and a few sweets and a handful of nuts in them. That was a treat for us because we didn't have them very often. Today it ain't a treat at all because they have plenty every day. That time of the day we didn't have much, so if we had a little bit extra when I was a nipper we were pleased. We appreciated it. Whereas today some of them they have nice new bike, nice new little pram, but in a week they're out in the garden in all weathers. They don't appreciate them to look after them. If we had anything, we have to look after it.

\*    \*    \*    \*

# Ashley Cooper

Farmer and historian, born 1952, Gestingthorpe, Essex.

*'It was like playing snakes and ladders.'*

At the moment we grow wheat and barley and beans and oil seed rape. We are utterly representative cereal farmers in the Sudbury area, circa 1992. I was born upstairs. And Dad came down and had a glass of whisky with the doctor. He doesn't normally drink, but that was his celebration. That was in 1952. I went to school in Sudbury and after I was about nine I went to boarding school in Bury St. Edmunds.

When I came home for my first summer holidays my father needed some help combining rye grass. It was cut with a grass mower before it was picked up by the combine and would sometimes get very lumpy. And the combine kept blocking up, and he felt if I walked ahead with a pitchfork I could help to feed it in. So at the age of ten I did my first day's genuine farm work. I walked in front of the combine helping to feed it in, and would sometimes rush round to the back if it wouldn't come out, to stop it blocking up. I was utterly ecstatically happy. I was also absolutely exhausted.

From that point onwards, from the age of ten, I fell in love with the notion of farming. And I've always seen it - sounds awfully pretentious - as a very moral thing to do. Some people farm because they want to make money, but other people farm because they want to farm.

The childhood work I did meant that I experienced farming when it was still in some respects rigorously unpleasant - a sugar beet field in an icy wind. It imprinted on me the full reality of rural life, rather than something that was too poetic.

There were awful things about the old countryside, the threshing machines which were terribly dusty, and the first combines I worked on were horrendously dirty. Ten years ago we got our first combine with a cab, and it was just incredible not to be sitting in a haze of dust the whole time, and spitting out great gobs of black phlegm and waking up in the morning feeling exhausted because you were so bunged up.

It had always been mapped out that I would leave school at sixteen after O-levels. That was the traditional thing that somebody going into farming would do. But just about the time that I was leaving school I began to have doubts as to perhaps whether that was the right thing.

But you can't have your cake and eat it. You can't have your parents committed to the farm at a juncture in their life when they could be thinking about taking life easier and me wanting to go and do A-levels and university as well. My mother and father had kept their side of the bargain by enlarging the farm. The dilemma was that at the age of sixteen, I was faced with the choice of either farming or not farming.

I left school. But I was very keen to continue educating myself by reading books from Sudbury library, all the great classical writers that I could, such as Tolstoy and Hardy.

Six months after I left school my father bought some more land, and more two years later. Then we sold off some land and got all seven hundred acres in one unit. By the time I was twenty-two big steps were taken consolidating the farm. And I began to be able to go away in December and January, when the farm work was quiet.

I regarded this as like doing A-levels because I went to different parts of the world. I went twice to India, I went to the Middle East, and once to Mexico, rucksack, back-packing journeys. It was a most wonderful alternative to formal education.

Then I went to some lectures on local history in the village, and I offered to write this five-side handout on the change in land use round here from the Second World War. Then I felt that it would be nice to have the memories of the village's oldest farmer, who was a chap called Bunny Hyde-Parker. So I went to see him. Then I felt that I ought to have the memory of one farmworker. And I rang up a chap called Tom Bird who said he couldn't answer all my questions. I ought to go and see another chap, the old thrashing contractor. He guided me to a blacksmith, until I'd spoken to seventy people and their wives. And obviously it was no longer five sides. It was fifty sides. And I decided to print it if I could afford it. And luckily the harvest was good and 'The Long Furrow' came out four days before Christmas.

If you costed your time it would be a mug's job, but it produced letters from all around the world which I keep, and I'm ever so grateful to people who write to me.

All this time I was still farming flat out. To me agriculture is still utterly fundamental. We have achieved so much in the last twenty years in terms of putting out of everybody's mind the prospect of a shortage of food, and it's been so disappointing that it has taken the politicians ten years to catch up with the opportunity that agriculture gave them. The community forest plantings, which they are now just beginning to talk about, could have started five or ten years ago.

I think the generation which removed the hedges - and in eighty per cent of cases it had to happen - was my father's. Because the Government subsidised you and you had this memory of being in competition with the prairie...Many of that generation of farmers were as embittered about their experiences in the Thirties as the unemployed of Jarrow were. They had seen their friends and neighbours walk off their farms and leave them. It was an untarnishable sort of bitterness.

When the Second World War broke out, there were twenty thousand acres of land derelict between Colchester and Haverhill. Whole tracts had just been abandoned. The first farm my father took over in Belchamp Walter had not been farmed for twenty years, because the prairie could produce cheaper than the small-field, rural economy of eastern England. It was more efficient. It can be mechanised more easily.

After the Second World War the Attlee government made a huge effort to put agriculture on to a sound footing, and you will not meet any farmer over the age of sixty who won't talk of Tom Williams, the Labour Minister of Agriculture, without affection - even if farmers traditionally are not going to vote Labour. There were minimum prices, grants for improving your holding, for building barns, for drainage, and also for hedge removal.

Now, the problem arose that the grants for hedge removal carried on, for probably ten years longer than they need have done. All my life I have been tarnished with the hedgerow destruction which went on in the Sixties, way before my time. I think Friends of the Earth perform a terribly necessary role.

We were faced with three major hurdles. First was the planting. I think it was '73, Plant a Tree: 74, Plant Some More', something like that. And we then had three severe droughts. '74 was very dry, '75 was drier, and '76 was the chronic drought. I planted about three hundred willows then, of which about ten per cent survived. There wasn't much expertise about tree planting at the beginning.

The second one was Dutch elm disease. Dad had bulldozed the hedges to make modern fields, but he'd left a horseshoe round the farm buildings, every one of which died. We lost seventy beautifully tall trees and about two miles of hedgerow. This winter we cleared up another three hundred yards of elm spinney which is completely dead. And we have one more to do. We will then have planted our last elm area up.

Of course having planted people say, 'Oh, well done'. And you feel rather cynical because the first bit is the easiest. It's watering them and weeding them; making sure they're growing well; making sure the rabbits aren't getting them; taking their stockings off.

Dutch elm was a sickening catastrophe. It made me very cross, because so much money is spent on things like packaging new versions of Coca-Cola or, pardon me saying, ladies' cosmetics, which don't do any good at all, and something which desecrated our countryside, no real effort has been made to get on top of it.

We then had the hurricane.

It was like playing snakes and ladders and going right back to the bottom again. Nothing had ever trained me for a hurricane. One of my neighbours said he walked round his farm with tears in his eyes for four days. It was just...you know, you couldn't believe that you could have two natural catastrophes in one lifetime. Although it was in a different league, it was like the first year I left school. Dad allowed me to choose the type of sugar beet seed we were going to grow, and we had a terribly dry summer and they didn't grow very well, and at the age of seventeen I just suffered interminably. It was like the world was going to come to an end.

Our loveliest area of the farm where we join the Belchamp brook was willow trees. They were semi commercial, because you sold some every twenty years, but it's only pocket-money. And every summer we go and prune them. It was almost like a day's holiday. You'd take a bag of sandwiches and perhaps a camera, and just enjoy it so much. And when I went down there it was like a bomb had gone off. There were in one area about a hundred and fifty just flat like a pack of cards. You know, you can't find words to express it really.

Of all the things I love, I love the countryside most. Whatever I've achieved in local history, I think I've achieved more for conservation. Coppicing is one of the most quintessential disciplines in traditional woodland management. For centuries woods were naturally coppiced. People would cut down wood for their fencing, hurdles, firewood. So it just happened naturally. But now it doesn't. There's a danger that one plant will come to dominate the others, and kill them out. So coppicing is - it's so important to get these things across - a life-restorative process. You should do it on a rotational basis every twelve, fifteen years. And it is particularly galling when you get criticised for it. There was an instance about seven years ago where a farmer did this in Norfolk, and a neighbour, I think a lady, came and put all over the hedge, you know, 'dog rose rest in peace', 'hornbeam rest in peace'. And this photograph got itself into all the national newspapers.

From 1940 to 1985, they were forty-five profitable years and from '75 to '85 was a fabulous time because there was money every year to re-invest, to do worthwhile things with, to buy tractors which had better safety or air filtration features, for improving your barns, planting trees, improving your holding. Right now we've probably got twenty difficult years coming.

Because, as a consequence of the improvements of plant breeding and agricultural science in the Fifties and Sixties, most grain exporting countries can now produce more than they need, and many of the Third World countries like Africa, where you would love it to go, can't afford to buy it. And the international politicians say well we must lower the prices of the products until such time as they cease to be in surplus. It will take another ten or fifteen years for the alternative uses for land to resolve the over-supply.

I don't want to bore you by being a typical farmer worried about his returns but our price for wheat is going down, and you keep thinking what huge amounts of money you have to find to keep your equipment in good working order. I think we're pretty baffled by it! My brother-in-law's a banker and he says 'Well do you get any return on your capital?' And I think the return you get is that you have a nice job in the countryside really.

*About 16 years old*

I've only got one full-time man on the farm now and another self-employed person for eight or nine months a year, and a student we get at harvest time. And there's my father here to help, a very typical sort of structure on this sort of farm. Until last year I did all the spraying and the combining and the drilling, and fertilising myself, and all the office work. This morning I was top-dressing, putting on nitrogen. There have been all types of students. The guy who's carting the grain now is quite likely to be studying to become a stockbroker rather than being a bloke who'll spend all his life on a farm.

We now all have these CBs. And radios in tractors. Which only happened about ten years ago. Before that it was a very lonely sort of day. Radio has helped an enormous amount. And the CB is fun, because you can call up the neighbours and joke with them, and it has more than anything I think brought a sort of humanity back into the modern solitary countryside.

I wrote some short stories - 'Tales of Woodland and Harvest' - in response to questions about how a modern farmer feels. There's one story which deals with a modern harvest. There are certain occasions when you're combining. It only happens three or four nights a year when, if it's very dry and there's a slight breeze just to keep the dew away, you can keep going till perhaps midnight or one or two o'clock in the morning. If you're a bit behind or a bit desperate you just grasp it. And it's always very memorable, because you're there by yourself with the lights of the combine rotating, broken up and defused. There are blue and orange warning lights. There's also an orange light on the top, which comes on when your grain tank is full. So you get a sort of stroboscope effect. And then when you stop, and the combine is quiet, it's suddenly...deathly still. And then you have this wonderful harvest moon just bathing down on everything. And that's if you like when you have the magic, sense of magic. And yet at the same time you're in the paradox of a huge machine costing nearly a hundred thousand pounds. But it only happens...occasionally.

I love the farm. The minute I've finished work I set off jogging, and I run right round it again. If the cards are down, the house would go before the land, and the land would go before the woods; the woods would be the last thing that I sold.

\*   \*   \*   \*

# Michael Raymond

House owner, born 1923, India.

*'The roof leaked a lot, and it was extremely cold.'*

I was born in 1923 in India. My father had gone out there because of the agricultural depression over here, when it was extremely hard for anybody to have any sort of living in the countryside.

He was born in this house. Then his father died and his mother could no longer afford to live here, and moved out. And my father, when he left school went to work for a cousin who had a coffee estate in India. My mother went out there in 1914 and got married in India. Meanwhile this house was empty for about thirty years.

When I was six and my sister eight, we came back to England to boarding school. Of course my parents had to stay in India, so we didn't see very much of them. The ship to India ...you know by the time you'd have got there you'd have had to turn around and come back again. I saw my father about every three years. Usually we spent our holidays with uncles and aunts and cousins. Then after a while my mother bought a house.

Finally my father retired in 1935, and came back to England and, as he had wanted, started living here, after those long years in India. And that was the first time that I'd lived here also.

My family came to Belchamp Walter in 1611, and lived in an old Elizabethan farm house I suppose it was, from the only picture we have of it, until 1720. Then they pulled it down and built the present house. And they've been living here ever since.

But then the war started. My father joined the Air Force. My sister joined the Air Force. And as soon as I was old enough I left Oxford and joined the Army. So we all split up again. But my mother stayed here and looked after the house, and started to farm.

It can't have been more than eighty acres then. My grandfather had borrowed a lot of money in Victorian times. Several of my ancestors were parsons in this parish and he was a parson and not very businesslike. The chief villain, though, if you could call a dear old parson a villain, was actually my great grandfather, who was a very benevolent character, and spent a lot of money on repairing the church and building the school, and various very worthy charitable objects, which he couldn't really afford. So when my grandfather died the bills came in and about half the land had to be sold, and a lot of pictures and furniture and china. Various ancestors in the eighteenth century were obviously avid collectors, and I think a number of them went abroad to Italy, and bought things there as people do and also quite a lot of Dutch furniture and pictures - all of which disappeared.

It was all sold in Sudbury for nothing. We still have the sale catalogues with the fearful prices things went for. We kept the family portraits because, a) there was an historical interest, and b) they were more valuable to us than to other people. But the ones by the very best artists, whether they were portraits or not, they all had to be sold. We had the house left though.

After the war I'd forgotten everything I knew at Oxford and I didn't see any point in going back to finish my degree. So I started working in the City, as there was no living down here. I worked at Lloyds for about twenty-four years. I had a family to support and children to educate. We used to come down for the weekends and help with the farm, but we lived in London.

As a few more old farmers died off we were able to get a bit more land back, about two hundred and fifty acres I suppose. But most of the land is still tenanted, and we won't probably ever get it back again to make a viable farm, because tenants have security of tenure for three generations.

Well, my father had an awful lot of things to do when he came back here, because the house had been empty for so long. It had no creature comforts and was very uncomfortable. The roof leaked a lot, and it was extremely cold. If we had dinner in the dining room we always put a coat on first before we went in. There's no heating there now except an open fire which heats the sky. We don't use it very much.

My father, with the help of a grant, managed to mend the roof in the Fifties, and so the house then became watertight. And he gradually cut back the jungle which had rather moved in, cleared a bit of the land and parts of the garden which had completely overgrown, and started to get it tidy again. But he didn't have enough money to employ as many people as the house and garden required or, indeed, requires. Then, at the end of 1973 I stopped working in Lloyds and came down here as my parents were getting very old.

My father did the roof. I've done the windows. Each of those stained glass panes represents a wedding in the family, gradually added over the years. I had to take them out to get them repaired.

One of the theories about the house is that the lovely pink facing bricks on the front are in fact Dutch. When the wool boats went down the rivers to the Low Countries who imported a lot of our wool, they needed ballast on the way back, and many people think that what they put in the ballast was their bricks. And it sounds a reasonable theory.

Well, as I say, the house is a lot of work, without the sort of help that was available when it was built, when there were large numbers of servants, all living in it. Now there are none.

Still the house goes on. We have about seven bedrooms going at the moment. There are a lot of attics which are stuffed full of old things, but of course they used to have little maids in Victorian times. There are four reception rooms, and a hall.

And of course we have a large garden. I don't know how many acres it is, it's just an awful lot of work. My wife was prepared to have a go at it. And very well she's done it. She's been particularly creative in the garden; she's completely changed and improved it out of all recognition.

As it's been a garden for some centuries it's built up its own fertility so we can grow most types of things except rhododendrons which need a very different soil. Of course we don't have as much help as one needs for a garden of this size, and we can't afford the time to grow very exotic plants. And in a garden like this you've got to have big clumps of things otherwise you can't see them at all. So we just grow as many bigger varieties as we can of plants that like living here. And it's got to be a rather wild garden. We have a lot of spring bulbs and things which grow virtually wild, snowdrops, aconites, daffodils, narcissus, and encourage them to grow on their own.

The house is open to the public, and the gardens. So you know, there is a standard which has to be kept up. In a clay soil, of course, roses are always happy. We've got a lot of old-fashioned roses that don't need too much attention, and don't get many diseases. With any luck you can give them a bit of space and leave them to it.

The people who come round are mostly parties of people like the National Trust, or historical societies. We have to open the house because of the terms of the grant my father received to mend the roof. There isn't an option, so we make the best of it. And although it does seem a nuisance now and again, the people who come here are really very pleasant and interesting and reveal themselves to be extremely knowledgeable about particular bits of furniture, or architecture or gardening. So that's very interesting for us, and we have learnt an awful lot from them.

If you want to get large numbers of people in you've got to spend a lot of money on lions, or aviaries and that sort of thing. And I think eventually you destroy the thing the people have come to see. So we just leave it as it is. It's not attractive to large bus-loads of people, but we don't particularly want it to be. We try and preserve it as an old unspoilt house and garden. People see the downstairs rooms that we live in, warts and all! And those people who like that sort of thing come and see us, and those who don't, don't.

I got the expertise to farm by forming a sort of partnership with local farmers. Farming, before 1984 was reasonably profitable in East Anglia, and it was profitable during the last war, but from about 1984 onwards arable farming has been heading downhill. Now it's a matter of survival! There was a shortage of food in those days, and there is no longer, for those who can afford to pay for it. Of course there are millions who can't, but they don't and can't buy the food. So although the food is needed on a global scale, on a local, or European scale of course there is a surplus.

The yield has increased enormously, with new breeds of plant, and the elimination of weeds by sprays, types of fertiliser, more efficient means of harvesting, ploughing, etc. Everything has improved at the same time ...which is partly the cause of the surplus. We sell it. It's just a matter of price. And the expenses, like those of any business, of course, have gone up with inflation.

I could go on for a very long time on the subject of fertilisers! I think the problem is largely misunderstood because the Press is always looking for a story. The romantic view of farming in say the Victorian age is so misplaced. People think that it was a glorious time, when there were no fertilisers, and farms looked like farms, and there were nice carthorses wandering around. It conceals the fact that the farm labourers lived in extraordinary poverty and discomfort. Yields were so low that no-one was really getting a good living out of it. And the housing of the ordinary farm labourer was, well frankly, slum-like. They would have all been delighted to have the machinery and the productivity that exists today. Having said that, of course, what prosperity there is now is due to the fact that labour-intensive methods have disappeared. Farming is no longer the principal activity in the countryside as regards wealth production. It's mainly produced by people going into towns and doing other things. So people are looking back nostalgically on something that was never really there.

BBC television drama is our best crop now! They use the house for filming one of their series. And we enjoy it. It's very interesting. They do the filming as quickly as they can, so they can pay us as little as possible. So the days they are here they work very long hours: arrive very early about six-thirty in the morning, with their catering truck, and leave as late as possible.

I used to shoot a lot, but I've given up now. I didn't think I was accurate any more, and I enjoy raising the birds and looking after them rather than shooting them really! We do have a lot of birds here. And a lot of plants. Because since we've run our own farm here, we haven't taken all the hedges out, and we haven't ploughed everything up, you know. We've got a lot of wild places. We've kept little woods and copses.

My son runs a shoot and, having a shoot, and being interested in raising pheasants, means that you're caring for and feeding all sorts of other birds who enjoy the habitat that you're looking after, and the food that you put out. Shooting, in fact, protects the countryside for a large number of animals and birds, because it is the same habitat that game birds prefer.

But I think it's a misconception that if you never killed or culled any birds or animals in the countryside you'd be better off. That you wouldn't be. If you're interested in raising birds at all you're fearful of the predators. And if you like to have wild birds around you have to keep an eye on the predators. Places like Surrey for instance, or places where you have a suburban atmosphere with never a gamekeeper in sight, you will have an awful lot of predators like magpies, who gradually rob all the nests of the robins and the thrushes and the blackbirds and, you know, very soon your balance of nature is very much out of true. I wouldn't say that I cull magpies, but you don't enjoy their presence!

We have a big variety of trees. But we've lost in the storms. We had a good deal of damage. We've had a lot of firewood anyway. But we heat the house with wood in a large outside boiler, and we consume an awful lot of wood. So we've got a use for it. Oil was expensive, and we had the wood, so we thought we'd better burn it. Of course it's quite a lot of work, hauling the logs. We've been burning things that have fallen down, and replanting, well,

since 1935. I can hardly think of any trees that we've cut down, unless they were dangerous. A lot of them are very old trees and of course they do fall down or get blown down.

We've done a good deal of planting as well - oaks, ash, cherries, maple. You can get grants for planting deciduous trees in this part of the country now - only pays for part of the expense, but it's a help. We've got an enormous number of sycamores. They regenerate so quickly. We'd be covered in sycamores unless we were careful.

My daughter, who's an artist, lives near Lavenham, not far away. One of my sons lives in Hertfordshire, one lives in America. He's an electronic engineer, and makes a very good living there. Married an American girl. Went out there when he was married. But my youngest son is now running the farm. He's joined a partnership with a distant cousin who also has a small farm in the village, so they work together.

I hope he will continue our work. But it's a daunting process. He's not married, and not every girl could want to live in a house like this, and manage it. It's not everybody's cup of tea.

The house, well it's been my life really. Whether I've lived here or not, I've always thought of it...because after you've had one family looking after a house for so long, it's a point of honour really not to be the one who sells the past.

\*     \*     \*     \*

# Chapter Seven

## TENDING THE MIND

One of the most radical social projects in British history has been the establishment of public libraries. The Anarchists embraced the idea of the public library, for it allows anyone to enter, walk up to the shelves, pick a book out and take it home. It is also a benevolently idealistic idea, for it assumes that people will return the books they borrow. At first many stalwart citizens regarded the whole project as sheer madness. If one indiscriminately opened the doors to the populace, everything would clearly get stolen. They turned out, of course, to be wrong.

We now take public libraries for granted, and the people who work in them are far from being seen as foolhardy radicals. Indeed, a classic stereotype of the librarian is of a grey, mouselike person living a decent but colourless life.

The establishment of a state education system is far more widely recognised as a significant far-reaching social measure. But again the stereotype of the public elementary school teacher, though different from that of the librarian, has not usually been an endearing one. 'The cane ruled the day' as one older townsperson put it, and though the imposition of discipline might in retrospect be approved of by older people, as children it didn't make them fond of those who administered it. Recollections of a heavy diet of rote learning have also in the past inhibited warm memories of school learning for many people. Since the 1960s, however, another image of the primary school teacher has emerged, permissive, innovative, 'child-centred'. Having spent decades castigating the narrow-minded authoritarianism of the old fashioned schoolteacher, the public now created a new bogey, the teacher who complacently presided over a decline in educational standards as the chief aim became to keep the children happy.

I had asked if she would see me and I suspect only politeness prevented her refusing. However, having agreed, **Anne Lockley** had decided to 'get it over with'. So here we were. But the prospect of offering an account of her career and interests aroused no pleasurable expectation in her. For she felt she had nothing to say that would be of any interest and her evident anxiety made me wonder whether I was imposing on her, but both her diffidence and anxiety proved unfounded. Once she began she described without any affectation, a lifestyle and set of interests which completely overturned the popular image of the lady who works in the library. Anne Lockley's story shows what our habit of pigeon-holing people can cost in terms of our understanding each other. A question then is whether her story makes us see her face differently.

Her total relaxation in the company of children was one of the most striking things about **Lee Loades**. Born of years of practice, she gave no sense of thinking how she should talk to them, what to say or the tone of voice to adopt. Those little signs of self-consciousness adults so frequently display when talking to children, other than their own, were absent. She seemed simply to enter the children's world. At the same time, and as her story confirms, she made no attempt to be like them. She remained a grown-up just as they remained children.

A photograph of her with children could help reveal her personality. But still photography can only freeze a moment. What her photograph would tell us about her would depend therefore on the photographer's ability to capture the feeling of a group in interaction with each other. This meant catching a moment when the angles of bodies towards each other, the poise of the heads, the direction of the looks between the figures, conveyed a sense of the quality of things happening before and after the camera's click.

# Anne Lockley

Library Manager, born 1950, Fulham, London.

*'We don't have 'Quiet' signs anywhere.'*

I was born London, in Fulham. My early childhood was spent a lot in the streets, rollerskating, playing football, knock-down-Ginger, you know, knocking on the doors and running away! From primary school I went to the secondary modern school. And at that time there were the Mods and Rockers. I was very much into that.

It was a vital part of life. We had to have whatever Twiggy was wearing that week, the particular type of clothes or colours that were in. If you didn't you weren't invited out, or you felt you couldn't go out. I felt very strongly about it. And so did the group I was with. Off we'd go to Biba every week. When I started work all my money went on clothes and make-up. I found it a tremendous pressure. You had to be part of the group, you had to go where they were going, do what they were doing, and to be part of them you had to look the part. I don't think that it's like that now: I hope it isn't.

You weren't allowed to even look or talk to Rockers, or like or look at motorbikes; it just wasn't allowed. Nowadays my taste in music is rock heavy metal. I go to all the concerts. Continually. I thoroughly enjoy rock concerts! I think it's so nice to have so many young people together. You're all there for the same reason, to enjoy yourself and to stand up and wave, and shout, or whatever. Which is different from a football match, where you've got two opposing sides. At rock concerts you're all enjoying the same thing, and very rarely get any trouble. I go not just to listen to the groups, I also go to watch the audience, because I love to see all these people, all enjoying the same thing without any problems. I go to Wembley and Milton Keynes and Donnington and Glastonbury.

There's a group of us. If there's a concert going they'll ring me up. Sometimes there's one car-load, sometimes there's two, or more. I'm a lot older. I like younger people. I thoroughly enjoy their company. They're so alive. I find some people of my age are quite happy - not that this is wrong or anything - sitting indoors. I like to get up and do things, rock concerts being one of them.

When I left school, I had no idea what I wanted to do. I got a job through the careers officer at 'Aslib', which is

the Association of Special Libraries and Information Bureaux', which was in Belgrave Square. And I decided this was definitely for me. I think most people think that everyone working in a library has been to library school, and is a librarian. I have just worked my way up. I'm a good organiser, making time sheets out for staff, organising rotas.

On a Saturday we will have well over a thousand people through the door. And that's just on Saturdays. And we have quite high issue figures, Tuesdays are about eight hundred. I should have more books here but I haven't got the space. So Sudbury's books are working very hard.

I have work experience people come and I always ask them, 'How do you see libraries?' And they still see libraries as places with 'Ssh, Quiet!' notices up everywhere. And just stamping books out, and maybe helping people choose a book. They can't see anything more than that. But I think libraries are trying to get away from that image. I think a library should provide a room where someone can study, but also it's nice to have activities going on in the library. In fact a lot of libraries now are quite noisy. You can hear conversations and the phone and the bustle of people around.

We don't have 'Quiet' signs anywhere. People use it as a meeting place, and I see part of my function is to be able to stop and talk to the elderly who come in for a chat as well as to change their book. It's nice to remember their name, and to say, 'Oh did your daughter-in-law come and visit you at the weekend then?' I see that as part of a social side to the library service, as well as providing a book and all the other information services.

I don't read a lot, I don't get the time. I've always got a book on the go, but it will take some time to get through it. I like non-fiction. I used to read science fiction when I was at school. Now I'm not interested in science fiction at all, totally gone off that. I've grown out of it.

I did a parachute jump. I thought to myself, I don't know, I am getting older, I'd better get out there and do these things I've always wanted to do. And a parachute drop was one of them, so I went and trained for three weeks, and then did two drops.

I can remember now sitting on the edge of the plane, and thinking, I can't go, I just can't push out. I don't know how I actually managed to lever myself out! But I did. Well you've got a row of people waiting in the plane, crammed on the floor, with knees up and pack ready, all waiting for

you. If I'd have been last I may have said 'Forget it', and got back in! But I was second to jump, so... I had to go!

I really enjoyed that. You're in the noisy plane, and then you push out. All of a sudden, this total silence. That was amazing. I started to talk to myself! It was lovely.

I would like to do some more, but it's the money. They're quite expensive. And I drive, but I haven't got a car. I just can't afford it. Simple as that! So of course it's difficult to keep these things up. At that time someone was lending me a car.

I used to work in Belgrave Square and do my shopping at Harrods. You can still buy reasonably priced items there.

I even used to buy furniture there. And of course they deliver. I moved here in about 1971 and I had stuff delivered from Harrods! I can remember the neighbours now!

It's very different here. But I love the countryside. I love gardening, I love walking. I go swimming once a week, and I used to go rowing on the river. I like the open space. Most evenings when I finish work I go home, put my jeans on and I go out for a walk. That was the type of life I wanted. I wanted to get away from the hustle and bustle of London. Now when I go back to it I can't wait to get back here.

# Lee Loades

Schoolteacher, born 1918, Downend, Avon.

*'...there were about fifty in each class.'*

I went to school when I was five, and I remember right from the very beginning finding reading extremely easy. And I always have read a great deal all my life. I went to grammar school and then to Cheltenham Training College in '36, and it was there I met my husband, who came from a real teaching family. His mother was a teacher. His brother was head of a very big comprehensive school in London, Muswell Hill. His sister was a teacher, and she married a teacher. My sister-in-law is dead now but she had two sons and a daughter, and they are all in teaching. So that's how it goes on. One of my sons - he's a teacher too, in Cambridge - he's head of a primary school, and his wife teaches.

When I first started teaching, I really wanted to be a pharmacist, but my parents were not very well off, and I thought well, a pharmacist, that will be three years' training, teaching would be two and we had to pay half the fees in those days. My parents scraped the money together, and we had a loan from the county.

In 1938 after college I went to teach in the same village outside Bristol where I was born. My first month's salary was eleven pounds ten shillings and for two years I had to pay back the loan. So of course my husband and I weren't able to save very much,

He was teaching in Sudbury. We wrote three times a week. I had a suitcase full of letters! But the war came along and he was called up and we thought, oh blow it, and we got married on forty pounds! He was lucky, because we were expecting the Germans to land any minute, but he got three days' leave. He came down to Bristol one day and we got married the next day. The church was full; the whole school was there; it was absolutely marvellous. And we were terribly happy. You didn't need money in those days.

We had one night at Portishead, and the next night we came back to Bury, where my husband was stationed. They'd fixed up with a couple for us to have two rooms but when we arrived we found...they hadn't got a bed. They thought my father-in-law was providing a bed, and he thought they were. So we had nowhere to sleep that night. Oh dear, what an ordeal! The next day we borrowed a bed, and a hand cart and my husband pushed this bed right

through Bury, surrounded by rude remarks from the rough soldiery ...because Bury was full of soldiers in those days.

In 1945 when my husband was de-mobbed we came to live in Sudbury, and I went back to teaching when Michael, the oldest boy, was eight, and Robert was five, and I could send them to school. I started teaching at the secondary modern school in Mill Lane in 1949. I went to North Street in 1959 and stayed there until 1978.

When I first went to North Street I found it extremely different from teaching in a secondary school. For one thing there were about fifty in each class. The school was crammed full. There was one big room with a curtain across, and there were fifty either side of the curtain. Can you imagine teaching in those conditions? I was lucky in the fact that I got a little room. There were forty-four in that class. They were such a big class in such a small classroom, that I had to push the desks back to get them all in, and when they were all in, to close the door, I had to pull the desks back again.

Before the war when I began teaching there wasn't a school meals service. But it had got under way when I started back in teaching. A lot of children stayed for school meals in those days because so many women were working. But North Street had no kitchen and the children had to march up to where Budgens supermarket is now, for school meals.

And the meals came in, I don't know exactly where they came from, some central kitchen. I shall always remember how horrible the suet puddings were. They literally glistened! And of course if it was wet you still had to march the children up to this place. And one thing that will stick in all teachers' memories is the smell of wet clothing. A hundred wet coats and wet plimsolls are not very nice. And of course you were on duty for the whole of the dinner hour with these children. In those days you didn't have helpers.

Then when we had the new hall at North Street School, and a kitchen, we were able to have our meals in that hall. And we had really first class meals, we had some excellent cooks. And then they started having helpers, dinner ladies, and they also had people to help supervise in the playground, which was a great help.

But I think it's terrible that they're closing down the casualty department at the Hospital, because there was hardly a week went by without some child did something terrible in the playground and had to be taken up to the

hospital to be treated immediately. I was myself! I was on playground duty and I was knocked over, quite accidentally, the child didn't do it purposely, but I landed up in the hospital having my nose stitched up!

My husband and I we were very keen on the NUT. In fact he ended up being County President. We usually went to Conference every year, and I always made a bee-line for the publishers' exhibition and spent about two days poring through books.

I'd always taught children, as far as possible as individuals. Even when I first started teaching and had classes of fifty, I made out work cards - so that they weren't all doing the same thing. And the head was very good; he let me

order what I wanted. I didn't like the idea of ordering sets of poetry books, for instance. I liked to have two or three of a lot of poetry books and put them round the room, so that the children could pick them up and read them when they wanted to. I suppose I was a bit way out in those days, but that was what I liked. I still think it's important that children should learn poetry. I think rhythm is terribly important for children. And I like modern poetry. I was also very keen on reading science fiction, because my sons were, and so was my husband.

When I started teaching at North Street I had the, in those days they called them backward children. Now they call them...oh dear, what do they call them nowadays? Learning difficulties. That's right. Then eventually, they stopped

*Wedding photograph 1941*

thought it was a bit sissy you know, but they thoroughly enjoyed it. I told them how terribly strong you have to be to be a man ballet dancer. I don't think they believed me, but once they went they realized it was absolutely true.

Now this is something that has saddened me a little bit. I know they say let a child write and express themselves. I'm all in favour of that. But I went through the era when free expression hit the secondary schools. Who was that woman? Shelagh Delaney wasn't it, the playwright. She'd only been to secondary modern as she said. That worried me when she said she'd 'only' been to a secondary modern... but she had produced these plays and she never worried about punctuation. And clearly somebody had typed it out and put the punctuation in for her hadn't they?

Anyway they said, 'Let's have free expression'. I used to say to the children, 'Look, it's very easy for me to understand your writing if you put a full-stop in here and there. Or it's a good idea to start a new line when a new thought comes to you'. I mean it's all very well for people to write ad nauseum, but how can you possibly understand what they've written unless they put a full-stop in somewhere?

A few years went by, and these people in the secondary schools were complaining you know. 'We're getting children who don't know how to punctuate. Why aren't we teaching punctuation?' It comes round full circle, it really does. Nowadays they're going to be far too rigid. I mean who wants to go back to parsing and analysis of sentences? It's so boring, isn't it, for children?

We do know a lot of people in Sudbury. My husband was twenty-one when he started teaching here in 1938, so his oldest pupils would have been fourteen or fifteen, and he'd be about seven years older. So there are people of sixty-five in Sudbury whom he taught. And I found people as time went on coming in and saying, 'Oh, you're still here Mrs. Loades. Do you remember when I used to do such-and-such a thing at school? If he's naughty, just you tell him off!' Some of the children I taught in Sudbury would be about fifty-six now. They have grandchildren and it's really nice to see them.

I don't think I'd like to be starting to teach these days, but I'd better not say any more! No, I'd better not. I thoroughly enjoyed teaching. It was hard work, but it's a very, very rewarding job. There's nothing better than seeing a child's eyes light up when they've grasped something, or when you praise them. I sound all sloppy, don't I?

streaming, which I was very happy about, because I don't believe in streaming.

But I used to have all the slow learner boys in the school, there were about forty of them, for art. Can you imagine? We used to have to cover up the desks with newspapers and little fishpaste jars of water you know. Oh dear! Luckily the Head was very kind to me and let me order all sorts of things for art.

And that's something I really enjoyed, teaching art. I used to tell the children in the morning what we were going to do in the afternoon and what equipment they could choose from, to let them think about what they wanted to use. And then they'd come in and choose. I put everything out on the tables before they came in so that no time was wasted at all. You can't afford to waste time in a primary school, Oh dear!

The age group I liked best were the eleven-year-olds, especially the boys. And one of my most cherished memories was taking the boys to ballet in Bury. They all

# Chapter Eight

# THE HEALTHY BODY

One of the most radical and enduringly popular post-war changes the 1945 Labour Government introduced was the National Health Service. The early ideal of free medical care has been significantly eroded and the service suffers from under-funding in the face of the increased sophistication of modern medical technology. Despite this general practitioners have steadily improved the quality of medical care they offer. Medical services related to preventive care have expanded enormously in towns like Sudbury in the last two decades. For services of this kind depend less on improved funding than on an enlargement of the medical imagination.

It is common knowledge that with this development the British health service has depended heavily on its Asian doctors and nurses. The Asian doctor, unknown in Britain in 1945 and more than a little suspiciously regarded in the Fifties and Sixties, is increasingly taken for granted in all English towns and Sudbury is no exception. **Kailash Sarda** is not only the longest established of these, his is now also the oldest practice in the town. He has run it for more than twenty years, a sizeable proportion of the town's population is on his list and his knowledge both of the town and its people is extensive.

His manner is easy and he does not look as if he would ruffle easily. It is indeed the kind of manner often popularly regarded as an old fashioned English one. Certainly Kailash Sarda appears to have settled deeply into the community. Meeting him on a summer evening outside his house, wearing shorts and watching the cricket across the road he appears completely assimilated. Talking to him, however, one discovers he has had a number of experiences very few of his patients would ever imagine. And he has a pipe dream. It is tempting to read into the slightly melancholy cast his face sometimes takes on, a fleeting shadow from the past. Certainly it seemed appropriate that the photograph we selected should be one that captured this look.

Quick speaking, bustling and cheerful, **Nita Sandford** is attached to the Sarda practice as a Health Visitor. She fits the image of the efficient nurse, but without the starchiness and unfortunate bossiness which has sometimes been associated with members of that profession. She is, in fact, a quiet progressive. She is also in her personal life tougher and more determined than people casually encountering the motherly style she displays in the photo. She has not only recouped on an inauspicious educational start and gained the qualifications she had missed out on, she has proceeded to add to them, joining that impressive band of women who, while continuing to rear their children and run households, pursue a university course as well. There are some people it is very difficult to read from appearances alone.

# Kailash Sarda

General Practitioner, born 1938, Tanzania.

*'Then it suddenly dawned on me, anyone could be in these shoes.'*

My father was an engineer. He had a building construction business in East Africa. In 1946, being traditional Indians, my eldest brother was taken by my mother to be married off in India, and I went with them. So we were there when India got independence in '47. It was horrifying, because of the partition, particularly in the Punjab, which was split into two. The Muslims went to West Punjab, which is part of Pakistan, and the Hindus moved east. A lot of people were massacred. Frightening? Oh God, yes! Definitely!

I don't want to go into too many details, and we were in India and in a largely Hindu village, so we were fairly safe. But a mile or so away, there was a village largely Muslim. And I remember a large group of elders from this Muslim village coming over to our village, and saying, 'Look, we've lived here all these generations, and we've been on good terms all along, why suddenly has this happened? It's not necessary.' And our elders said, 'Yes, of course, carry on as we always have'. The next morning, word came round that these very people had packed and gone. Because they were frightened. The village was empty. When the Hindus in our village found out, a frenzy for some reason struck them and they all charged down the road to this village, and started looting and setting the houses on fire. For no apparent reason. Sheer madness.

And there was a horrible incident on the outskirts of the village. I saw these local people grab ...there were two men, two ladies, a babe and a toddler. They stopped these people going to the village, saying, 'Who are you?' 'We are Sikhs and these are our wives.' 'We don't believe you. These are Muslim women; you are probably taking them away to Pakistan. You're providing them with safe passage. Where are their bangles? We don't believe you. You are a traitor.' And they kicked these men and chased them away. And they took these two women and the children to the fields. And I followed them. And I'm not exaggerating; the babe was thrown on to the ground, and axed right across the face... you can't imagine it. A human...and I was nine years of age.

Then it suddenly dawned on me, God, next they'll be grabbing me. I was a foreigner because I was born in East Africa and these people didn't know me from Tom. And I'm not a Sikh. My hair was short. There was nothing to distinguish me from a Muslim. I didn't wait to see what followed, you know, to the women. I ran like hell!

We used to hear all these tales, train loads of people coming from the other side, they'd all been slaughtered, or a train load of people going there, and they'd been stopped and... It was horrific. But once you get into politics there's no end to it. We keep away from it.

But then my brother got married and we came back to Tanganyika in '48 leaving my other two older brothers in a boarding school in Simla. They came back in the December on the three-month school holidays. In those days travelling took about twelve to fourteen days coming from Simla, catching a train down to Bombay, and then waiting for a day or two to catch the boat. Crossing the Indian Ocean to East Africa took up another ten, twelve days. And when they went back in March or February '49, I went with them. So I was in Simla from '49 to '55.

The school was founded in 1857 by a former housemaster from Rugby. Prior to '47, about ninety-five per cent of the boarding students were English, and five per cent at most Indians. But of course after the partition a lot of the English left India. And when I joined about seventy-five per cent of the students were Indians.

It was a traditional English school. About seventy per cent of the teachers were English and only about thirty per cent Indian. You wore your uniform, and you went to church in the morning. I was a Hindu. But whatever religion you were was irrelevant. You had to go to chapel. You had to. I don't personally think it converted many of the students to Christianity. But that didn't stop me participating. I quite enjoyed it, singing the hymns. History was a mixture of English, starting about Henry VIII's time, and some Indian history, not current Indian history, all pre-British arrival, I think we must have come as far as about 1550.

The school's still operating. Strange as it sounds, I loved it and was very happy there. But my younger brother hated it. He used to write letters home saying, 'I'm going to run away.' That made Mother anxious. If he runs away in India she'll never find her son again! So he came back.

It was during boarding school that I realized the privileged position some people had, and the masses of poverty. Simla is at a height of about seven thousand feet. It's very cold in winter. From about mid-December to March it's more or less snowbound. So we used to come down on the train. We didn't see our parents for sometimes four years at a time, because it was too far to travel. But we went down to our village, where our ancestry were farmers. And on the day we left school, we were given packed lunches, sandwiches and bananas. Of course we had had enough of school food... throw the bananas to the monkeys, there were loads of monkeys there, and the sandwiches to the beggars. You'd rather enjoy that, chucking the damned things to the beggars. Then I realised, anyone could be in those shoes. I could be one of them. I was fortunately born into a privileged family. I thought this is ridiculous, behaving the way I am, throwing things. I think that more or less decided me that I wanted to be a doctor and help humanity.

But my family were mainly in the engineering profession. My eldest brother came to Cambridge and did engineering, my next brother came to Oxford and did architecture. And my father wanted me to be a chartered surveyor. But Mum said, 'Son, you do what you want to do.' So I went in for medicine.

I came over to England to do my A-levels and I tried to get into Oxford or Cambridge, but I didn't have any luck and ended up in Trinity, Dublin.

My brother, who did engineering, married an Indian girlfriend and family friend he met during one of his trips back to school. My second brother was taken to India to get married, and there was another Indian girl there from Uganda. Her family was looking for a boy for her. They got to like each other, and they eloped to London, and got married in Oxford, at the Registry Office. All hell broke loose with the parents up in arms. But they lived happily ever after. I met my wife in the later part of my medical student days. She was a nurse in the same hospital. She's Irish and we got married here, in Sudbury.

This affected my desire to go back to India and help the poor. I had to think about my wife now and I thought in all fairness I should settle down over here. And Suffolk seemed a nice place.

I'm not the oldest doctor in the town but I've been here the longest. I came in October '69. It was a small practice with about fifteen hundred patients. I was on my own. This was the surgery and we lived upstairs 'above the shop'. And I knew all the patients.

There has been quite a transformation. As the practice grew and with the changes in the National Health Service, various ancillary staff were attached. We've had a nurse fourteen years. My first partner, Dr. Patel, who's also from Dar-es-Salaam, also an Indian, married to an Irish girl from Dublin, came in 1971. Then in 1981 I took over another practice. We had a list of about five thousand then, and he had a list of about three. So that increased the workload considerably, and obviously we had to expand in space too. By good fortune next door became vacant, and we were able to incorporate the two semi-detached houses into one surgery complex, more or less like a fully comprehensive health centre. Even prior to that, for say fifteen years, we've had two health visitors attached. They look after the children, give mothers guidance regarding nutrition, hygiene; look after any eye or hearing problems. Apart from that there is a community nursing sister for the people who need home nursing care.

So we have four doctors and a list of just over eight thousand patients now. More than ninety per cent of the children are immunised, the same with cervical cytology. There is a small proportion of ladies who don't like cervical smears and you've got to respect their views. But on the whole they're aware of the risks and come and have it done. The recent change in the National Health Service and the new contract, where we are paid largely depending on whether we meet our target figures has made us more aware. And we have met our targets.

Also we're having more health promotion clinics, asthma, hypertension, anti-smoking, alcohol advice, dietary...we have about twelve clinics, apart from our normal consultations. Then we have anti-natal and family planning clinics and... I've also been doing some occupational medicine work, looking after two of the local factories, employers and employees. Which is different from general practice work and I find it stimulating and interesting. Sometimes my patients tell me, 'Oh God, doctor, you're busy', and I say, 'Well, I enjoy it. I don't enjoy you being ill, it's just that I enjoy my work.'

I like to think of myself as a relaxed, friendly chap. Whenever I meet patients I call them by their first names, and try to explain to them medical ongoings in laymen's terms. I'm very happy with my lot! We're settled here. Oh yes, yes. Our ways are set and the children are progressing.

By '76 we had had three of our four children and we only had two bedrooms, no dining-room and a small kitchenette. The surgery list was expanding and we needed more room. Eventually we saw this house in Friars Street, which has a fascinating history, because it's been a GP's house since Victorian times. It used to have its consulting room and a small waiting-room about five by twelve, with benches on either side. People have told me that if you sat, your knees touched the person opposite, it was so cramped. And there was a door between the waiting-room and a little dispensary at the back, where they used to make their own potions, and a cubby-hole with a door you lifted to dish out your medicines. It's actually a Georgian house with a Victorian white-brick front. It faces the cricket ground so you've a lovely view, and it's five minutes' walk from the surgery. It's very convenient!

Yet I still have the desire to have a Range Rover and a luxury caravan. The caravan would be a mobile clinic, and go around India for three months in the year, and help people in rural parts. I come from the Punjab, and that's the area I'd go to. How practical the idea is I don't know, but you could do a lot of preventive medicine there.

# Nita Stanford

Health Visitor. Born 1945, Belfast.

*'I always say that the babies haven't read the books.'*

I've been interested in nursing from an early age, because I spent a lot of time in hospital as a child. I had pneumonia and things. Then...I don't know why, but I got this idea, around the age of ten or eleven, that it would be exciting to join the Royal Air Force. I don't know whether I actually thought I would get to fly planes or what. I think it was listening to the Flying Doctor on the radio at that time; it seemed wonderfully exciting, you know, people dashing about all over the place. So, at the age of seventeen I decided to join the Air Force and do my nursing training and then go off and join the flying doctor service in Australia. That was my idea, as a teenager, of an exciting life!

Unfortunately life didn't quite work out like that! I did join the Air Force at seventeen. But I couldn't begin my SRN training because by law you've got to be eighteen. I had been accepted but unfortunately my mother had a coronary. I was the only child and Mother was a widow. So, back home I went to Belfast to look after Mother.

I couldn't wait to get away again having been away. So once my mother was well enough I wrote off to about eight or nine different hospitals to begin my training, and Chelmsford happened to be the first one that accepted me. So I ended up doing my nursing training there. And while there I met my husband, and we got married and set up home in Chelmsford. And from that we moved to Great Yeldham and I had two children.

During my student nurse days I had been aware that when people came into hospital and you looked after them you only saw one side. And you were dealing with a fait accompli: they were already ill. Alright, you could help to put it better. But I was of the impression that it would be much better if they stopped getting ill in the first place. Also I liked the idea of meeting people in their own homes, on their territory, rather than always on mine.

I didn't do anything about it because a) I hadn't got the necessary O-levels and b) I got married and had children. But then as I was just doing part-time work I decided I would start doing some O-levels. But I got side-tracked because somebody suggested that while I was doing them, 'You could do A-levels Nita, and why don't you go on to university? Everybody else is going.' I was with a small group who did A-levels together. They all went off to university. I said no, I wouldn't go, because university was only for clever people. But they seemed to survive and the following year I was feeling there was nowhere I could progress just working part-time, so why not get some qualifications? So I did apply, and went to Essex and did a degree in sociology.

It was quite exciting. It did make the brain hurt at times, when you're not used to doing that thing. I enjoyed it because it made one question every assumption that one ever had. It was extremely stimulating and very hard work. Especially when you've got to dash home and look after children, then as soon as they go to bed start studying. I suppose my only regret is that, going in as a mature student with family responsibilities, I couldn't join in a lot of the other interesting things that were going on. It was basically go to lectures, go to the library, and home again. Although I made some friends and met some interesting people.

It gave me a lot more self confidence, because being ill a lot as a child I had missed out on schooling and I'd left school at fifteen with no qualifications whatsoever. And there's always this niggle at the back of your mind: what could you have done? So from that point of view it was very good.

And it made me question a lot of things. I actually had to think about them and justify them. But I don't think it changed any of my views and beliefs radically. It didn't change me from a Thatcherite to a Marxist or anything dramatic like that. There was no Road to Damascus experience either way! But it was quite an experience.

So then, when I finished university I applied for health visitor training. And that was much more difficult to get on because it's a complicated procedure. But anyway, I did my health visitor training at Ipswich in 1983, and then came to this job. I have been here ever since.

I like the variety of people I meet, from all stratas of society. But I think the thing I enjoy most is meeting the ordinary young mum who perhaps hasn't got an awful lot of confidence in herself. To see her grow in confidence, and from being slightly terrified at the beginning actually to enjoy her family, it's very nice, yes, it is.

I think there's always need for health promotion. Look at our rates of death from coronary heart disease, one of the highest in the world. We have had various market stalls where the health visitors have actually been out to give advice and promote health. Those are the sort of things

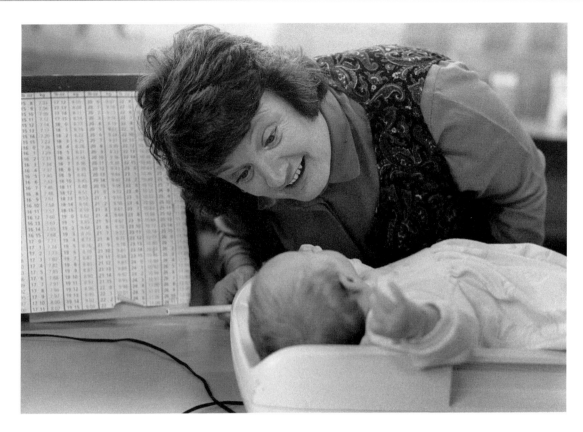

that we need to expand. And I still think that despite the good work that is being done in the schools, parenthood comes as an awful shock to a lot of people, the reality rather than what the books say. I always say that the babies haven't read the books. It would be nice if they'd come knowing what they were supposed to do, but unfortunately they don't.

The weaknesses of the job ...? If I could give everyone on my case-load a nice home, a job with a reasonable income, I could solve an awful lot of health problems at a stroke. It can be very frustrating when you know there is nothing you can do. You can give support, and write letters to the Housing in support of people's housing applications. But the Housing people are under so much pressure. And there's not a lot we can do about getting people into employment unfortunately. It would be lovely to have a magic wand sometimes. But unfortunately, that's life, isn't it?

There's too much paper work, which I am notoriously bad at and hate doing, but I realise it is essential to try to do it. Every year I think I spend more time doing paper work. That frustrates me, because I feel I should be out there.

I feel there are some people who are still slightly wary of us because they think we are going to take their children away from them if they don't do things like we say. One of the things I always make very clear to people right from the beginning, is that I am a nurse, I'm not a social worker; I'm not going to inspect their house. People have asked me, do I want to look at the drains! Do I want to look at the room the baby's going to sleep in? I say, 'I'm not here to lay down rules. I will comment on safety factors'. If they haven't got a fire guard - that's for the child's sake - one has to comment.

It's not the sort of job where you see dramatic changes. In a hospital people come in ill, and hopefully you see them go out well, and they say, 'Well thanks a lot nurse, I feel a lot better'. The sort of thing that pleases me is that perhaps a mum will ring me up and say, 'Can you tell me...?' That pleases me, because they've got enough confidence in me to ask. Another thing is if you've seen a family through a fairly tough time like a bereavement, and you see them come to terms with it and pick up a normal life again, even though obviously they still haven't forgotten.

I went back to Belfast for the first time in twenty-two years last year. I've got no close family over there.

# Chapter Nine

# FOR YOUR COMFORT AND CONVENIENCE

There is a group of people in our society whose working lives are spent servicing the home, smoothing the domestic round saving the rest of us time and trouble. Cecily Stebbing and Annie Newman have worked for extended periods - one as a domestic, the other as a home help. George Cooper is a postman and Peter Byham is one of four generations of milkmen. We take for granted the services these people provide, though we would miss them sorely were they to disappear. Yet despite the comforts they supply, these people have traditionally had little social recognition.

Badly paid and working horrendous hours under poor conditions, women who went into service often escaped into alternative jobs as soon as they could. Factory work offered more freedom and greater independence. But factories were not to everyone's taste. The two women here describe lives in which the considerable periods spent working in other people's homes are by no means remembered with distaste.

**Annie Newman**'s character is marked by a deep stoicism and absence of rancour. Physical disabilities have marred her entire life and some people will find her portrait which captures the blank gaze of her eyes, painful. She also tolerated conditions many people would have rebelled against, and derived considerable satisfactions from being a home-help. For she clearly took her role very seriously in the rearing and training of the children she looked after, and in time came to feel that under different circumstances, she might have made a good teacher.

For **Cecily Stebbing** there were also real satisfactions attached to domestic work. Acquiring her own house only late in life, there was pleasure in being left in charge of someone else's, and ensuring that she kept it looking beautiful. It seems appropriate that a major feature of her photograph should be her hands which, in a natural gesture, she clasped in front of her.

**George Cooper** is a jovial man and his portrait with its unaffectedly untidy posture captures a sense of cheerful relaxation. He is also a man of surprises. At the same time as living up to the children's book illustration of the friendly postman, he has literally travelled the world, is an enthusiastic bee keeper and an organic gardener.

**Peter Byham**, by contrast, is not a story-book milkman but a successful businessman. Though he recalls driving cows through the streets of Sudbury, the milk now arrives in container lorries, he sits in an office and secretaries arrange the rounds on computers. The Byham family's ability to keep abreast of the times has led not only to a profitable business with a sleek Jaguar parked alongside the milk floats, but made them virtually the only milk delivery firm in the town. Yet they continue to operate from the original site and until a year or so ago Peter Byham lived in the same house as his grandfather with the milk crates stacked next door. Indeed he only moved out in order to let his younger son move in.

# Annie Newman
Domestic, born 1915, Sudbury.

*'...people have told me since, I should have gone into teaching.'*

I arrived in one of those little Victorian bay-windowed houses, seventy-six years ago, January 1915. I remember the Armistice of the First World War, because that evening my mother took me down in my perambulator to see the lights of Sudbury, which I'd never seen before. I particularly remember the two gas brackets outside St. Peter's Church were lit up. And to me as a small child that looked absolutely wonderful.

When I first went to school you wore white pinafores over your dress. They had to be washed and starched and you had a fresh one on each morning - a lot of work for Mother! I often wonder what the children of today would think of the clothes we wore. Because on our feet we usually wore woollen, hand-knitted stockings. And then there were button or lace-up boots to the knee, ideal in the winter. And you had perhaps a flannel petticoat on underneath your dress, which wasn't always comfortable. The stockings used to be itchy too! And in those days the hair was usually long. You either had it in two plaits or you had it drawn back from the face, and ribbons put at each side of the head, tying it back.

I went to school in North Street. Girls and boys were kept separate. We were let out at one time in the morning and afternoon, and the boys afterwards; we never played together at school in those days. We had a good schooling with history, geography, and arithmetic. And we also were taught sewing until we got to twelve. Then we used to go one day a week to learn cookery and cleaning of silver. I've always been grateful for my schooling, because in those days it was thorough. And we had pleasant times as well in school.

But we used to have what they called drill, which was physical exercise. And I used to fall over backwards; I think chiefly, although it wasn't recognised then, the arthritic condition was already in my hips. The teacher would say, 'Hips firm, knees bend'. And of course I'd get down to a certain position and then, whoops! off she goes, back! So she thought I was a naughty little girl and as a punishment, I used to have to stay in after school, learning poetry, or writing it out, 'The Lady of Shallot' and Wordsworth's 'The Daffodils'. Also one of Tennyson's about statues on the terraces, and peacocks strutting by. As a matter of fact, I disliked poetry in those days, but now I just love it. Whether I didn't get into the rhythm of it, I don't know.

But it's a ridiculous way of making a child behave properly. In those days, teachers hadn't got much imagination. They didn't go into the question of why is this child falling over every time I tell her to do that? I don't think it would happen these days, because there's so much checking on children's health isn't there? We weren't taken to the doctor's. There wasn't the money. When the rent was four and six a week you had to pay a half-a-crown to the doctor before he'd come out, and in those days my mother was working for sixpence an hour. But when Mother did take me to the doctor's because of the pain, he said, 'Oh, that's growing pains, she'll grow out of it.' You see there weren't X-rays in those days.

I would have loved to have learnt to swim. There was an old bathing pool, which was a piece of the river partitioned off. But my mother was afraid of running water. I never knew why. So, not to cause her stress, I didn't go swimming. Then nine years ago I was in West Suffolk for the arthritis. They used to put me in the hydro pool each day. It was a joy to get in there.

I was very close to my father, who used to take me for long walks. He was a keen man for herbs. He used to point out different herbs, what they were used for. We would collect yarrow and he used to dry it and make a tea if anyone had a bad cough. If a horse broke or bruised its leg, they put a poultice of comfrey on. And I myself drank comfrey tea when my leg wouldn't heal, and I do believe it had some help. He would make up white oils and men that used to play football would come up with their small bottle and ask him for a pennyworth of embrocation oils, to rub on their stiff legs. There used to be a salve he made, that used to help heal an open wound if you fell down or scratched yourself. Of course there's all sorts of herbs we don't see in the hedgerows now, because of the sprays they use.

Sunday morning I used to go to Sunday School, and again in the afternoon. And Mother would go to church in the morning, with Father, and then we used to go for these nice walks in the evenings. Especially on Sunday evening in the summer, father used to like to go out. In those days you would hear the bells from all different churches. Often he'd say, 'Now you listen, there's Lavenham Church coming in, and that's Cornard'. On a still summer evening it's surprising what you could hear. There were no noisy motor cars or aeroplanes to disturb the quietness.

He was a keen gardener and he also liked to look after his chickens. People kept chickens then. It was a means of having an egg supply come into the house. We had a hen

run, but with plenty of room. And a hen house so they could have shelter at night. He used to put me in the hen run and tell me to collect the eggs. And we had a cockerel that used to chase me, and to this day I can't bear it if a bird comes near me and flutters.

At Christmas I always had a stocking, but I never had a Christmas tree. And I had a dolly and a funny little wickerwork pram, with a wooden handle and two little wheels. I can remember my mother taking me to buy it. That was a Christmas and birthday present. My birthday is in January, so I always had Christmas and birthday together - through lack of money.

When I was nine my father died. That was very hard on my mother. She used to go out daily doing domestic work. There were two ladies she used to go to, and there were no days off in those days except she used to have Sunday off. But I never went short of clothing or food. My mother was a good manager and she made all my clothes.

After school I went into domestic work too until I had to give up in 1950, because of my sight going. One family, the gentleman was manager of a corset factory. I think I was with them six years. Another worked in the tax office and one had his own little business. It was six days a week, eight till five. Saturday afternoon perhaps I could get done an hour earlier, so I could get home and do some shopping.

They were long weeks and very hard work, because there weren't the sophisticated washing machines, or vacuum cleaners. You got down on your knees with a hand brush and dust pan. And you did all the washing by hand. For the children. And the sheets and pillowcases. Then you put them through a great big mangle. Being a short person, sometimes it took me some pushing! And we ironed with flat-irons. Oh, it was a great occasion when they had electric irons.

My mother and I did our own washing on Sunday morning. No, I didn't think of it as unjust that some women were able to stay at home and also have me in to help, not a bit. It was the way of life. And you managed. I suppose some people would think it was hard, but it was just a way of getting bread and butter. And I'm very grateful that I had that sort of work, because I think that's taught me to cope with life. I appreciate now things that are done for me.

I worked at Gainsborough's House as a chambermaid when it was a small hotel. Some retired people lived there and one of the church organists Dr. Thalben-Ball stayed there for a time. But they also used to take in weekly guests. People with children would come on the train or by car for the week.

My work would entail getting there about half past seven, to go round with the early morning tea, and I'd usually finish about eight o'clock in the evening. If you had Sunday off, you didn't have a day off in the week. Christmas Day afternoon, perhaps you were lucky and got off at three o'clock. In those days workers weren't looked after like they are now. We just treated Christmas as another day really. You couldn't do anything else. We got in perhaps an extra piece of meat, and had a Christmas pudding. But there wasn't money to buy Christmas presents in those days!

But I liked the job. It was a way of earning money. I did it, I think, for three years, until the management changed, and the new manageress brought in different staff. I went back as a mother's help then.

If possible I worked where there were children of toddler age, so I could help the mother look after them, because I was very fond of children. And I was always fortunate that the mothers let me correct them without interfering. I went in daily and I'd stay until the family didn't need me any more. Then I just went and found work somewhere else. No, I don't know where the children are now. They've all moved away, and their parents have gone.

In 1934 I started the first Brownie pack in this town. I realized then that I could control children and get them to do what I wanted without shouting. In fact people have told me since that I should have gone into teaching. But there weren't the help in those days for you to do that sort of thing.

In 1954 my mother and I moved to a little two-room cottage in Suffolk Square. They've built flats there now. You stepped into a living-room from the garden, and there was a bedroom, and the landlord had built a little kitchen on the back. You had a tin bath, and made do with that. My

mother died in 1961. I'd looked after her and done all the cooking so she was only in hospital a week before she died. But I went into a home then.

My sight had been going peculiar since I was about ten years old. It's something to do with the retina. The veins at the back of the retina haemorrhage, and that produces scarring on the retina itself, and so no light can get through. If it happened now, I could have had laser beam treatment and that would have sealed the veins. But fortunately, going blind has never bothered me. Now, losing my hearing, that was a terrible tragedy to me. I still get in a bit of a panic when my hearing aid battery goes dead. I know I shouldn't, but I just can't stop myself. I think it's because, not being able to see, I lose contact with people when I can't hear. You feel as if you're in a cage, and there's no light coming through.

My hearing went quite suddenly - through the arthritis. One day I just couldn't hear. It was Harvesting Sunday. I'd got the service on, and I'd had a fresh battery in my radio and I had to turn it up high. I thought, oh, the battery's not working. Then a friend came in, and said, 'For goodness sake, turn that down!' And she was shouting at me, 'Whatever's the matter?' I said, 'I can't hear.'

It's distressing when you can't hear properly. You're straining to hear, and you try your hardest and then somebody says, 'Oh it's no good talking to you, you can't hear'! That's one of the most shocking things I think to say. People don't think of the pain they give you, sometimes. I have learnt to build a brick wall between me and the next person, if you know what I mean. But my disablement has taught me a lot. I know that often when people say things, they don't mean them. You have to remember that. But it hurts.

I naturally would love to be able to get up and walk out like people do, but I know I can't do it. Everybody tells me that I'm a very patient person but I think it was my father that taught me that. Because if I went to him and said, 'Dad, I can't do this,' he'd say, 'You go back and have another try. Go on.' And that's right; if you try hard enough you can usually find a way round it. And I think that's what's helped me to cope.

People go out such a lot these days, don't they? The helpers here sometimes say, 'When I leave off at six o'clock, we're going out for the evening'. They will go to a public house. Well I must admit I've never been in a public house in my life! No! I do think sometimes it would be a good thing if young people today had to weather it a bit more, and learn to save up for things.

# Cicely Stebbing

Domestic, Silk Factory Worker, Hospital Orderly, born 1909, Long Melford, Suffolk.

*'I really liked the housework best.'*

We were eight children in the family. I was the youngest and we were fortunate enough to have a three-bedroomed house although of course you rented them, you didn't buy them. My father worked at the flour mill. He used to get up at six o'clock and go to work, come home at eight o'clock for his breakfast. Then he came home to lunch, and in the afternoon, when I was old enough, I had to take him a flask of tea, and he used to come home from work at eight-thirty in the evening. All those hours! He did work hard; he said he'd never ever want any of his sons to do the job that he'd done, a flour miller. He used to say he wouldn't bring drink into the house on account of his children, but he thought he was entitled to a drink in the pub, a half a pint.

I always had long curls, done in ringlets. I used to twist the hair round a bit of rag. And when the hair had gone round it had to be tied at the bottom. We used to have these spin tops and hit them with a whip, and hoops and hit them and run after them. And my sister if she had any sweets given her during the day, because we didn't get many sweets, she used to save them and give us one each. And we used to play games in bed because my youngest brother and my next sister, we used to have to go to bed about half-past eight. We used to imagine we were rich, and I had all lovely things, lovely dolls' prams, all in the mind.

We didn't get much on our birthdays. Christmas, well, by the time I came, being the last child, I think my mum had got a bit fed up with it, and I think I used to put things in the stocking myself! Because I didn't get anything in it. Put an orange in my stocking before I went to bed. But we managed. We didn't have much luxuries. We never went out for the day at the seaside or anything like that. But we always had enough to eat, and my mum was ever so clean and tidy.

We had to walk to school. It was a long way, and of course we didn't have any wellingtons on or mackintoshes, when it was raining. But the schoolmistress was ever so strict, she said, 'You won't melt, you're not sugar. You come to school, raining or not'. We had to go. I didn't like school very much. I wouldn't say I was a dunce but I'm not what you call brilliant. I didn't do very well at school. I had one sister who could have done well if she'd have had the chance to train for something. But you had to go to work to earn a bit of money to give your mum for food.

I was thirteen or fourteen when I left school. I hadn't got a bicycle. I couldn't even ride a bicycle. So my older sister and me, we went to work at a branch of the corset factory that used to be in Sudbury They had to have different needles and cottons and bindings sent in from Sudbury, and I used to have to check to see that everything was coming in and they never got left without anything. I used to feel important doing that. I think I earned seven shillings a week. And I had to give it to my mother. Then they closed down. That was when I went to the Gainsborough silk weaving on a warping machine.

I got a very old second-hand bike then and I rode into Sudbury. There I met this boyfriend, and he said, 'That old bike's not safe for you to come to work on. I'll pay something down at the shop, if you can manage to pay each week'. So I was very lucky, I got a new bicycle.

My sister and I hadn't been at the Gainsborough very long, when we found out that Mr. Sayers had been married and as they didn't ask the staff to his wedding he gave a party up at his house. We had charades and a nice meal. I liked that job. But we went on short time, and we had to have three days at work and three days on the dole. That took our money down a bit, and we was bored doing nothing. I get fed up if I haven't got a nice lot of work to do, you know. So I left.

Because I like housework, I went to Mrs. Clover. They'd got three children, and they said, 'Do you like children?' Of course I said yes, because I wanted to get the job. But I really liked the housework best. I stayed there a good while. I lived in, but I used to get homesick. When I saw the girls going home from work to their mothers, I wanted to go as well. So she used to say, 'Well you can go home every night on your bike, if you like'. So I done that. And I carried on with that kind of work until I got another job in another factory. But in the end I left the factories altogether. I loved housework, but I wouldn't sleep in like my sister. I used to go daily. I used to have one nice job. There was a shop in Sudbury the name of Butterworth. And his wife helped out in the shop, and she used to be out all day, and she used to tell me what she wanted done before she went. I was happy there because there was nobody in the way. And that was a lovely house. I done it just how I liked and when I liked. After that I used to be on the wards at the old hospital, cleaning again. It was quite nice working there.

After I'd grown up we used to go to Clacton or Felixstowe

for a week in a boarding house but my mum and dad never went for holidays. I went to France once. I was staying at some seaside place and you could go for the day over to France, Calais. Cor, coming back, that was terrible. I was sea-sick! Oh dear! I don't go for holidays now. I don't really want to. It's funny how you settle down as you get older.

When my dad retired we moved to Sudbury. Somebody put a word in for us, and we got a council house - not a new one, an old three-storey. Of course they're modernised now, but they wasn't when we went there, they hadn't got anything modern. The toilet was right down the bottom of a long garden. My mum and dad they lived there for several years. They're both buried near there and I got left in this big house. So when I got to the age of sixty - because you can retire at sixty can't you, although I went till I was sixty-five - I wrote to the council and asked if I could have a modern bungalow. I told them how things had been, and how I'd looked after my parents until they died, and I wanted to live in a smaller place. And they let me have one, straight away. Of course I'd never lived in a modern house with a bathroom and all that before. We never had a bathroom until I moved into that bungalow. All them years you know. It was a long time, wasn't it?

That was a nice little bungalow. I had everything; I had carpets. When we were children we didn't have carpets. We had lino all the way round and mats, but we'd never had a carpet or a settee or anything like that, we just had ordinary chairs. But we was clean and tidy and respectable!

And I had a dear little garden at the bungalow. Lovely geraniums in pots in the porchway. Most of the people used to grow vegetables, but I used to grow all flowers. I didn't grow vegetables! The soil was so good. I used to have lovely gladioli, and you'd often see me walking along taking them to somebody. Yes, I liked that. I liked living there all right. I lived in there several years.

Then one of my sisters, she was ill. I had a letter come one day from her neighbour to say that she was pretty queer and could I go. Of course I went. Just before I went my doctor told me not to overdo things. Of course I never thought any more about it, but that was what made me have the stroke. I went against the doctor's orders. And that's how I came here.

I had to give the bungalow up to come in here. It nearly broke my heart, it did really. Because I'd got everything just how I liked it, after working all them years. Oh dear, I had to get rid of everything. I just let them go cheap.

*In the centre, the youngest of the family, about 1914*

When I go out now I often see somebody in the town, she says, 'Oh, your bedroom suite, I'd never had a bedroom suite before'. Yes, she was so pleased. She always mentions it when she sees me out.

But I could see that the bungalow wasn't for when you get older. It would have been too much. I've been here a good few years and I don't regret it, really, because everything is done for you. And I always dreaded when I got old, getting dirty you know, and untidy.

When I first came here that was November. I kept looking at the garden. And when it got fairly warm I didn't say nothing to anybody, I went to the shed and got the hoe and the tools out, and I worked out there for a long while, nearly all day. Nobody said anything to me. I thought, you know, I'd get told off because I didn't ask. Well at the end of the day, the matron said to me, 'Thanks for weeding my herb bed', So that was all right. It's a lovely garden, isn't it? Bill, he does all the odd jobs, and he does the garden, and he's made that lawn and those lovely round beds where the flowers are, tulips.

\*　\*　\*　\*

# Peter Byham

Dairy owner, born 1936, Sudbury.

*'...your business was only as good as your cream line.'*

The business started in 1913, seventy-eight years ago, with my grandfather and one cow. There were twenty-two milkmen in Sudbury, then. So it was very local, you just supplied the streets near you. Then as the older milkmen retired we took the rounds over. Now there's just ourselves in Sudbury. We employ twenty milkmen on twenty rounds, plus office staff. So the business has changed out of all recognition.

At the beginning it was very basic, hand milked into a pail, and delivered warm, actually straight from the cow. It was two milkings a day, which it still is, but also two deliveries a day, morning and afternoon, because the keeping quality was so low. Often the milk was sour by morning. So, that was quite a hard type of business. But there again it was a regular income, which wasn't easily found.

We had a twelve gallon churn on a three-wheel barrow, a lovely thing, brass taps, brass caps, and the stirrer, at the top, to agitate the milk to keep the cream fairly level. It was pushed by hand. And on the front handles of the cart there used to be two-gallon cans, and the churn taps was turned on, and milk put into the cans when required. And they had a pint and a half-pint ladle and you ladled out of the cans straight into the jug at the door.

Later the milk was put through a cooler, a ribbed aluminium steel contraption, with cold water running through the inside, to cool the milk down. That was the beginning of the single delivery. And we started to go a bit further out in Sudbury. We then had a three-wheel bicycle, with a tray on the front, which would carry about four to five crates of milk. It was quite a bit of weight to push round.

The first cow was kept here, in a small yard. And with all the Common Land around us, everybody had grazing rights for which they paid the Freemen of the Borough. So to start with our cows grazed on the Common Land. Then, as we got more cattle we purchased another yard and two meadows. And as we increased further my grandfather rented other grazing land from farmers. In the finish, we went to about a hundred head of cattle.

Our herd was mainly a mixed herd: Fresians for bulk, Guernseys as a good intermediate and a few Jerseys. So we always maintained a good cream line, even in winter

which was important. Mixed herds are nice, and produce a good product, but they are obviously not so profitable. Fresians are the most profitable, because you get the bulk but of course you get a reduced cream. Now that doesn't matter.

To feed the cattle we used to lease a farm to grow mangles and so on. But it became difficult to get feed after the war, and we were finding it hard to keep the cattle in the condition in which they should be kept. So that was when we decided to sell the herd and buy milk in from farms who had bigger areas to graze. We used to pick up about twenty-five farms in about a five-mile radius, which is quite amazing today, because they're all gone. It was more profitable to go arable and a lot easier. When you have to get up early mornings, and do two milkings, a farmer can think, well, I'll just grow cereals,

When we had the farm we had Suffolk Punches, about seven or eight, for ploughing and harvesting with binders. They were lovely animals. And we had a horseman of course. We did have one tractor but that was as far as mechanisation went. Mangles and sugar-beet, that was all done by hand. We employed about three men delivering milk, but they also did farmwork. There was hay-making to be done, and crops to be lifted. So the men not only started early, they were still working at ten o'clock in the evening, summertime. It was a hard life, no doubt about it.

A milkman's day consisted of about sixteen hours. They was up early, milked the cows, then delivered. Then the cow-sheds had to be maintained, and the cows grazed out and brought back again, and the whole process was done again in the afternoon, and in the evening. And with cattle you have always got cows calving. Oh, I remember we having calves! And to lower vet bills, basically most of the calves were born with just my grandfather doing it himself.

When I was a youngster we hardly ever saw my father. He was at work before I got up, and he was still at work when I went to bed. My day is about eight until five. It's mainly office work, because the rounds today, they're a lot larger and need a great deal of supervision. We now have a computerised system which has greatly assisted us but has brought a lot more work into the office than when the roundsmen did their own bookwork.

We used to do the processing here, bottle filling and washing. Then legislation came in that milk had to be pasteurised. So we got it pasteurised elsewhere. Then the ruling came that milk must be bottled where it was pasteurised. So we had to get pasteurisation in, or finish

bottling, and my father decided then that we would buy in bottled milk.

We started off with one cow, supplying about twenty households; we're now supplying about ten thousand households. The main competition we have nowadays is the supermarket chains. We have had to accept that they take a large slice of our business. But, thankfully, the majority of people still like their milk delivered to the doorstep, preferably in a glass bottle.

Back in the old days your business was only as good as your cream line! And if your cream line wasn't what the customer thought it should be they'd darned soon tell you quick. The deeper yellow the cream, the better the product in the customer's eyes. I believe that still is. But that's another thing. And if someone else had a better colour cream line than you'd got, you had to work very hard to keep that custom. It goes against all today's theories. Nowadays, I suppose fifty per cent of our milk sold is semi- or fresh-skimmed. It may revert again.

A few years ago, supplying people's cream needs left a lot of skimmed milk nobody wanted. It was virtually given away to pig farmers, Now, we can't produce enough fresh and semi-skimmed. It's ironic really how it's changed round. But we're eating as much cream. That's the funny thing about it. People want low fat milk but cream on their Christmas pudding and for the fruit season, for strawberries and raspberries. Everybody's conscious of what milk they're drinking and yet they still want cream to make a fuss of themselves.

Fresh milk is a totally different product to pasteurised. It has a totally different flavour, and I must admit I didn't like pasteurised at all. But your palate accustoms itself to it, doesn't it? I must admit now we mostly have semi-skimmed ourselves now.

We stopped Sunday deliveries about ten years ago. We work a six-day week now. The thing was the keeping quality of the product has greatly improved. But the main reason we done it for was because it was getting more difficult to recruit staff. They used to have a day off on a rota system. But the thought of Sunday work frightened a lot of people. And we double up on the Christmas Eve, so the staff can have a day with their families on Christmas Day, which is quite important. It does make a lot of work the day before Christmas Eve and Christmas Eve, and indeed the day after, but I think it's worth it to get that day off at home.

The official starting time is five in the morning, but Peter, who gets all the loads out, he starts at three. The gates are open at four, and there's quite a few start at four o'clock. So the majority of the customers get their milk by break-fast time. And that's what people want. And I think that's what led the supermarkets to buy milk. Because if the milk is not delivered by the time the wife goes to work, it's left out all day, and summertime that's not very good, unless they come to an arrangement to find a shady spot. So it is important to get the milk on the doorstep at a reasonable time in the morning so it can be put in a refrigerator by the time the wife goes out. The problem is that you've got to have your rounds large enough to be profitable but everybody wants the milk early. And if you start too early in the morning we get complaints of the noise from the customers.

Two of the men have been here thirty, thirty-five years; And we have another two who have been here about twenty-three years I think. And quite a few between fifteen and twenty years. You have a turnover of course. A lot go.

We've always lived on the premises. I went to school in North Street and then to the secondary modern school. That's where I done my schooling. And here's where my two sisters and myself were born and brought up. I moved out four years ago. But my older son, Nigel, lives here now, so it's a continuation of the family living in the same house. Grandfather, Father, myself, and now my son. And both my sons are in the business; my eldest runs the dairy and my younger son runs the bakery shops we've opened. They're also convenience stores open eight in the morning until nine in the evening.

My grandfather spent a great deal of his time on the Sudbury council. At the end I think my father was running the business. He was asked once or twice to be Mayor but his wife just didn't want to be involved with the Mayoress role. So it was unfortunate for him because he thought a great deal of being a councillor. He pioneered the sewage system in Sudbury. That was one of his pet things to get done. But he didn't actually become Mayor. I'm chairman of the Eastern Division of England for the dairy trade, but I'm not really into committees. It seems to take a long while to get a decision which you could probably make yourself in about five minutes, so I don't tend to get involved with committees, whether it be the council or anything. I don't think I would like council work.

When I was young I used to hand-milk. I used to love it, milking and driving the cows to the meadows. I think though the cows I used to milk were picked out. They were the older gentler ones. No chance of being kicked! The only thing you could get was a sting in the face with their tail come around. But some had to have the hind legs tied with a rope. I've seen cowmen knocked across the cow-shed quite a few times. And the milk pail and everything went! Fortunately no serious injury, but it's not very pleasant. They're temperamental beasts. It's funny, you'd have a regular cowman and if another person went to milk, the cow very often knew right away, and would lash out.

It doesn't seem possible now that we used to graze part of the Common Land, the People's Park, where they're going to build the new hospital, and there's all the arguments about at the moment. We used to graze that with cattle. And it doesn't seem possible that we used to drive forty or fifty cattle through the town and the Market Hill, twice a day, one man at the front and one at the back, and I used to go along. And that wasn't an unusual sight. Other dairymen were doing it. They wouldn't allow it now. That was part of the re-organisation of milking, the cattle couldn't go on the highway, they had to go from farm to meadow, meadow to farm.

# George Cooper

Postman, born 1926, Bermondsey, London.

*'I listen to Radio 3 or a talk, and I'm quite happy.'*

My childhood was spent in Dagenham. Father worked in a factory and we were pretty poor. I didn't enjoy school very much; I wasn't very academic. Then the war came, and in 1939 my brother and I were evacuated.

We were all taken by bus down to the Ford's jetty in Dagenham, where the iron ore and coal used to come in. And we were put aboard a paddle steamer, hundreds and hundreds of us, and taken round to Yarmouth. It was exciting. I wasn't at all apprehensive. We stayed the night in a school on straw palliasses. Then we were taken to a little village called West Beckham, to the church there. There must have been about thirty of us, all sat on these pews, and the people who were going to look after us, came in and selected the ones they wanted. Some wanted girls to help with the washing up and the ironing and cooking.

Anyway, some lady came and picked us up, and we were taken to this house. And there was oil lamps. No electricity or gas. Sewage was a bucket. I helped with the harvest, rushing around with a stick killing these rabbits that ran out of the corn. It was a marvellous time. And I made friends. I wasn't unhappy at all. Then there was a threat of invasion, because of the Dunkirk affair and we were transferred to a place called Cheadle. And I stayed up there with my brother in a doctor's house. We had servants and maids. It was marvellous, a real different way of life. Because we'd roughed it in Norfolk.

Then my parents came up and they could see that we were going to get moved again, and they didn't like the idea of us being shifted about, so they took us home. Just as the bombing started! We'd been evacuated to avoid this! Anyway, as soon as we came home, bombs were dropping, and we were in the shelters. But after a few months we didn't bother to go down the shelters, they were such dreary rotten places to go. We just stayed in our beds. Then I left school and went as an audit clerk in an accountant's office in London until I became seventeen, when I volunteered for the Royal Navy.

I was in the D-Day landings as a signalman on a landing craft. I could see everything that was going on. It was more exciting than frightening. The sea was full of ships; never seen so many in my life. I was very young you see. When you're a little bit older you realize the awfulness of it, and what could really happen to you.

When I got de-mobbed I went to work with my father in Bermondsey, in this paint factory. Then I began to get restless. I thought this no blooming good. And one day I took a Saturday off, and went down to the Royal Docks. I just walked in, and the first ship I saw, I walked up the gangway, asked where the chief mate's office was, and went in and said, 'I want a job on this ship'. So he said, 'Well, what can you do?' I told him I was in the Navy, so he asked me if I knew anything about seamanship? 'Very little', I said, 'I can handle ropes a bit.' 'That's not really good enough,' he said, 'What was you doing in the Navy?' So I told him I was on landing craft. And he straightened up and looked at me. He said, 'I was the commander of your flotilla during that landing. Here's a chit; tell the shipping office you're employed - as a deck boy.' I was twenty-one. Deck boy! But I was at sea. So I went back home, and told my dad, 'I've got a job on a ship. It's called 'The Highland Chieftain' going to Buenos Aires.' 'Oh, that's all right', he said. 'When are you going?' I said, 'Tomorrow night'. He couldn't believe it! And I was away the Sunday night, to South America!

I went everywhere after that. I used to come home and think of a place I'd like to go, like Australia or Africa, and then I used to go to the docks and find a ship relating to that place and join it. Oh, it was lovely. Yes, it was the most natural thing for me to do, to go in the Navy.

Then I met this girl I was evacuated with and we became friendly all over again. And I did a trip to India on this trampsteamer. It only did five knots, and was the most dreadfully slow thing you've ever been on. Eventually we got to Calcutta, and sailed for Australia. We came down the Indian Ocean, through the Strait of Malacca, past the enormous Philippines to Cairns in north Queensland. For six blinking weeks we was on that. Homeward bound, we left Fremantle, and went to Dakar in West Africa. It used to be called French Equatorial Africa I think. That was seven weeks. We had Christmas and New Year and we were still plugging on. Dreadful it was. Hit bad weather and I was out in it all the time and I became unwell. I couldn't stand it. I cabled my girlfriend to put up the bans for us to get married.

After we married I stayed on another twelve months. Then suddenly I realized I'd had enough. So I said to my wife one day, 'I'm not going back any more'. And I applied to the Post Office and I've been a postman ever since. Thirty-five years.

I did eleven years in Romford. By then we had three children and another on the way, so I wrote to every house

agent in Norfolk and Suffolk for properties that had four bedrooms, an acre of garden, and was near Norwich, Ipswich or Sudbury, so I could transfer you see, and still work. We finally found this place. It had the acre of garden, and I bought three more acres along the river. And we've got five bedrooms. We had two boys and two girls, so they had a bedroom each. I don't think you could better that. Just imagine, I was brought up with my brother in the same bed, let alone the same blinking room, and all these they had their own rooms. Now they're all married.

Sudbury's been interesting. I used to sit in the Post Office canteen and look at all the roofs, jiggly and lop-sided and old. Now they've sorted them all out with the government grants. And when we first came down in '67, if it rained, you got quite a drowning because all the gutters were rotten.

But the job has changed very little. The only difference is the increase in the quantity of mail. You get these mailshots now. So they've reduced the size of the walks for each person. I start at four with the sorting and get back about eleven o'clock. The afternoon deliveries are done by other postmen who work from eleven to seven.

I talk to most people. I'm always having a chat, and people begin to know you if you're friendly enough. If you're lucky, you get called in for cups of tea. There used to be a blind person, I used to read her letters for her, bills, the lot, read them all! And once I had a letter addressed to 'To the postman who delivers down Trafalgar Road.' When I opened it, it said, 'Will you please call at No.14, and ask the lady to answer the letters I've been writing to her for the last six months.' It was her daughter. So I knocked on the door and I said, 'Your daughter wants you to answer her letters!' 'Oh, I will, I will,' she said. Wasn't that amazing.

Another place, it's a farm, and there's a lovely labrador there. I used to open the door, and give the letters to this dog, to take to its master or mistress. One morning I opened the door and gave the dog this letter. And it ran away! It was another dog from a farm further down! I don't think they ever did get that letter.

We do get bitten, but I think it's really a question of your approach. I usually crouch down and the dog comes up to me, or just backs away. I think if you stand over it, it becomes afraid. There's a chap here, I think he gets bitten every month. I've only been bitten two or three times. My own fault mostly.

I don't do anything with the extra land I purchased, although I am going to keep sheep on it. But I'm a keen gardener. Not very good, but I'm keen. I supply my children with onions, they're so easy to grow. Every time they see me they say, 'Don't offer me any onions.' I also grow tomatoes. The wife and I went on a holiday in Greece, and we had these salads. 'They're lovely these tomatoes,' I was saying. So what I did, I got a serviette and picked the seeds out of these tomatoes, and I dried them and I grow these big tomatoes now. Great big things, they weigh about a pound each.

I don't use anything in the garden that's not organic. And I get surprising results. Mostly weeds! Because anyone that grows organically and says he doesn't get weeds is a liar. You don't spray so you don't kill the damn things off. You just have to keep pulling them out. But I take the radio with me. I like classical... so I listen to Radio Three, or a talk, and I'm quite happy.

I also sell honey. It started by my reading a book by some lady who kept bees. It was an interesting story and as I was going through I was thinking, 'I could do that, yes, I reckon I could do that.' So I sent away and got this box of bees by rail in 1976. I went up to Bury St. Edmunds railway station and picked them up one night. Delighted I was. I'd never handled bees before in my life.

I carried on from there. A person down the road who belonged to an agricultural institute approached me one day and said, 'There's a course on bee-keeping at the College, one day a week. Are you interested?' So I went to see the postmaster and persuaded him to let me use up

*c1938*

a day of my leave for every day I went to this college. I used up all my leave, and I learnt quite a lot. I was fascinated by it. And various people came to me, 'I've got a swarm of bees in my garden, will you collect them?' So I used to collect these swarms and with the swarms I got from my own garden, I got these colonies. More than I could handle. I had to cut down. I've about ten hives now down on the meadow. There's a ditch there where they can drink. Bees must have water. People who keep bees on farm land must put water around in trays. And I sell the honey. Sometimes I get a lot and get a lot of money, sometimes none! Because if it's dry early in the year bees pack it in and prepare for winter when it's still July.

I got stung a lot, of course! I used to put the veil on and carelessly tie it round my neck, and the bees would get in. Now I've got a proper suit. But the wife she's got the tweezers ready even now, to pull the stings out of my neck where I can't see them. It's painful when they sting you, but it goes. And you've got to disregard it. If you worry about that you'll never be a bee-keeper.

# Chapter Ten

## ON THE MOVE

**M**echanised transport is now a central feature of modern life and there is a running debate about what forms we should encourage from the point of economy, convenience and environmental pollution. Yet despite decades of pleading against the motor car on all three scores, the number of cars on the roads increases annually. And short of implementing legislation to stop it, we can look forward to more and more people having their own car.

When people lack a car taxis are the next best option for getting round modern British towns. In seeking to approach a broad cross-section of the population of Sudbury it seemed appropriate to include one or two people whose working lives were bound up with the motor car. Ken Hall owns a service garage in the town; Elsie Elliston ran a taxi-cum-hire-car for many years.

**Elsie Elliston** loves the land and the animal world and her car has been her means of raising the income to realise these loves. So she has taken enormous care of it. As a result one car has lasted her the whole of her adult life.

After fifty-five years it is not often taken out now. But though it largely sits in the garage, it is still road-worthy. We examined the engine. We climbed inside. The leather upholstery is now shiny and dark with wear in places and the driver's seat has had to be recovered, but it remains comfortable, and the exterior still gleams black. The garage, its windows hung with cotton curtains, faded but clean, and everything arranged ship-shape, continues to give good service. We toured the acre of garden, mostly given over to vegetables and fruits. A greenhouse contains a beautifully nurtured vine, the fruit painstakingly thinned out so that every grape reaches the same size and each bunch is perfectly shaped. We also visited a variety of hutches and pens housing Elsie Elliston's animals and birds. Finally we went down to the stables and the horses and to walk briefly on Elsie Elliston's 'own acres'. Though she does not now get up as early as she used to, she had been up since about six and would go to bed around midnight. Most of the tour was done at a semi-run, pausing only to dig up vegetables, gather tomatoes, shut pens, feed animals.

Elsie Elliston has created a world which absorbs her emotionally and imaginatively. Though its demands are beginning to tell on her, her appearance seems scarcely to have changed over twenty years judging from a photo which had appeared in a local newspaper article.

At one level **Ken Hall** seems almost a cardboard cut-out Cockney. He clearly enjoys presenting himself as sharp witted and pugnacious. He uses expressions you thought only stage Cockneys used and then embroiders them richly with expletives. His zest for life makes him an attractive figure. His assimilation into, and appreciation of, the small town where he has landed up cuts across the smart street-wise Cockney image, as does the note of uncertainty which just very occasionally creeps into his voice, and hints at a potential for self-scrutiny which is not part of the stage Cockney's baggage. His portrait shows him as slightly bullish, the line of his skull showing through his close cropped hair. At the same time his eyes are narrowed with a question.

# Elsie Elliston

Hire-car Driver and Riding School Proprietor, born 1912, Sudbury.

*'I knew the North Circular like the back of my hand.'*

This was the site of the original leprosy hospital. When that was demolished these houses were put up, and Grandad came and brought Mum when she was a fortnight old. Then when Grandma died Mum had to bring up the family. And when she married, she still lived here. I had two sisters and a brother, and we were all born here. I've been here all my life.

My dad was a farm worker, and he always said he reckoned it was the farm workers what want a bathroom. It wasn't the high class; they never did the work; it was the poor people. I knew Dad wanted one and I said, 'When I go to work, if ever I earn some money...' But we were renting the house then so I also thought I'd go to the trustees and ask would they put a bathroom on. Oh no! They hadn't any money. They couldn't do that. So I said, well, if I put it on, will you allow me to stay on if anything happens to my mother, because she had the tenancy, not my father or me. So that's how I come to put the bathroom on.

Later on, of course, the trustees decided to sell the house. They had to put it in the paper for six months, to make sure they got the highest bidder. You can imagine what turmoil I lived in, in case somebody came along who bid higher. I would have been heartbroken. Anyway, in the end, I was able to buy this house and next door.

I don't go in for machines in the house. When they had the Horse of the Year Show on telly my friend, Mrs. Bampton, would always invite me to go and watch it. And when she left Sudbury she said would I like to buy it. So I did, and we had television till my sister died about five years ago. She loved it. When it packed up I thought I should miss it, because I used to like 'Emmerdale Farm'. But when I went to buy a new one all they'd got were these black plastic things, and I said no no no, never. It's got to be a bit of furniture, or I wouldn't. And I don't miss it. I don't want one. I think it's such a time waster. And the noise when you go into some people's houses and the damn thing's going! It's unsociable. Then again, my cousin comes down, and it's 'I've got to go now because there's so-and-so on'. I'd hate to be a slave to something like that. As it is I don't have to worry about coming in to watch. I'm free.

And I've got that little wireless but I hardly have that on now.

From a child I always loved the garden. It gave me my one ambition which was to walk on my own acres one day. There's a big farm on the hill behind here. I knew the farmer so I used to go there blackberrying. You could stand up there and see all over his farm and fields. And I thought, one day, if I can, I'll get my own land. And the car was the answer you see. That was the means of me having money. And that was how I come to buy my land. I've got fifteen acres down the road, beautiful meadow land. Oh yes, it was the car.

My brother, he ran a taxi business, and if you get one job you get two, and he said to Mum one day, 'You know, if you could lend Elsie the money she could help me out.' So that's when Mum bought the car, in 1936. It was £301, all handed over in cash, which was amazing because that was a lot of money in them days. I was nineteen when I had the car. Then I did the jobs and paid her back.

I did a lot of war driving. It was funny, you never worried about the fares. Some of these airmen when you dropped them off at midnight they hadn't the money and they would go in the camp and bring it back. You never doubted them, and not once did they ever let me down. You wouldn't do it today, would you!

It was registered as a taxi, but I did a lot of private hire. It was nothing for me to get up in the morning and go down to Southampton and back the same day. We used to do quite long journeys in them days. And I used to go up to London a lot. I knew the North Circular like the back of my hand. Father Moore often used to have to go up to the Cumberland Hotel, after tea sometimes, so I used to take him and wait and bring him back, or leave him one day and go back and fetch him another. And I used to do all the maternity jobs in Sudbury, because the women would prefer a woman to take them, you know. And most of the weddings too. I had some lovely good class work.

I've just had the one car. It's been five hundred and fifty thousand miles. That's the equivalent of going round the world twenty-five times. It's amazing. It's been looked after though. Every time I came home at night, it may have been snowing whatever, I always washed or wiped it down and looked in case somebody had dropped a cigarette end in it. Well, it was the only means of earning any money.

I never really liked the car hire though, because you lived by the clock. The diary was full and, you know, every hour

there was something to do. I gave it up when the stables became a good proposition.

I was always mad about horses and it was my dream to have a pony. When I was, oh, more than twenty I went and had a few lessons. And you'll never believe it, I got a pony. I acquired it after I got the car and got the money, you see. I'd had it for two years, and I still daren't tell my parents, because I think I would have been killed. Anyway, they found out. But they were quite happy, because I didn't neglect my work for it. I used to get up early in the morning, and someone I knew allowed me to rent a little meadow and use this yard and stable. And of course, wherever I go it has to be tidy: I like to be just so. So I tidied this up and I cleaned the stable and they were rather impressed. And when all the land came up for sale I was

given the offer. And that's how I come to have my fifteen acres.

Of course I couldn't afford to have all these acres without making them pay. But someone who had a pony asked if I would keep it, and I managed to accumulate a number of ponies like that and eventually that's how I built up the riding school. I must have taught hundreds and hundreds of children.

I was always gardening as well, of course. I used to take the stuff to the shops, but it's ridiculous, the price they give you, and what they make on it! It's much cheaper to sell at the door, and it gives me more pleasure. And of course there's not so much now. I've cut down a great deal, because I feel I'm only running myself into the ground now. But I don't like to see the ground stand idle and I like to get rid of my surplus.

No, I've never been away. I've been out with the car, but I hate the sea. If I had to take people to the sea for the day I'd spend it polishing the car, or something. But I've never had a holiday because I had animals to look after.

I've got a pair of doves. If it was three o'clock this afternoon, they'd both be in here. I make a cup of tea and one sits either side there. My sister used to talk to them. And I've two tortoises. One of them was my mother's and the other one belonged to my friend, and when she left Sudbury thirty-two years ago she gave it to me. One must be over a hundred, the little one. He's waiting for me now. I shall wake him up and feed him soon. The bigger one has gone to bed in his house.

I've always had animals, all sorts of animals. I used to have lovely dogs. There's a photograph of one up there, a spaniel. My last two dogs were shelties. I love shelties. They're not too small to be silly are they? I've had some beautiful cats. We had Honey here. She's died now, but I've got a big ginger called Arthur down the stables. If I had rabbits we used to sell the babies. Everything I always had, had to pay its way.

I've still got four ponies and four horses. Actually, the only ones what are really mine are three that are very very old, that remain from the school and are just resting their days out. Then I've three or four liveries and I keep a pony for my granddaughter and one for her friend, Karen. Both the girls get down here half five, and feed and water the horses, so I needn't get down till about eight. I'm generally up at six or earlier, but I have an hour or so in the house, before I'm down the road to turn the horses out. When I get there Karen goes home to get her husband to work and get the baby up. Then she has to take her baby to a babysitter, you know, because she works at Babergh Council. Susan's a good girl too.

I hope they'll be able to carry on, because eventually somebody's got to carry on after me, haven't they. I can still get on a horse and I could still ride. It's the getting off. But I don't ride. I've got so much responsibility left with me for the land and the animals that if I did anything daft or fell, everything would be at a standstill wouldn't it? It used to worry me a geat deal, it did. But I've got Susan and Karen working now in such a way that I'm quite happy. They respect the land and love the stables. I don't know what they'll do with it all, but they wouldn't part with the horses, and I can't see the land going.

*Photograph from the East Anglian Daily Times*

# Ken Hall

Garage owner and Stuntman, born 1924, Stepney,
London.

*'I've been as happy here as a pig in shit.'*

I was born Skidmore Street, Stepney. That's the East End
of London. My grandmother on my father's side - this is
going to sound comical - was the most beautiful little
Chinese lady. My grandfather on my father's side was as
Jewish as a bagel. But on my mother's side, plain, down-
to-earth Cockney. Unfortunately, when I was eleven my
mother and father were divorced. My brother is two years
younger than me and we went to live with Nan and
Grandad on my mother's side, and they brought us up,
because my mother took a job as the manageress of the
Imperial Hotel, Russell Square, which was a live-in job.
My grandad was a diamond, he was. His name was Sam.

I went to school in the East End. Didn't do very well. I can
hear the headmaster now, 'Hall, you are an idiot! What are
you?' 'I'm an idiot sir.' And I will admit I wouldn't know
an A-level or an O-level if it hit me in the mouth. But when
I was nineteen I drove my Rolls Royce into the school
playground, and went and sorted out that master. 'Do you
remember me sir? Hall, the idiot! I haven't done too bad
sir, have I?'

Today, in fact I often make a boast, you name the word I
can't spell, and I'll give you fifty pounds. My writing, I'm
told, is practically perfect. All learned since I left school.
No pressures. No bullies. Because believe me there were
some bullies at that school.

When war broke out I was nearly sixteen, and thinking it
was great fun, put my age up to eighteen to get into the
Navy. By the time I was eighteen I was smashed up. I'd
spent twelve months in Naval Hospital and was
discharged medically unfit, weighing seven stone. I was
snookered on the North Sea, running out of Scapa Flow. It
wasn't as romantic as I thought it would be. It was
terrifying, to put it bluntly, and any man who says he
wasn't afraid is either a liar or a raving lunatic.

The one advantage I did have when I came out of the
Navy, was that the war still had another two or three years
to run, and there was plenty of opportunities for somebody
like me, who was a bit slippery, a bit quick on the uptake.
I hit upon the idea of starting my own chauffeur-driven car
hire business. My wife, Vera, has been my partner all my
life and with the help of her dad I bought a car. Being a
disabled ex-serviceman I was granted concessions, and I

got a petrol allowance and Hackney Carriage plates. And
I went on in leaps and bounds, from one to two cars, then
two to four, and so forth. Then I started employing people.

I acquired a few unusual cars, and a friend said, 'Why
don't you put those into the film business?' I said, 'Good
idea'. So we did, and I saw this stunt. This bloke come
flying out of this window and landed on a load of air boxes
and mattresses. I said, 'Christ, and they call that a stunt!
I'd do that for nothing. It looks like he's having fun!' I
thought I was whispering, but I've got a very loud voice
and the bloke heard me. So he came over. 'You're
prepared to put your action where your mouth is, mate?'
I said, 'Every time, mate.' 'Right, you're on!' Next thing
I know, I'm in Equity. I still keep my Equity ticket going
even today.

I did become one of the top stuntmen in the country, but
there was no such thing as an all-round stunt man. When
we did 'Rififi', they called for a guy to walk across a wire
from one building to another. So the director said to me,
'Now look Ken, this is what I want you to do'. I said, 'Get
stuffed! You've got no chance!' My speciality was behind
the wheel of a car, on a motorbike, or a light aircraft, a
boat, anything mechanical was my forte. But let me try
and explain myself to you. If we went into one of your
flash restaurants, where everything on the menu,
irrespective of what you had, was a set price, lobster
thermidor, steak tartare, pie and mash, I'd have the pie and
mash. That's what I like. Like I like my wife's meat
puddings and her bread pudding.

My one extravangance was my Rolls. That was my love.
And it was done for a purpose. When I lived with my nan
and grandad down the East End, I'll never forget it, there
was a crowd of us standing on the street corner and this old
Rolls went by 'Cor! look at that! I'll have one of them one
day.' 'Yeah? Hark at him! Cor, you've got some bleedin'
chance. Hear that! He's going to have a Rolls Royce one
day!' Well I got it.

And up until three years ago I was never without one. And
this is the comical bit. All the time I lived in the East End,
my Rolls never got a scratch, never got touched... Down
here, three years ago, my Rolls got vandalized. Forever
after I was paranoid. Terrified to leave it anywhere. It was
making me a nervous wreck. One day we were visiting a
mate of mine and he said to me, 'What the bloody hell you
keep jumping up for?' I said, 'I'm looking...' 'For God's
sake get rid of it,' he said. 'It'll drive you mad.' So we sold
it.

I've always been into bikes. I've got a motor bike over
there now. The only thing that annoys me is having to wear

*Posing with Audrey Hepburn*

a silly bloody crash helmet. We've both got crash helments. But I hate them. I go out of here without a crash helmet on, I'm nicked. A Sikh goes out with a towel wrapped round his head, and that's legal.

And the seat-belt law. Maybe it's good, maybe it's not, I don't know. But law! It should be a matter of choice. You want to be an idiot, don't want to wear a seat-belt, that's your privilege. Too many boody laws. Sure, children should be safe, children should be belted in. I'm not arguing against that. And I'm not saying anybody who wears them is a sissy. I'm just saying it should be a matter of personal choice. But don't keep imposing on people what you've got to do and what you haven't got to do. Though certain things I do tend to agree, like them or not, we all have to abide by. You need services. You want your dustbins emptied, you want your streets cleaned. So you pay, which I do, you know. But twenty-five years ago I'd have been one of the stuff-the-Poll-Tax rioters, up the front.

My two older daughters moved down here about two years before we did. My youngest daughter wasn't married then and she missed them, because we're very close. There's hardly a day goes by that we don't see all of them. One day she said, 'Daddy, why don't you sell up and move down there?' I was terrified. 'Who the bloody hell do I know down there?'

But eventually we did move. And when I'd finally got shot of everything in London I had exactly enough money to buy this garage. Then I looked at Vera and I said, 'Here, we've got the bloody garage. We've got no money for petrol.' And I had to go and borrow three thousand quid from the bank to put the first lot of petrol under the ground.

Now I wish I'd known about this place forty years ago! I say I'm a Cockney; I'm not, I'm a Suffolk man. This place has been kind to me. This is my home. All my family are buried in London. Not me, I want to be buried here. This is the place where we've known peace, tranquility, no flash boys. In London I don't think I had any friends, I had acquaintances. I was too wary of people. When anyone came I'd wonder what they were after. What a terrible way to be. Down here, I walk up to the bank and if I don't pass at least twenty people...'Hello Ken', 'Morning Ken'. Do that in London and they say, 'Crackers! He's going along saying hello to everyone!' Have an attack in London, they'll step over you, say, 'Oh, he's pissed', or they'd go down your pockets while you lay there. Not here. This is a good little town.

I don't like getting dressed up any more. Upstairs there's forty-odd beautiful suits, each one in its own zip-up wrapper. I've lived here for twenty years, I don't think I've had a suit on four times. Up there, you had to have your Rolex watch, your gold chains, your rings and all that jazz, otherwise you're doing bad. And it was a load of bull. If the truth was known we'd have all liked to have said, 'let's turn it in!' The motor game up in London, it was a game of anything you can do, I can do better.

What brought it home to me, one day, I went to get some spare parts and I took the wrong turn. Bugger it! Where

*In character for a studio portrait*

sandwich. So if I never had two fights a week there was something wrong. I've been here twenty years, I've never hit...it's getting boring! I've never even had an argument! I tell you it's been the best years of our life. I shall never forget my ex-partner's words when he knew I was moving down here. 'What the bleeding hell do you want to go down there for amongst all them carrot-crunchers, working for ha'pennies and pennies?' We only talked about it the other day, didn't we Vera? I said 'Those ha'pennies and pennies, they've mounted up a bit, haven't they love? And them old carrot crunchers, they haven't been a bad lot have they?' My old man had an adage. He turned round to one of his mates one day who was running down some people out in the country. 'Mate,' he said, 'If you ever want to find a mug out in the country, be sure and take him with you.' And boy he was right.

\*    \*    \*    \*

am I? Then all of a sudden I thought, what am I getting excited about? It's a beautiful day. I slowed down to about twenty-five mile an hour, and I thought, now where can I see anything like this in London? The trees, the birds, the flowers, the corn growing, the gorgeous countryside. And I suddenly appreciated what I've got. If somebody - it's hardly likely to happen - but if somebody came in here tomorrow and offered me two million pound for this place on condition that I went back to London, I'd tell them to get stuffed! No way! These have been the best twenty years of my life. I've been as happy here as a pig in shit.

It's a totally different world. Three times last week different people came in. One bloke opened up his... 'Oh blimey, I'm sorry Ken,' he said. 'I haven't got a cheque left.' 'It's OK, you owe me fifty-seven quid.' 'Well do you want me to leave the car here while I...' I said, 'Take the bloody car!' Now in London... 'Cheque? Barclaycard? What are you, a comedian? Pound notes, or you leave your bleeding car here'. You do not trust a living soul. And if you do, you're not a good fella, you're a mug. And the word goes out. 'Oh, he's a right mug down there!' Not, 'He's a good old boy.' And in London as I would never knuckle to nobody, if they got flash they got a knuckle

# Chapter Eleven

## LAW AND ORDER

The image of the English JP which has come down to us through historical records and literature has generally been unflattering. Classically depicted as a member of the gentry, arrogant, narrow or stupid or a combination of these he is seen as defending the interests of his class with scant concern for the principle of justice. In **Betty Bone**'s wry description of how she received her preliminary invitation to sit on the Bench, one seems to hear a faint echo of that world. The modern JP's role, of course, is more circumscribed than originally. More importantly, Betty Bone's account reveals a serious concern and sense of responsibility for her work.

Her photograph shows a small woman with an alert expression against one mass of possessions she has acquired as part of her home building over the years. If one interprets this photograph solely by reference to the visual evidence it is much less provocative than when accompanied by a reading of the text. Similarly the text without the photograph of the speaker's domestic interior seems much flatter.

Historically the JP pre-dates the English policeman by a considerable margin, the Force only being established in 1829. Since then the image of the policeman has varied significantly by class. For many of the middle-class the policeman has featured during this century as a benevolent figure; the English Bobby in his comical headgear directing the traffic, helping old ladies, befriending lost children. By contrast, the old industrial working classes, now fast disappearing, have commonly rejected this image. Classically the police have been recruited from their ranks, the Force offering the possibility of upward social mobility. But as the police have often been used to control industrial action, many working-class people have seen them as enemies.

The policeman has long been a ubiquitous figure of the television screen. In the long-running BBC series of the Sixties, 'Dixon of Dock Green', the lead actor, Jack Warner, had a square-cut face which broke easily into a genial smile and both his figure and deportment radiated reliabliity and good nature. Today the television policeman continues to fight the battle against vice night after night, in stories people watch casually as they relax. Now, however, the police are depicted in a variety of guises. Few any longer include straightforward geniality and in a marked number of cases the difference in manner and outlook between the cop and the villian is blurred.

Most recently the police have been at the centre of the real life drama of the TV news, as a series of serious police cases have come up for review resulting in the overturn of a number of long-term convictions and leaving the police's image deeply tarnished.

**Clive Shipley's** story covers the career of one small-town policeman. Stories like his probably remain as common as stories of the unscrupulous or overzealous within the Force. To complement his account of a steady rise through the ranks we include pictures of a young man with his young bride and a father with a young family, alongside a contemporary portrait.

# Betty Bone

Justice of the Peace, born 1922, Acton, London.

*'Of course, I was absolutely amazed.'*

We'd never heard of Sudbury, Suffolk, but we came down from London one wet, windy Sunday to look for this wholesale grocery business called Braybrook's. Well, we drove around and couldn't find it anywhere. It was cold and miserable, and everything was closed and absolutely dead quiet. And we sat there, wondering what to do and decided we'd have one more look round the town. And this time we came upon a little square, Acton Square it was. And there was a bright little corner shop, very nicely painted, and clean and tidy looking, and there was obviously what originally had been a stable block and store-rooms out the back, that was the wholesale part. And the sign over the door, 'Braybrook's'!

We bought it. Sudbury was a most delightful little town, to my way of thinking, then, 1948. Just down the lane from our business was the cattle market, and behind the cattle market on a Thursday they used to have an auction of furniture. It was all piled up in the open. Too bad if it rained! They'd sell the cattle and the pigs and sheep first, then the furniture.

We bought this thatched cottage, my dream cottage it was, having lived in London most of my life. And of course I was looking for furniture, so of a Thursday I'd be in on the weekly bus. And that was a great social occasion. It would stop at all the cottages along the way, picking up Mrs. So-and-so. They would always wait for whoever was a regular.

And I'd make a bee-line for the auction sale. Oh, I used to get some incredible bargains. I can well remember a very pretty set of shelves with a glass backing. I was terrified that it was going to go for a lot of money. When it came to this lot, there was dead silence. The auctioneer finally said, 'Come on, who will give me a shilling?' I said, 'I will'. And I got this set of shelves for a shilling. And it is still in my drawing-room now, with various little pieces of porcelain on. And very pleased I am with it.

As time went by it became very expensive to send a traveller out, round all the little village shops. So my husband, who was a very forward-thinking man, opened the first cash-and-carry at the bottom of Ballingdon Hill, which was an immediate success. The old people in the village stores of course grumbled about having to come and fetch their stock instead of having it delivered, but they got used to it. And by this time of course cars and petrol were more readily available.

I really didn't have a job after I married. I had two children and the thatched cottage got crowded and we moved to 'The Limes'. But I'd never got involved in local politics, never had thought about even going on the parish council.

By this time, though, we had got London overspill in the area. It was all started up by CAV of Acton, W3, who had got a small factory here. Now, I was born in Acton W3, and as I say, I was very pleased to leave London and city life for the country. Anyway, now, to my dismay, were all these Londoners, suddenly living all around me again!

The GLC in conjunction with the local district council built these vast estates of houses, but did absolutely nothing about leisure activities or amenities. All these folks came down, with a job it is true, and a roof over their heads, but very little to do in their spare time. The powers that be realised that they'd just got to do something. And they decided that the best thing would be to get a community centre built.

The local council said that they would contribute a certain amount, but the people themselves had got to raise the rest. So they called a meeting, and to this meeting they had quite a lot of politically-minded folks arrive. And Cornard was pretty evenly split. The Labour people would be mostly all the newcomers, and the Conservatives would be the original inhabitants. They managed to get enough volunteers for a committee. And then they had to get a chairman. Well, whoever one side proposed as chairman, the other side refused to have! And it was absolute stalemate.

So they decided to end the meeting, and re-convene the following week. And in the meantime, they would try and think of somebody that would be acceptable to all. And I was the one person they thought of, not having been involved in local politics, who might be acceptable to either side. So somewhat reluctantly I agreed, went along to the next meeting, and of course was voted in unanimously!

What it really involved was raising money. We had various schemes. One of them was selling bricks at a

pound a piece. A lady called Mrs. Newton, was a great worker in this respect. She said, 'Now come on, we've got to draw up a list of all the people in the town and around who would give us a nice little sum of money'. And on my list to call was Mr. Alan Phillips, a local solicitor; so I went to see him, and he very kindly contributed, bought so many bricks and said what a good idea it was. And that was that.

But what I didn't know was that Alan Phillips was the Clerk of the Court. And one day he phoned me and said that he wanted to discuss something with me, but it couldn't be done over the telephone, would I please come down to his office. Well, I wondered what on earth he wanted to discuss with me that couldn't be done over the telephone. So I got down there as quickly as possible. And he said, 'Now I'm going to ask you a personal question, and depending on your answer is whether we go any further'. This is mysterious I thought. 'What is it?' I said. He said, 'Are you fifty years old yet?' 'Indeed I'm not Mr. Phillips!' said I. 'Right' said he. 'Now I can tell you what it's all about. I wonder if you've ever considered becoming a magistrate?' Well, of course I was absolutely amazed. I said, 'No way! Never thought of it'. 'Well,' he said, 'I think you might make quite a good magistrate.'

So he filled in the form. And in due course I was told that I'd been accepted and I had a letter from the Lord Chancellor's office. Having gone to what was then Quarter Sessions, and sworn the oath before the judge, to administer justice without fear or favour, it was suggested that I sat in as an observer for a few times. And then I was sitting on the Bench.

I had my training from Mr. Alan Phillips. We'd very often finish round about twelve o'clock. And he would say, 'If you've got a few minutes, we'll just go through... such-and-such a point.' So I'd listen for about a quarter of an hour. And I had a residential weekend at Ipswich, and there was a biennial conference at Cambridge, where we all met up for a weekend. That was it. You learnt by experience, as you went along. There's a lot more training now. And it's all a great deal more difficult in spite of the fact that it's completely voluntary as far as pay is concerned.

When I first was appointed there were always far more men than women as magistrates. It's not easy to get young people as magistrates because of course they're too busy earning a living. And the women, whereas in my day it wasn't the norm for women with young families to have a job, nowadays it is, and it's not all that easy for them to get time off.

But it's extremely interesting. Fortunately, though I can be very concerned whilst I'm dealing with a problem, I am one of these people who can switch off. Otherwise you would come home and probably have sleepless nights wondering whether you'd done the right thing. Sometimes it is very difficult to know what to do. And you are not told until you give your decision the defendant's antecedents. So it's a great relief when you have a case you find difficult to make up your mind about, and come to the conclusion that it's Guilty, then the prosecuting solicitor produces a list of previous convictions...as long as your arm! If it had been a completely clean sheet, you might have had qualms about your decision. Another thing that is a great help is that you always sit at a bench of three minimum. It's not so worrying if you have two colleagues to discuss the thing with. And if one is the sole dissenter, you don't feel so badly when it comes to the result.

One difference I find nowadays is the time it takes to deal with offenders. Particularly if it's a Not Guilty plea. When I was first appointed perhaps it would take a month between the first appearance in court and coming to trial. I don't know how many times they have to come to court before they come to trial now; so many things have to be done.

The sort of case that worries you is when you have a group of young men, I wouldn't say a little gang, but they all know one another, and all are under twenty-three, twenty-four. Two youngsters will be involved with another two on one burglary or...taking a car, and then two or three more will be involved in another bit of villainy. And they're all sort of bound up. Some are far more serious than others. We keep adjourning while the police gather evidence. And you have to decide whether you can remand them on a conditional bail, so that they can remain in the community, or whether the likelihood of them committing further offences is so great that you'd sooner have them in custody. And you know very well that if you do put them in custody, they're going to meet up with all sorts of very much more hardened criminals. In fact you don't really want to put them in custody at all. But if you remand them on conditional bail and they commit further offences, then that puts the whole proceedings back, because these further offences have to start at the very beginning of the system and go through all these adjournments and advance disclosures, and sometimes it takes eighteen months to get the thing heard in Crown Court, and by this time the witnesses have forgotten all about it!

You can't say you enjoy it, but, I think one appreciates, you could say, the privilege of attempting to decide the right treatment for the particular offender.

I've always been interested in needlework and the WI had a course of classes in canvas work. I didn't really apply myself to it, but then a friend of mine suggested that we went to a WI weekend on embroidery. So along I went. Well, I did a fair bit of painting in those days, and she said, 'Why don't you join the embroidery school? I think it would tie in with your painting.' So she proposed me, and I went to every day school and class there was.

Now, you know, I thought it would be very nice to have an occupation that I could sit at of an evening, in front of the television set. But as time has gone by, with all this dyeing and painting and the rest of it, embroidery's got nearly as messy as the oil painting was!

My grandfather was a goldsmith in Clerkenwell and my mother was born in central London. But goodness me, I'd never go back to London now.

\*     \*     \*     \*

# Clive Shipley

Police Superintendent, born 1937, Burton upon Trent, Staffordshire.

*'I'm not sure I can persuade my wife to move again.'*

I was born the youngest of three boys. My father died when I was three so my mother was left to bring three children up just at the time of the war. Later my mother remarried and when I was eleven, we moved to Suffolk, which was her home county. I didn't get on too well with my stepfather, so I lived at home until I was fifteen. Then on leaving school I also left home and lived with an aunt and got a job as an apprentice motor mechanic, served my apprenticeship and then at the age of twenty-one years I was called up for National Service, and joined the RAF for an extended period of three years.

We were constructing airfields and I went to Libya and from there to Cyprus, at the time of EOKA. A very nice island indeed. Never been back since, but always have the intention of doing so. My job was to drive a bulldozer and keep the snow clear from the top of Mount Olympus to Platros. We went to Aden and Sharjah from Cyprus, and so I travelled quite a bit in the RAF, and always have rosy memories of that. I think you tend to put the bad memories behind you and remember the good times. Anyway, I was de-mobbed having attained the dizzy heights of Senior Aircraftsman, which is about two from the bottom! I came back to the garage. Then in October '61 I joined the police service.

I'd never aspired to be a policeman. Like most people I'd viewed them from afar. What happened was that I worked in a garage next door to H M Inspector of Constabulary, and I was made redundant because the garage was closing down. So I decided I'd have a stab at being a police officer and I went next door and and explained I'd got a young child and was recently married and wanted security for my family. So they got in touch with the Chief Constable and I joined the Suffolk Constabulary.

I did my training at Eynsham Hall. It was a bit of a shock to the system, because I didn't realize the police service was so regimented. The discipline was quite severe. My last memory of Eynsham is of the top table where all the brass used to sit. My last morning there somebody had seen fit to fill their sugar bowl with salt, so they spooned that into their cups of tea. I didn't actually do it, but I did get the blame for it. Eynsham Hall had a long drive. It must

have been half a mile. My punishment was to carry my suitcases to the end of the drive, then walk back, pick my car up and go and pick my suitcase up. I knew who had switched the sugar, yes. But I didn't say. It was worth it just to see their faces as they drank their tea.

Anyway, I eventually moved to Long Melford as a beat policeman. Policemen worked a six-day week then. And because there was no radios you used to have to keep fixed points. You used to cycle to meet another policeman at a telephone box, in one of the other villages. That made sure you did your patrol you see. So at eleven o'clock at night I would cycle to Glemsford where I'd meet up with a Cavendish policeman. That was a fixed cycle. Your section station, which was Sudbury, knew you were to be there and if they had a message for you they rang that kiosk. If the phone went and you were not there you could be in trouble. Plus the the Inspector from Sudbury could take it in his mind to visit these locations, and you never knew whether he was going to turn up. So you used to hang about this telephone box for about ten minutes and have a chat with your mate, and then cycle off again.

We used to do a lot of walking and cycling. Now people ask me, 'Where are the policemen? We don't see a policeman.' That is mainly because of the other duties we have to do, which in my day we didn't do. And now we can only work them for a straight eight-hour shift; there's no question of them starting at nine in the morning and finishing at midnight. That has changed, and probably for the better. Police officers I think, like the the rest of the community, deserve modern treatment.

We used to get things done by the Ways and Means Act. Now we are bound by police regulations. I well remember one evening. There'd been a sharp frost and we'd had three or four accidents in succession. We couldn't get anybody out to do anything and this was obviously going to go on, and we got fed up with this by about one o'clock in the morning. The fellow I was with knew a guy who worked for Suffolk County Council and his lorry was loaded up with grit and salt. We couldn't get him out, but he said we could borrow the lorry. So we ended up with my mate driving this lorry and me standing in the back shovelling salt and sand on the road. We gritted the whole road that night. He was singing away in the cab and I was shovelling away at the back. We would have both got sacked I think if the powers that be had known. But we didn't get any more accidents! Nowadays youngsters would not even dream of doing that, and I wouldn't encourage them.

So that was Long Melford, and we had two more children,

I don't know how my wife coped because my son was born, and two years later my second son was born, and a year later almost to the day my daughter was born. So she had two in nappies at that time; a hell of job when I think back.

I then moved to Sudbury as a Detective Constable. Young detectives were just expected to work all the hours that God sent, whereas nowadays, they are entitled to overtime and get it. Superintendents don't get paid overtime, because we get a fat salary to start with.

A few more moves and I was promoted to uniformed sergeant at Eye, in East Suffolk. Eye in those days had a reputation as a bit of a rough place, and our wives were subjected to a certain amount of abuse. And policemen's children at school had a bit of a hard time. Anyway, we gradually became more accepted. I had a very good social life at Eye and both my wife and I became keen outdoor bowlers.

All these moves that I've described to you my children were being taken out of school each time, and starting at fresh schools. The one regret I have is that my three children probably under-achieved at school. I don't think they were ever going to be brilliant, but the constant disruption had a detrimental effect on their education, there's no doubt about that. We moved to Lowestoft for example. My son had just left school, and I got him an apprenticeship with a firm of builders and my wife got a little job. And six months to the day I got a call from my Chief Superintendent saying you are being promoted to Inspector. That was very good news. But at Felixstowe! I said, 'Hang on a minute, I'm not sure I can persuade my wife to move again.' Anyway, we discussed it, and decided we would. But it was a lot of upheaval, and I'm sure the children suffered.

My early memories of Felixstowe are of flooding. In the middle of the night, I got a telephone call saying, 'We've got a flood arouser, you'd better come down'. Well that meant not much to me. But I went down to the station and got in this big Transit van, and my sergeant said, 'I'll take you along.' The tide wasn't quite in but the waves were rattling up the prom and then suddenly one came right up the beach and just went over the van as well. I said, 'Are you sure you know what you're doing?' He said, 'Everything's all right sir.' But I said, 'Get this bloody van off here.' I could just see us getting washed away!

There was a lot of flooding that night. I've got memories of standing in Manor Terrace four or five hundred yards in from the beach, and the sea was up to my thighs. My

*Honeymoon 1959*

sergeant had the only pair of thigh boots in the police station. I'd got wellingtons on, and water up to my thighs! So I'd got it wrong somewhere. I finally got into bed about 5 a.m. I always remember the distress of people, waking them up in the middle of the night and the waves coming into their homes. We had about three foot of water in a lot of houses. It was a surge tide, where the previous tide hadn't gone out completely, and was being held up by the winds when the next tide was coming in.

From Felixstowe I went into Complaints and Discipline, a different job altogether. We hear a lot about people believing that policemen shouldn't investigate complaints against themselves, but I can vouch for the fact that there is a very thorough investigation done by policemen about policemen. We certainly don't want bad apples in our bale. Then I was promoted to Chief Inspector at Ipswich. Again a bit of a traumatic experience. A totally different style of policing to anything I'd encountered before. A lot harder. Plus we had football policing when we were first erecting barriers in the grounds, segregating fans, meeting them at a railway station and marching them like a herd of cattle down to the ground. Putting them in pens for the duration of the match, and then escorting them back to the railway station. They were hairy times, a lot of aggravation and a lot of arrests every fortnight, and up to two hundred policemen for a game.

Difficult place to police, Ipswich. Quite a high ethnic population, Afro-Caribbean and Asian. We used to get a fair amount of trouble from the young blacks, a lot of them unemployed at that time. But gradually I think we educated our young policemen a bit better in community relations.

Then a sideways move, to the new Police Complaints Authority. The old Police Complaints Board were very much a toothless organisation, but the Authority have the power to direct that a police officer is disciplined, even against the Chief Constable. People, as I said, say policemen should not investigate themselves. The Police Federation, that's our union, resisted this until a few years ago when they suddenly said, 'Well, if that's what you want...' But it hasn't come in and I think the reason for that is a financial one. It would be so costly. Then I returned to Sudbury where I really started policing as the governor.

There's a lot more disorder now. The young officers' job is more difficult though we've got excellent radio contact. But youngsters by and large have less respect for authority, and they certainly question a policeman, which is perhaps not a bad thing. But a lot of people seem to think that policemen can do exactly as they want. Nothing could be further from the truth. We have to work within the law, and if you don't you're likely to be complained about and have that substantiated against you. So I think policemen now are more careful than they were.

In the past if you went to a dance at a village hall and there was a fight, you could arrest someone without too much fear of them turning on you. Now we often have to teach our young policemen, 'Just weigh up the situation; don't get into something you can't get out of.' I believe there is a more relaxed attitude, both in the home and at school now. And I don't think that's a good thing at the end of the day personally. I think a certain amount of discipline is necessary. But perhaps that's an old-fashioned attitude, I don't know.

But I also think things went on and were not reported because they would have got very little sympathy. People didn't like to believe some things happened and probably turned a blind eye. The incidence of sexual assaults on children has increased dramatically. I think a lot of it comes out through the schools now, you know. They do talk about things to their teachers that perhaps they wouldn't have done years ago. And it is a difficult decision I think for a child, particularly a young girl, to complain about that. The stigma that's attached to that is quite terrific, isn't it.

And certainly assaults by husband on wife are treated far more seriously now. Again the same applies. A few years ago females would just not report that sort of thing, and would make excuses for injuries they'd got, wouldn't they. So I don't know that it's more prevalent now but certainly it comes to notice a lot more. In fact we've just had a Force policy reiterated, that we treat those incidents as if they'd been outside the domestic environment. The difficulty is that we will get called to an incident where perhaps a husband has given his wife a beating that night and she's full of anger and pain, and wants something done about it. We arrest him and she makes her statement. Then two or three days later she's had second thoughts and wants to withdraw the statement. That makes life difficult because we've charged the man and he's to appear before a court.

I can well remember the miners' dispute. I had to go up to the coal fields on two or three occasions as a Commander with groups of police officers. They used to stay up there a week. Quite horrific scenes. Charges against policemen. Policemen in full riot gear with their shields and helmets and staffs drawn. We were sending policemen up there from Suffolk to do that. Then they were a week back on the beat, and we were asking them to be community officers and friendly to people. Very difficult.

There's not many realistic TV programmes about the police. I mean 'The Chief' isn't realistic at all. A chief constable as autocratic as that wouldn't preside very long, because he'd have the whole of the Force in uproar. Plus he gets involved in all sorts of things that a chief constable just would not get himself involved in. I mean, in the case of Suffolk, he's got twelve hundred officers to do that sort of work, and he just doesn't get involved. There are one or two programmes that are a little bit true to life. 'The Bill' for instance is not bad.

I think most people if they can't get an answer elsewhere to a problem that needs some fairly urgent attention, end up bringing it to us, because we won't turn them away. If it's a Saturday night and nobody else is prepared to turn out then we will  - and often get ourselves in muddles doing it, because we get involved in things we shouldn't ought to. But you cannot say to someone at the other end of a phone who's distraught and wanting help, 'That's not our job. Goodnight.'

# Chapter Twelve

## POLITICS  AND  CITIZENSHIP

**P**olitical life is not for the faint-hearted, for public attitudes to politicians are commonly ambivalent and often hostile. A popular view, for example, is that politicians are self seeking, untrustworthy and power-hungry. In a democracy, of course, not even the most powerful positions guarantee their holders freedom to effect all the changes they wish. Nevertheless, some positions carry more power than others and the opportunities for politicians to realise what they think should be done will depend on the authority invested in the office they attain. Politicians naturally like to occupy the more powerful positions and they have a tendency to jostle and manoeuvre for such positions. This inevitably gives them a bad name.

At the same time people constantly turn to their elected representatives expecting that they will help them to effect changes in public amenities or offer them personal help and advice. The public is  not always consistent.

Historically Sudbury was one of the rotten boroughs, the prototype for Eatanswill in *Pickwick Papers*. Things have changed since then. And latterly, with the reorganisation of local government in 1974 much of the Town Council's power devolved to Babergh District Council. The town, however, still retains its Mayor, a Council and a small budget. It is notable in having had the first Asian mayor in the country and Howard Singh has since served a second term. He is a member of the Conservative Party but the town does not consistently favour one party.  Over the years the Council has, at different times,  been evenly divided between the two main parties, overwhelmingly Tory, and, in the most recent elections,  overwhelmingly Labour.

A number of people in this book are involved in local politics so that  there is a certain arbitrariness about the choice of people for this chapter. The three people who are included differ in party affiliation, personal history and general interests for the question of what motivates people to get involved in politics is complicated. Yet they have something in common. Howard Singh and Elizabeth Wiles share a feeling that certain kinds of civic action should be taken and that given the opportunity they will see it is and they derive satisfaction from that goal even though it demands time and energy without monetary gain. George Reynolds is a newcomer to the political arena, but judging from his work with the British Legion, he too seems similarly motivated. The image of the hard-boiled self-seeker does not fit any of them neatly.

They are caring people. **Elizabeth Wiles** acknowledges her sense of hurt when the electorate rejects her, as they have more than once. But she recognises that in politics you must be prepared to take knocks and carry on without bearing grudges. Whether she is in or out of office she keeps her files up to date and the telephone busy in the office-cum-front-room of her small terraced house. It is important to her that the public see her as motivated by principle. If this earns her a reputation for being contentious she is happy to pay that price. What she does not want is to appear 'wishy-washy'.

Talking to him in his suburban semi-detached house, **Howard Singh** displays  less flamboyance. The story of his leaving home and coming to England rather gainsays the placid set of his face and speech.

**George Reynolds** is a political newcomer but his story reveals a man prepared to fight tenaciously until he gets what he regards as his due. He had thus won the right to continue to inhabit his post-war pre-fab years after all the rest had been pulled down, and then to buy it. The house is now a living example of the adage that an Englishman's home is his castle. George Reynolds opening the pages of *Great Expectations* would surely recognise Wemmick's Fort as the work of a fellow spirit.  For George Reynolds has transformed the strictly utilitarian little house designed with a view to putting a roof over people's heads in the immediate post-war years, cladding it with coloured stone, giving its windows diamond-shaped leaded panes and adding a rich red-brown finish to the door and porch. And around it he has created a garden. In the strictest sense George Reynolds' home is a mini paradise. Through the summer his pots of geraniums and miniature roses bloom with a lavishness and brilliance usually found only in the illustrations of seedsmen's catalogues. He has settled on plastic ducks for the little pond - perhaps for reasons of practicality. But the thick clump of water iris is vital with life, a mass of exquisite white blossoms finely tinged with blue. And dotted around are a number of formally clipped trees. For George Reynolds has not allowed the loss of an arm to stand in the way of his practising topiary. There is also a little windmill. And much else. The energy harnessed to the creation of this garden suggests the Town Council might have acquired a useful new member.

———————————————

*Elizabeth Wiles*

# Elizabeth Wiles

Town Councillor, District Councillor, County Councillor, born 1936, Southampton, Hampshire.

*'There's nothing I like more than getting a problem and solving it.'*

My early memories are of wartime childhood in Southampton. For a great deal of the time we lived in an air raid shelter my father built. The house next door was demolished, and I went to school one day and came back, saying, 'The school has gone.' And my mother said, 'Don't be silly darling!' She thought I was making up stories. And I said, 'Yes, it's not there any more.' After that I spent only half days at school until the war was over. We didn't have many toys. I can remember the first time my sister and I had a balloon. She went and popped hers. Then she took my balloon and popped it on the holly hedge as well. I was so unhappy I screamed. Then I got smacked for screaming.

After my father had gone to war in India, and my mother was an air raid warden, and we only had half-day education, there were long periods when we just roamed about. The boys next door were horrible. I had a dolly with an open mouth, and they used to put spiders and beetroot in it. But we used to have gangs and that was quite exciting, because we used to trek off on our own, and had great adventures, because no-one ever said, 'Don't, that's dangerous.' On one occasion, a child fell down one of these blooming bomb craters and we had to rescue him.

When I got to eleven I went to grammar school then from there I went to Edinburgh University, and did Modern Languages, because I couldn't think what else to do. I think really I should have done anthropology or something like that. But there you are! And I came down from Edinburgh and went back home. By now we lived on a smallholding outside Southampton, and had pigs and chickens and grew strawberries. It was quite nice.

Then one day my father said, 'It's about time you went and got a job.' So I went and got a job as secretary in a boys' boarding school. The chap who owned it was an MP. I went to work for him because he was a Labour MP and then found he'd swapped sides, and become a Tory MP. I remember typing these wretched speeches and saying to him, 'That's not on, you know, you shouldn't talk about people like that.' At the same time he was a very pleasant man to work for, but we did have battles royal. Eventually

I went to London to work at the BBC as a secretary on 'Radio Newsreel' and the 'Today' programme. And just when I thought I was going to make a career of that I met my husband, and we set up house in Putney, and had children, and that was the end of my career.

My husband was born in India and he'd travelled all over Asia. So I visited India and that was nice. He ran a travel magazine, and wrote books, and I helped. I'd have the baby sitting on the floor, and type his manuscripts. His family came from East Anglia and in 1975, we decided to leave London and come to Sudbury. I remember it was raining and we walked, in the twilight, up Cross Street, and I thought this is a most awful place. You could see people's television sets winking in the houses as you went along; that was about the most exciting thing in Sudbury. But Sudbury's done us well, and I hope I've done Sudbury well.

The politics came after my husband died. I suppose it's foolish to think that I in any way influence what happens in Sudbury, but it might be that I do. But how I got into politics is quite interesting. I met someone from the children's play group in a supermarket one day, and I said, 'Who's standing in our ward for the Labour Party?' 'Actually no-one. It is not possible to take that ward, and therefore no-one attempts it.' So I said, 'Well I will do it.' So, I started, and in 1979 lost heavily. But in 1980 there was a bi-election and I went for it, and won.

And I've stuck to that ward. It's very attractive to go to an easy ward, but I've always kept faith with people. So in 1980 I won; 1983 was a very unfortunate time when Labour was not popular and people were more willing than not to slam the door in your face, which is very unkind. I lost that time. In '85 they felt sorry for what they'd done to me, and they sent me to County Council. So I thought I was all right, and I was happy as Larry, and in 1987, I put forward again for the District Council, and they threw me out. In 1989 they took me back as County Councillor for Sudbury. So I've had this see-saw with people. I've been County Councillor for Sudbury for six years, and I've recently been put back on the District and Town Council.

I had dreadful hassles with the Labour Party in Sudbury when the SDP came into being. I can remember on one occasion they said to me, 'We are sending you to Coventry.' And I said, 'But you haven't spoken to me for six months!' And they said, 'No, but now it's official!' Now people from the SDP are coming back to the Labour Party. So things don't last for ever, and you can't hold

grudges because politics is like mountaineering; you make steps together.

I can sit in County Council and in one morning we will spend perhaps ten million over four years, or three million on something for four or five years, and think nothing of it. With the Town Council you're haggling with ha'pennies. But the Town Council is what people relate to. And we have to value people. I pray that we do. If we don't I would be very upset.

When I talk about praying I suppose I ought to mention the church. One of the semi-political things that I first did when I came to the town was to join the church, The other thing I've done is to be secretary of the Babergh District Trades Council. And from there, chairperson of the regional Trades Union Equal Opportunities Committee.

My political memories start with an election in Southampton in '45. I must have been about nine. The local headmaster was putting up for Labour and I said to my mother, 'Who did you vote for?' And she said, 'The best man.' In my judgement the best man was this Labour chap. So for many years I thought... when apparently my mother had voted Tory all her life, and she is still a dyed in the wool, really up and down Tory. And so was my father. But anyway, I made up my mind which side I belonged to, and I haven't changed. One of the first things I did when my husband died was to join the Labour Party and decide to do something. I had the freedom then, and I felt that was one of the things I wanted to do. I just believe in getting the best for people, and I believe that the Labour Party is the party which will do that.

There's nothing I like more than getting a problem and solving it, though lately I've realized that it's very bad to take some people's problems away. You have someone who is worried about a pothole. Now you go and fill that pothole in, and that person has to actually think up a new problem, something else they can complain about. You've taken away their reason to be alive. So you have to be careful not to take away their problems too quickly.

One very significant thing in the town was the miners' strike in '84. It seems surprising that Sudbury was affected by the miners' strike, but we used to stand up there with the miners from Nottingham, and they would speak to the people. And a lot of people in Sudbury had links with the mining communities in Kent and up north. So we had collections of food and raced up to the strikers with it. I can remember there was a dentist who came along and he said, 'The most awful thing would be if you couldn't have your favourite toothpaste', and he brought a collection of toothpastes and toothbrushes. So everyone thought about what they would most lack if they were in that situation. It was a real fellow-feeling thing. I still get Christmas cards from miners.

On the other hand, after the case where some people got killed because two miners threw a piece of concrete over a bridge - it was very nasty - people were actually walking sideways up and down in front of us saying 'Murderer!' and spitting in my face. And that was dreadful. Yes, in Sudbury, they spat in my face. And people said, 'We will never vote for you again Mrs. Wiles.'

But in '85 they returned me to the County Council. It was a surprise to us. We were a very small group in Sudbury at that time, the Labour Party. But I think people admire courage, and conviction.

During the miners' strike I couldn't go home and see my mother. I think she would have shouted at me. So I just stayed away from her. I go and visit her now. My husband's parents are Tories too, so I really didn't know what my children would do. We just let them be. And now my daughter's a Labour Councillor, and Edward my son, he's fiercely Labour, so it's a good family unit. They don't go to church, they refuse to go to church, but at least they vote Labour!

At the moment, I'm highway spokesperson for the County Labour Group. We have a budget of something like twenty-three or twenty-four million pounds a year and you get all these men, road contractors, saying, 'What's a little woman like you doing being interested in roads?' But it is very important obviously to have roads that are safe and footways that people can walk down without falling on their faces. At one stage in Sudbury we had almost an epidemic where people were falling down. It got to three

*Town Councillor 1980*

or four a month until I called in the County Surveyor, and said, 'Look, we've got to do things.' And we started to make things better. And that's something that I've been able to contribute to the town.

Of course another thing I'm interested in, and was voted in on in 1985, is to get a by-pass for the town. We've got a by-pass to the north of the town, we need something to go up to the west. But the problem with Sudbury is that it's surrounded by the most beautiful Water Meadows. And the reason I was tipped out in 1987 was that I don't take votes for nothing, but try and tell the truth, and I saw that the price of a by-pass in Sudbury was to eat into the water meadows. So people are stomping up and down, and there will be a public inquiry, and they will all do their nuts and get really upset and in the end the by-pass will be built. And it may be that I will lose the next election on it, because they won't like it.

The other issue at the moment is the fifteen million pound hospital the NHS is going to provide for Sudbury. We had a campaign because they were closing down our maternity services, and we lost it. They took away our casualty service. Therefore they feel they have no need to replace these because they don't exist. But I don't think the people really understood that we will just get a geriatric unit with outpatient facilities, a few GP beds, an ambulance station, and an X-ray unit.

The trouble is people seem not to be able to react very quickly. You go round saying, 'Look, I think you ought to be thinking about this', and they don't see the urgency. Then, when it's happened, they start to make fusses. I'm in the chair at the Sudbury Library Users' Association, and we have very nice talks every two months. But I've heard that the library is not big enough, and that something will have to be done. Now people will start in about five years' time, throwing up their arms and saying, 'Save our library!' And so I started the ball rolling yesterday, saying, 'We've got to think about this now, and look at making better use of the space, or finding a new site.' That's looking ahead ten years. But if people don't start thinking about it now, they'll get someone imposing solutions on them. So, I thought I'd done a bit of good last night.

I don't have a job. I've done a lot of things, but I've never been paid for them. That means I'm not tied. Because when you do things you get paid for it, you lose out on freedom. If I want to do something I can go and do it. And the other advantage I have on some councillors is I do my council work full-time. I get up in the morning, and read my post, and the papers. That may last till eleven. Then I can go up to town. And I will take forty minutes to walk about a hundred yards, because I talk to people all the time. Whether men would want to do that I don't know. I think possibly not. I'm a great gossiper; I pick up things and listen. I listen perhaps more than I talk some days. Always on the listen, always...not sympathetic, just listening, so you've got your finger on the pulse of Sudbury.

Of course the latest thing we had was the ambulance drivers' strike. The ambulance drivers were really non-political; a lot of them hadn't really thought about politics at all, or unions, and they were suddenly confronted with this strike. In Sudbury, the owner of a local pub actually gave an empty shop to them, and they opened this shop to sell goods that people had donated. I spent weeks down there. It was lovely, and you got quite close to these people, who were starting to talk politics.

Then came the day when we all went to London, courtesy of the Haverhill Fire Brigade who paid for the coach, and we took the fire brigade with us. It sounds daft, but I was quite worried about the ambulance people. They seemed entirely innocent, these dear people, and I was worried they would get lost. Some of them had never been to London hardly. So we marched to Trafalgar Square. Then suddenly, with all the speeches going on, one of these chaps said, 'Mrs. Wiles, Mrs. Wiles...' And I thought, 'Oh God! one of them's died!' and I ducked under some barrier and shot through, to see what was going on.

And there was Neil Kinnock. And these people were saying, 'This is her! This is this wonderful woman from Sudbury! You must shake her hand.' Terribly embarrassing, you've no idea! But Neil Kinnock was very good, and had great presence of mind, because he actually smiled and shook hands with me. And all the television cameras were on him, so the next day they rang me up at home and said, 'You're on telly!' I hadn't seen it so I had to go round to the ambulance station on my bike, and see myself on telly!

When my husband was alive if you had come into a room and seen the both of us, you wouldn't have noticed I was there; I would have been like wallpaper. There was no way I could compete with him; he was very much the star of the show. And a very lovely man as well. But when I was first elected to the District Council in 1980 some man said to me, 'Have you any experience of local government?' I said, 'No.' And he said, 'How do you think you'll get on?' And I just said, 'Very well.' I had absolutely no idea that I could do anything like that, you know. And I just went from there. People would say to me, 'Would you like to make a speech?' And I'd think, 'I don't even know how to turn a mike on, but yes, I'll do it.' Oh Sudbury's my home now. What's more, I've known Sudbury very intensely because I've had to study it.

I've got a nice life really. I don't have to be beholden to anyone, and that's good. To be able to be your own person and decide what you want to do is a rare privilege I think. I have to do as my children say sometimes, and they will be quite severe with me, so there are bickerings and arguments. But it's a nice household to live in, with four grown-up people, not always, but generally, living together in basic harmony.

*   *   *   *

# Howard Singh

Town Councillor, ex-Mayor, Quantity Surveyor, born 1935, Trinidad.

*'If there's something to be done I'll try to do it if I can.'*

My grandparents emigrated to Trinidad at the turn of the century, as farmers. My grandfather had a sugar cane plantation and dairy and as a child I would sit with him on the river banks, while the cattle grazed, and he would tell us stories about India, which was fascinating. My father was converted to Christianity by missionaries and became a school teacher. But he had nine children and he found that teaching didn't keep his family, so he started his own transportation business, and then he had a taxi fleet, and in later years he bought an estate. That's when I decided to come to England, because I didn't see myself running a fleet of lorries or taxis or going back to the land. I came to England in 1956.

I booked my passage, with my mother's consent, and only ten days before leaving told my father. In fact, I told him on my twenty-first birthday. He was not at all pleased or happy. Nevertheless he wished me well.

I started studying politics and economics in England, but quickly felt politics was a rotten business and gave it up. Then I thought I would like to have an acting career. I went to a method school of acting in London, and took a few bit parts. But I couldn't put up with the starvation in between, and decided to find myself a proper job. So I became a quantity surveyor with the Greater London Council and studied in the evening for my qualifications. I also got married. My wife is English and when she died we had been married almost thirty years.

We lived in London, but when we had children we decided we couldn't go on living in flats. And just by chance in the evening paper there were some houses, which seemed reasonable to us, in a place called Sudbury. We then discovered that it was the town where my mother-in-law grew up, though my wife hadn't known. So we came to see the town - well we didn't, because it was so foggy we couldn't see anything - but we decided we'd take the house anyway.

At that time the Greater London Council were busy trying to encourage councils up and down the country to house people from London. But everybody who worked for the GLC in London wanted to stay there. But as we chose to live out here and I was able to get my job transferred. I became responsible, together with a host of other people, for the town development schemes around Sudbury.

We started living near the development scheme and I soon became itchy, because there was very little to do in the neighbourhood, and so much needed to be done to make people's way of life better. I discovered that people coming in from London wanted to use telephone boxes and there weren't any. And we hadn't a community centre. So I decided to do something about it. I consulted my then MP who said, 'The first thing you could do is become a local councillor.' That was 1966. In 1967 I stood in the council elections, and to my amazement I topped the polls.

This no-one thought was possible, because I was always told you had to live in the area for about thirty years before you were accepted. But I had decided if I was going to become a councillor, I should go and visit everybody and tell them what I had in mind. And they voted for me! I've not been aware of racial prejudice, but what I do know, of course, is that I have had to work twice as hard as everybody else in order to get half as much, if that makes sense.

Well I first became a councillor in 1967, so I've been one for about twenty-four years. In 1980 I was asked if I would like to become Mayor, and I accepted. I think I was successful because they asked me again in 1988. The mayoral chain is one of the most interesting I've seen. It's a delight to wear. You really feel honoured wearing a chain of that beauty.

I have represented the District Council on the Eastern Region Sports Council and chaired the Environmental and General Services Committee, and the Tourism Sub-Committee.

As a councillor you can claim travelling expenses and you get an attendance allowance. But from April 1st, a number of people are going to be paid in various ways. We need a wider cross section of people as councillors. I think the next move is to have paid councillors like MPs. My only worry about that is that then you will get the professional councillor, rather than people who just work from interest. But we will have to wait and see.

I stand as a Conservative but once the election is over my decisions are not ruled by party politics. I act just for the benefit of the people I serve. If the day comes that some

political party tells me what decisions I have to make I will need to think again about my career.

I have involved myself a lot with the town, because my belief is, if I am going to live in the town, there should be facilities for us to use. And there's no point complaining if you don't do anything about it. So if there's something to be done I'll try and do it if I can.

One of the first things I felt needed to be done in the new housing development was to have a community centre built. We used to go round every week, collecting. It was a challenge; but we got it built. Then when my son was an age to join the Cubs, I took him down and was horrified at the condition of the building, and soon put the idea forward that we should have a new one. It took several years. In fact it was not until I was Mayor the second time in 1989, that the building was opened. It's rewarding to see things that one had an involvement in come to fruition.

By 1975, the Greater London Council were finding that too many people were now moving out of London, and they wanted to reverse the trend, so I was then asked to go back to London to work and I commuted daily for about twelve years, Then in 1986 the Government decided to close the Greater London Council. I think it was the right decision, because the Council was becoming too political and one-sided. I finished with them anyway in 1979 and we decided to go into selling knitting yarns, tapestries and needlecraft. We then started two other shops, and decided to run a business in earnest.

I have been back to Trinidad. I have some brothers and sisters still living there. I also have two sisters and a brother in Canada, one brother in New York. And we have a daughter who is married to an Australian and now lives there, so the world is becoming a very small place as far as my family is concerned.

*Mayor of Sudbury*

But this is my home, this is my country, this is where I live. Even when it comes to cricket, I never support the West Indies, I support England, because I've lived here longer. Maybe that's unusual but I think the way to get the best out of the environment you live in is by being part of it.

# George Reynolds

Town Councillor, Designer, silk factory, born 1919, Sudbury.

*'I think that I shall learn a lot that I didn't know before.'*

Gregory Street, where I lived, was the slums of Sudbury. They were old weavers' houses, covered with wallpaper made of newspapers and plastered over with distemper, which was nothing more than coloured chalk and we were infested with fleas. We used to cope with the fleas with 'Keating's Flea Powder'. It was an ideal killer. If you didn't have Keatings you got covered with bites.

Nobody had much money. There was a saying in Gregory Street that if you paid the rent two weeks running the landlord would want to know where you got the money from. He didn't often get money every week. They were terrible times, but they were also great times, by the fact that everybody mucked in and helped each other.

I went to North Street school. The cane ruled the day. But I don't think it did us any harm. When I left school I went to Armes & Son. They were mat makers from King's Lynn who came down to Sudbury. And several families including mine came down with them. My grandfather, my mother and my uncle worked there. For me it was too much. I stuck it for a fortnight. It was like living in Charles Dickens' day, with the old gas-lights and the dust, and you couldn't hardly see anyone. And the tallow what they put on the matting it was...I never did collect my pay, so I suppose they owe me a few bob now!

From there I went to a big estate and became a thatcher's mate for about five years. There were no combine harvesters, and everything was stacks. We used to thatch the stacks to keep the rain and the elements out, until the thrashing machine came round and thrashed the corn.

I liked working on the land. But the money was not very good. I think I started off with ten shillings a week and I had to give my mother five shillings. I had to do that because my father died of wounds he got in the First World War, and she brought the three of us up on her own, and therefore I had to give her the five shillings.

I can remember going for my first pay day at the great house and standing in front of the boss and receiving the first ten shillings. I happened to go in there with my hands in my pocket, and he said, 'Take your hands out of your pocket and stand decent!' So that was my first taste of authority. Which was useful later in life. Discipline in my life has been one of the greatest things, and I don't think

I've come out of it too bad. When you see hardly any discipline today, you wonder why they didn't keep conscription up. It made them come out men, they didn't come out yobbos or layabouts that you see about today - no disrespect to them, of course.

During that time I joined the Territorial Army, the Suffolk Regiment, and when war broke out we were called up and I went to India. We were actually in Cape Town when Japan declared war on America. And I went up into Malaya and got caught in the battle. I had my arm, most of it, blown off. The first thing that came to my mind was my mother, whether I'd ever see her again. Nothing else came to my mind. I can remember that very vivid. Then a friend from Haverhill came with the scissors and cut the rest off. It was as easy as that. And I had a cup of tea, and that was that. Now I can talk about it but it was not very nice at the time. Then on the last day of the battle for Singapore I got captured, and shoved in a prison camp.

I spent three years in prison camps. The Japanese theory was, if you didn't work you didn't get any food. I was in the low-class work. They shoved me in the nurseries raising small coconut trees, palm trees, tapioca. That was a part of my life now that I like to forget. But I never go a day without something comes back. Because I lost so many friends out there from round here. So I really am exceedingly fortunate. And I came home and I thought, why me, why did I come home and all the people got killed or died of beriberi, or cholera? Why me?

When I came out I couldn't pull the straw into yellms. I had to learn a new trade. And we used to go on the beer at the different pubs for quite a while, Then one day our colonel, who lived in Sudbury, saw me and said, 'Reynolds, it's getting time you had a job. Go and see Mr. Kipling'. So I did. In the prison camp I'd got hold of a pencil and paper and made sure that when I came home I was going to write just as good with my left as I did with my right hand. So I joined Vanners and became a silk designer. And I've stopped there. I said to my mother that I was never going to work inside again. And I finished up inside thirty-seven years!

Well I came home, I got married, and I lived with my mum a few months, and then they were building prefabs for the ex-service people because there was not a lot of houses about. And as my wife was in the forces and I was in the forces we were given this house.

I've been in it ever since. I used to rent it, The council was after me at one time because they wanted to pull it down. They offered me any house in Sudbury that was new. But we didn't want to go, because it's ideal here. I wrote to the Environment people and they said, 'Of course you can buy

your own house'. So I was not in the Council's good books. But that doesn't matter. If you don't try to do anything you'll never achieve anything. That's the trouble with a lot of people I think. They talk, but they never try to alter things themselves. And they'd be surprised sometimes what they can do actually, if you keep at it.

When I came out of the army, I thought to myself, I've been exceptionally lucky, so I joined the Royal British Legion, and now I'm their Welfare Officer, I love to go round to the old ladies, mostly widows. I go to probably about nine widows to one widower. A lot of widows lost husbands after the War through various wounds they got during the war. I also go to about ten ex-service women who were in the Wrens, or in the WAAF or in the ATS.

I like to go for a drink, and I heard so much about the council, what they do and what they don't do, I thought to myself, well if you can't beat them try to join them. So I put up for councillor, and I got in this last time. And I think that I shall learn a lot that I didn't know before. And I think that that's what a lot of people should do; they shouldn't moan about things, they should try to join them, and find out what really happens, instead of moaning and not knowing what really happens.

I went Whit Monday down the Six-a-side. Of course they knew I was on the council, so I was immediately stopped. They said, 'You're just the man we want to see, because there's no B good asking anybody else. You're on the council. Now do something about it'. The Monster Truck Show that was on their field four or five days before had made great ruts on the football pitch so they had to play at the side of the pitch, where the grass is long, which spoilt the game. So yesterday I went down to the Free Press and they took a photograph of the ruts. You'll probably see me in the paper tomorrow.

Gardening is my hobby. I've always been drawn towards things that grow, like corn and flowers and the trees. Who made them? Who could make something like them? I think it comes from when I was just a little boy. My father was a gardener and we used to go to the shop next to where we lived and buy a penny packet of seeds, and he said, 'Scrape a row in the ground and put them in, and see what happens'. Now I've got so many flowers, and three greenhouses and they're full that watering them is the main problem. If you don't water them they'll all keel over. So once you start gardening you've got to keep at it really.

I've not had a lot of money. I don't think riches really is the thing. I think the main thing is your health. You can be a poor man but healthy, and you are just as rich as any man with a fortune. Because they're not necessarily healthy. And, after all, if you've got a mansion, you can only sleep in one bed, and in one room each night; you can't sleep in thirty rooms.

By the time I came back after the war I'd travelled about twenty-five thousand miles. I think I've done enough. You have to have money to travel really and I think being a prisoner of war put me off. I've no inclination to travel at all, anywhere. No fear. I know it's not right and of course if anybody would want to travel it's up to them. But I think Sudbury's an ideal place. We are surrounded by meadows, with all the numerous shades of green, especially at this time of the year. Just imagine living in a tower block, twenty storeys up, without this scenery we've got.

## Chapter Thirteen

# GOD AND GOOD WORKS

The English are not great church attenders. Americans and Europeans go to church much more. But though England is one of the most secular countries in the contemporary world, there is a nucleus of people for whom religion remains a vital part of life and most small English towns retain a variety of churches.

The son of a Church of England vicar, **Peter Hollis** went into the family business, becoming a parson himself. For nearly twenty years he was rector of St.Peter's and St.Gregory's. He is a small, very straight-backed man, who speaks thoughtfully but fluently. He has not risen high in the church hierarchy but one imagines he has never tried to. Not because he feels there is a special virtue to unworldliness, just that his interests have driven him in other directions.

He might at times seem a bit of a firebrand to some people, joining campaigns for nuclear disarmament. But talking to him it is not his inclination but his concern about moral and religious propriety that comes across. He is an intellectual and his theological reading is extensive. In his quest for religious understanding he shows a delicate fastidiousness and makes no secret of his reservations about contemporary expressions of religious fervour. Old parishioners and acquaintances generally, remember him as a man of practical kindnesses. He left his successor to enrich the musical offering of the church.

Tall and gracefully built **Faith Widdicombe** knows about spiritual need and has a strong religious conviction both through her loved mother's upbringing and by temperament. Her spiritual explorations eventually brought her to the Quakers whose simple, austere style of worship seemed to be what she was looking for. Yet she continues to tussle with belief and one suspects she will always find it difficult and puzzling. But if belief presents problems, good works do not. Our need to help the poor and badly treated in the world is unproblematic for her. Her photograph, taken at a small mid-week meeting, aims to capture a sense of style more than a likeness.

Religion is fun for **Glenda and Bill Dixey** and the Army absorbs a lot of their time. But they also live full lives outside the church and enjoy that too. Because we commonly read a great deal from a person's clothes we decided we needed to photograph them both in their army uniform and in other dress. So we start with a joint portrait of the Dixeys in uniform. They posed themselves formally for this, Glenda spontaneously linking arms with her husband. We then offer two other pictures which present very different images. As a group these pictures raise questions about our interpretation of individual photographs.

# Peter Hollis
Rector of the Church of England, born 1920, Hull, Yorkshire

# Anne Hollis
Rector's wife, born 1928, Paris, France.

*'We were rather a cut below what was expected of us'.*

PETER: I enlisted in the services in '39 when I was nearly nineteen. After the war, when I became a parson, I was a curate in Birmingham, and eventually I stayed there for sixteen years and then came to Sudbury. I always regarded myself as not belonging to the place; partly because as a parson, you know when you retire you've got to move out of the house, and normally you move well away from the parish so that you're not in the way of the person who moves in. But having lived here well over twenty years I've realized that I do belong here, and I don't belong in the East Riding of Yorkshire where I grew up. I spent a day in Beverley, looking at house prices, and it suddenly came across me, I don't belong here any more. And then I realized that I really belong in Suffolk.

I became a parson probably because my father was a parson and although he was very liberal and didn't push religion down your throat I suppose I grew up with the idea I wanted to be one. And by the time the war started I'd got a place at Cambridge, with the idea of getting a degree - because you had to get a degree in those days before you could go to theological college. But after seven years, and serving all over the place, my views changed considerably and I didn't really know what I believed. I came out of the Services and had to go to a selection board, where they decide whether they want to accept you as a parson.

I don't suppose he was an old man, he was probably in his fifties, but he looked an old man to me. He interviewed me and I said, quite honestly I don't know whether I believe it all or not. But if it's true, then I want to be a parson, but I said I shall quite understand if you reject me, and if you do that my next priority will be to go back to Africa where I'd been in the war, and try and join the colonial service, which still existed in those days. And to my amazement I was recommended for further training for ordination. But I suppose since then I've always been a person who asks lots of questions. I think doubt is a great stimulus to thought.

I think what happened is, I grew up in the army. I was sent away to a boarding school, and with that kind of background you leave school terribly naive - well you did in my day - knowing nothing about people at all. My children, who all went to State schools, are far more mature at eighteen and nineteen than I was. And as I grew up I grew out of a rather childish view of religion really.

I had a very easy war because I spent all my time chasing it and never catching it up! I joined the East Yorkshire Regiment, but the CO refused to post me overseas, he said I was too young - I was nearly nineteen. And after a year I thought, this is no good, so I asked to be seconded to a unit called the King's African Rifles in East Africa. And I went there, and then from there we went to Madagascar, because that was a French colony. But they were suspected of allowing Japanese submarines to go there. So we did some heroic landings, expecting to be fired on from all sides, and they just shook our hands and said good afternoon as we came in! So after another year or so I thought, well this is no good, I must try and get to Burma. I was very romantic about it all. So I went back to East Africa and eventually out to India and from there to the Burmese border. I think I hitch-hiked the last bit in an American aircraft - and within a fortnight the company I joined came back to India! So, I gave up after that.

Of course I was very lucky. But if you're young and you're in a war you expect to be involved in the fighting. I felt I really ought to justify myself by getting involved in a battle. I thought I was chickening out by not being. But I was very lucky really. I had a lot of travel at Government expense!

Then I did three years at university, two at theological college and was ordained in 1951. I'd got to know a chap in Cambridge who I was very impressed by, and he left and went back into an ordinary ministry in Birmingham. So I said would he be willing for me to go as one of his curates when I was ordained. And he agreed.

One thing that has influenced my life as a Church of England parson is that most of my time in Birmingham was spent on housing estates, when the post-war building was going really fast. My wife and I moved into a little council house as they were building the remainder of the estate. We had no church, no hall, no nothing. There were no shops, not even a pub, but just houses being built very fast. To begin with we had a morning service in our front room, and a little evening service in someone else's house nearby.

It made me think very hard about what you really needed in terms of ceremony and all the rest of it, when we started very simply like that. It affected me very much. Then eventually a school was built, and we held services in the school, and then a church hall was built, and then eventually the church itself.

But if you're working as a parson on that type of housing estate, it comes over fairly strongly that you've got no status whatever! And when we were there the Midlands car trade was booming, everybody had jobs. Unemployment just wasn't known. And they would work weekends if they possibly could, to get a bit more pay. And they regarded people like myself as doing no work. I remember well calling at a block of flats, to talk to a family about a baptism. And on one occasion, when the husband came in to have a chat, he said, 'Do you know I saw some grown-ups coming out of your church the other day'. So I said, 'Yes'. He said, 'I thought only children went to church'. He wasn't trying to take the mickey, that's just how he regarded the church. Another occasion, as I was going out from seeing a family about a christening, the husband said to me, 'You've got a right job for a convalescent you have!' In other words I was really doing nothing.

The thing that struck me about Birmingham was that a lot of Northerners had moved down there for jobs in the Fifties and I got the impression that nobody was proud of the place. It probably wasn't true of the proper Brummies, but so many people weren't born there. I mean if you were born in a place like Bradford you would think that was the first place God ever made. But Birmingham struck me as a place where the one thing people wanted to do was to make money. There used to be a saying that a bloke would do his brother over for a second-hand car. This may have been quite untrue, but my impression was that a lot of them were just making money as hard as they could, and nobody seemed to think very much of the place itself. I enjoyed being there because I learnt so much about people and how they lived and the difficulties.

The estate finished at twelve thousand people, which in Birmingham was a small parish. Being an entirely new place, what needed doing was some kind of community sense building up. Although we only had a very small congregation, the Methodists started in a hall not far from us and between us I think we probably provided the leadership for things like Scouts and Guides, and grown-up clubs. I think we saw the role of the church more as a means of serving the community in this way, of building up some kind of feeling for the place so people felt they

*A 'Clergy Against the Bomb' march - Fleet Street 1984*

belonged. When I came to Sudbury there were stacks of organisations, and the church felt very much on the sidelines.

Well we felt we wanted a change. I've always felt the Church of England appointment system was bad. It is still the old-boy network. What they ought to do is to advertise vacant posts in 'Church Times', short-list and interview like they do for any other profession. But they don't in lots of places. A bloke I knew moved to Sudbury, when we'd been in Birmingham sixteen years. When this chap was about to retire, he wrote to me and said would you like to come to Sudbury.

Well I'd never heard of it. I didn't even know where it was. But we came over to look at it, and when I eventually came to be interviewed by the Bishop., I was most impressed with him, and I thought I'd like to serve under him. And so that's how we came to Sudbury.

ANN: We'd expected to go to work in the North.

PETER: It was quite a shock when we came to Sudbury, to be called Rector this and Rector that. I found it difficult to get used to. I expected to be regarded as an outsider. I'd always heard unless you've lived here thirty years, you don't belong. But I was amazed how incredibly friendly people were. I remember I had to make a little talk when I first came. I felt I would be treated like a West Indian immigrant arriving in Birmingham, but it was quite different. They were very friendly and supportive. It was a lovely place to work in.

ANN: We felt embarrassed to begin with to have such a grand house. And to be treated respectfully, a thing that had never happened to us before. Peter had a verger didn't you, who was extremely respectful. And I remember not long after we'd come, I was scrubbing the front doorsteps, which were covered in moss at the time, and the church warden came by and he was shocked! The rector's wife couldn't scrub a front doorstep, I mean this just wasn't done! We were rather a cut below what was expected of us. And of course we sent our children to the local schools, which apparently hadn't been done in the past.

PETER: We had every intention of leaving the area when we retired but sadly the housing boom was beginning in 1986.

ANN: We were always behind in the market. So we try to keep a low profile. But it would be better to move right away, than to feel that you shouldn't be here because you suddenly have to cut yourselves off. It's like a bereavement. I found it extremely painful leaving our Birmingham parish too. When we left Birmingham and came to Sudbury, and I looked round at all these, well rather upmarket people by comparison with the housing estate where we'd lived, I didn't see how I could possibly settle down here. It was a lovely house, the children had a real garden for the first time, but basically it's people that matter, and the people that mattered to us we'd left behind. And again, when we left this parish, it was extremely painful. Basically the parish is your family. Peter has never expected me to do any particular thing as the Vicar's wife. But you're married to your husband, put it that way! You can't escape it. You're a public figure. And your children can't escape it either. So you don't make close friends, because it could be difficult if you developed a vicarage clique so to speak. But on the other hand, well you get very fond of everyone who belongs to the church.

PETER: Theologically, I'm an 'Honest to God' man. I couldn't go along the evangelical line. But I think one good thing about the evangelical end is that some of their more thoughtful leaders are beginning to see a relationship between religion and politics, which at one time they'd have nothing to do with. I think they're beginning to see more importance in relating to social needs, rather than just 'giving your life to the Lord' as you might say.

# Faith Widdicombe

Quaker, Amnesty International member, born 1925, Harrow, Middlesex.

*'...You're up down, up down, when all you want to be is quiet.'*

I grew up with the background of a public school which was quite fun. My father was a house master at Harrow and then when I was about six he became headmaster at Bryanston, which was a very progressive school, and had only been going six years then. My father always seemed rather an exceptional person to me. And so did his wife, my mother. But he was so bound up with the school that we didn't see much of him. She definitely had the biggest influence on us, through her life and her loveliness.

I went partly locally and partly to boarding school. I kept a diary at that time and noted all the films I went to, and when my younger son, Adrian, was growing up, and I criticised him for watching the television, I read back into my diary and found I was doing exactly the same things, but I'd completely forgotten about it. It was very salutary. There's a lot to be said for writing diaries! Anyway, then I went off to the Central School of Dramatic Art and did a couple of years there. I didn't finish the course because the war was on, and I taught at a prep school for a little while, and then I had to go and look after the headmaster's house because my mother was very ill. I never actually joined up in the end.

Afterwards I went as an au pair to America for a year and a half with somebody who worked for the United Nations. She was the daughter of a person called Baroness Budberg, who escaped from somewhere like Estonia, having swallowed a huge necklace of regal pearls which was all she possessed in the world when she got over here. She was also a close friend of H G Wells. She was a great character, and the first woman I'd ever seen drinking neat gin!

The trip got America out of my system! It's never come back! Oh, there were nice little bits. Washington was gorgeous, and the highlight was going to the art gallery there. It was so spacious. Every picture had its own space, so you could appreciate it. Normally you get hundreds of pictures all crowded together, like at the Royal Academy. There was this wonderful painting of a woman by Vermeer. It was so peaceful. That was really the loveliest thing about America, as far as I was concerned. And also the shock of seeing modern art like Van Gogh in the real

rather than on postcards. That was really an eye-opener, and exciting too. I also went as an au pair to Florence for a year and a half, which was quite marvellous and stimulated one's interest in the arts.

Then I got married and went to Good Housekeeping to learn to cook, because that's one thing I'd never done. And we moved here to Suffolk, and lived in Hadleigh until about ten years ago. We came here because it was nearer for Nicko to get to the special school.

I've got two sons. I lost a daughter first. The natural childbirth I'm afraid wasn't very successful. Anyway, Nicko came in 1958, and at first it was a shock. He's spastic and mentally handicapped. He was two months early and very tiny, and I said at the time, is this going to affect him. They said, well, it might make him blind. It certainly didn't do that. But a friend next door had a baby born the same date Nick should have been born, so I could see that things were not right. However, he was a beautiful baby, and has always been a lovely thing. Then Adrian came along about two years later. I was in the hospital with Adrian being born and Nicko having fits at the same moment. He had a lot of fits when he was young, and he's just started having them again, though only infrequently.

But we were very spoilt when Nicko was born in that we had help in the house, an absolute gem of a person who adored Nicholas and guarded him as a grandson. So a lot of the burden was rather taken off one.

I think I accepted what had happened, but my husband was overwhelmed. It gave him a deep shock. And one did have to completely change one's hopes and fears. Of course one hasn't had anything like the worry that people with normal children have; no sex problems, drugs, smoking, none of those have arisen. So one's been relieved of great worries one might have had. Because when you come to actually look at families, nobody escapes without some worries. Sometimes they're more obvious if there's a handicap like Nicko's, but every family, even with the most lovely, bouncing, healthy children, have probably got something worrying, haven't they?

I never felt ostracised with Nicko because he looked lovely; it did make a difference. People...it's all wrong, but they don't like these in-a-way, ugly little mongol children, though they are so lovable. One's terribly sorry for parents whose children haven't got some lovable sort of qualities. It must be terribly worrying. I know Nicko will fall on his feet when we go. But I know somebody who's got an incredibly sad child, very large and difficult,

and I know he's very concerned who's going to really love him when they go.

Leslie, my husband, was a founder member of the local Mencap and it's a very flourishing society; the parents are all so involved.  Belonging to Mencap one's got much more aware of other people's greater difficulties.

Adrian went to a lovely prep school. It was where my father went. I do think he did enjoy it after the first term or two. I hope he did. But of course we'd always thought he'd go to Bryanston, and we signed him on. But when it came to the end of the prep school he said, 'No, I've been away enough.  Nick's been at home, I don't want to go away again to boarding school.'

And that was disappointing because I think he would have got an awful lot from it.  The local school that he should have gone to was at a very low ebb educationally and I think he might have mixed with not the highest sort of denomination so we thought we must find one with a bit more intellectual stimulus. So he went to a Catholic school. But it turned out to be an extremely dry sort of place . You just learnt and took your exams. No expeditions. Whereas Hadleigh High School, which I became a governor of, were going here there and every-where. He got his exams, but he didn't stay on for A-levels even. So yes, I think he would have got a lot more out of life if he had gone to Bryanston, or perhaps a good local school. But ...there we are! And I'm very, very glad we didn't insist he went away again. If he wanted to be at home, that was right.

I'm not bright; I'm not intellectual, although I was brought up in a very intellectual school. But my mother was always giving one confidence. She always looked for the best in everybody, to bring it out.  At her funeral a great friend spoke and said she was really a mystic. Certainly she was lovely beyond anything. And her faith was always there. On the other hand she was very down to earth. She was lovely with the new boys. Wonderful letters after she died from old boys. She played a quiet but major part in the school, in the way a headmaster's wife would. And she had a really good mind. Every time I went down to see her she charged my batteries, and I came back feeling all renewed.

I joined the Quakers about fifteen to twenty years ago in Ipswich. Leslie's not a member. It's not at all his thing. He loves music but he's only recently really started going to church. When I was in Italy I almost became a Catholic! I think we had enquiring minds about religion. With my mother  you  couldn't but be religious. Obviously we weren't happy with the Church of England, and I used to get bored in Church of England services, the fact that they never stopped talking and you're up down, up down, when all you want is to be quiet. It just appealed to me, the simplicity of the Quakers, and not spending all the money on churches. There can be problems. In one Meeting House I've been to one person snores loudly throughout, every time. Well of course that's very difficult. And at one time we had a person who had just come out of a mental home at Ipswich, who used to read long articles out of 'The Times'.  But in Sudbury there's none of those problems. We've just got a few people who talk...not frequently and we hope they'll say something because it's interesting, though there's complete silence sometimes. I find one's got an awful lot of questions still to ask, and to be convinced. 'Lord help thou my unbelief.' A lot of questions are very difficult to find answers to.

I can't remember what actually clicked me off to join Amnesty, except that it met at the Quakers in Ipswich - and it meets at the Quakers here. One feels it's so impor-tant that I can't understand why more people don't... But everybody has their own thing; they can't all be doing Amnesty. We've got between fifty and sixty people who are paid up members, and about ten people come to the meetings, not nearly enough to do all the things that are demanded of us. But there's one person who is absolutely exceptional and takes on the lion's share.

A lot of prisoners we've had have been released though we have come across an impasse now with Syria. I don't know if I can remember them all. An Argentinian we had was released.  This was in the dreadful times of Argentina. Gosh, you do learn a lot about geography when you join Amnesty. We had a Turkish prisoner who was released. We sent them quite a lot of money, and got him on his feet. We had a Vietnamese, we had a German.  She was released. And we had an Algerian. I had a letter from his mother. She had two sons both standing up for human rights, one in prison, the other in the desert somewhere, not actually in prison but banished. We wrote back but we never heard any more from her.  And he was released.  I was also writing to a chap in Uruguay. He came over.  The Bristol group had adopted him. He made me this brooch. He had colossal parties over in Bristol.

I've made several hundred pounds for Amnesty through doing cards; I make Christmas and greetings cards and sell them.  I think we have to do what we're best at, and I'm better at doing that than writing letters. I do write letters, but not as arduously as some. The cards are really my contribution to Amnesty. We raise a lot of money in Sudbury; we send a thousand pounds a year to Amnesty, which for a small country town is quite good. But Sudbury is pretty generous.  They're always having collections, aren't they, for something.

# Bill Dixey
Builder, Salvation Army, born 1947, Bulmer, Essex.

# Glenda Dixey
Play-school worker, Salvation Army, born 1949, Sudbury.

*'Some don't even realise that it's a church.'*

GLENDA: I went to North Street Junior School and it was there that I heard some girls chatting about their Sunday School, and I was intrigued and thought I'd like to go. My parents didn't think it was a good idea. My father tended to think 'Barmey Army'. And he didn't want that for his daughter. Anyway, I persuaded them, and I thoroughly enjoyed it. I took part in various Sunday School activities. It was an effort to get my father to come along but he came because he was a good father. Then he found he felt at home and my parents started to attend the senior meetings and decided they'd like to make a commitment, in the same way as people are confirmed in the Church. In the Salvation Army one is enrolled as a soldier. You promise, apart from trying to lead a better life, you won't smoke, or take alcohol or drugs, anything that's classed as unclean. But they have never worn uniform. When I was about sixteen I decided that I too would like to become a soldier and I was enrolled and got a uniform.

There's a lot of emphasis on music making and hymns which we call songs and choruses. The choir is called the Songster Brigade. I'm a member of the Songster Brigade. And I used to be a member of a rhythm group called The Proclaimers, and we went to Bulmer Village Hall for the Harvest Supper one year. And there was this young man serving the cider.

BILL: That wasn't the first time I met you dear!

GLENDA: Wasn't it? It's the first time I remember meeting you! And to cut a long story short we started going out together. And Bill used to come to the Army Sunday evenings, and play the organ at the Church of England in the mornings.

BILL: I wouldn't say I'm that talented, but I like playing the organ, and I liked playing for the Songster Brigade and gradually found I was enjoying the Army more, and getting more out of it than a lot of the church meetings. How long ago was it, I was made a soldier?

GLENDA: It was about five years I think.

BILL: Yes. I've got my 'Articles of War'. When you're made a soldier you get a piece of paper called your 'Articles of War', and you sign them at the bottom. I've got mine. You can have a look at them. Before I went to the Army I associated it with people who were a little bit dim. But in actual fact, most people in the Army are more talented musical wise than a lot of other people. A lot of people who play in Silver Bands started in the Salvation Army.

GLENDA: Even now, Bill goes back to play if he's needed at the Church of England. And at Christmas time we've still got that link with Bulmer Church, in that the band and Songsters always join with them for the annual carol service. We got married actually at Bulmer Church. We had the band and organ playing together; the choir and the Songsters singing together, and the flag and the cross processing together. We had the Church of England vicar marry us, and the Salvation Army officer read the scripture.

The main difference I think in the Army form of service from the churches is that if there's a lively piece of music and a chorus, the congregation would clap along and you'd have the timbrels playing and the drum would be going. It's a freer type of worship.

Sundays are very busy. We have half past ten to half past eleven our meeting. Then we're both Sunday School teachers from twelve until one, which means rather a late lunch. Then we're back again for the evening meeting at six-thirty. And quite often there's something else on in the afternoon, perhaps a visit to one of the old people's homes.

BILL: The group will go and just have a half an hour with songs and a reading, getting the old people to join in.

GLENDA: At Christmas time it's very, very hectic because the group are asked out a great deal, mid-week as well as Saturdays and Sundays. Everyone seems to want the Salvation Army at Christmas, so come Christmas you just feel like flopping!

In February we have our annual appeal. I don't like going to someone's door with a collecting box, because I always think they probably can't afford to give anything, But you get mainly a positive reaction, and many people say, 'Oh, the Salvation Army, of course we'd love to give', I think most people think of the Salvation Army for its social work, to help the down-and-outs, and drug addicts. Some don't even realize that it's a church, which I found quite strange at first.

And going round we sometimes find people who are lonely, or they may have had a husband or wife walk out. And quite often one of us goes in and just has a chat or you

say a word of prayer with them.

BILL: It is very rewarding.

GLENDA: And occasionally they open the door, 'No!' Slam!

BILL: We have a pretty good spirit down at Sudbury and there's always somebody who'll shake your hand or have a word with you. And that does make a difference. I mean if somebody comes into a place and they're not made to feel welcome, they don't feel like coming back.

GLENDA: I've heard people say that they've been along to a church, not necessarily Church of England, and perhaps no-one has spoken to them. Well they're not likely to want to go back are they?

The uniform? We wear it on Sunday. We wear it when we have a formal singing engagement. We generally don't wear our bonnets to sing; we find it easier if you haven't got anything restricting you! I think generally people are proud to wear it. Because it's quite expensive so you've got to think hard about it. If you want to join in the Songster Brigade, or the band, then you need a uniform, because when we stand up we stand up all dressed the same. Members of the congregation, some wear a uniform, but if people are soldiers and they don't want to wear uniform that's fine. There's no pressure on them. And some people don't feel that they want that commitment, or feel they still want to have a drink. So there's that choice.

We don't go in pubs. Obviously we go out for a meal, but we would have a fruit juice or something. It doesn't mean we don't enjoy ourselves. In fact quite a few people have said to me, how can you act like that when you're sober!

It's sad that some people can only feel relaxed when... But if people want to have a social drink that's fine. I don't agree with people drinking and driving. But in moderation it's... And I put brandy in the Christmas cake, because the alcohol content goes once it's cooked. You have to interpret it for yourself. But certainly, I don't find it an embarrasment at all not to drink. Obviously the Army, from the time it was started, was connected with helping alcoholics, and their families. And it wasn't thought that you could be drinking on the one hand and helping these people on the other.

I also run a play school with a friend which meets every day. We have twenty-five at each session. So it's quite noisy, but... rewarding! I was a legal secretary before I had the children, but I don't feel I want to go back to legal work at the moment. I've worked at the play school twelve years, first just as an ordinary helper, but now I run it, and I'm doing a training course at college on a Thursday evening. Also I work for Bill's building firm in the office, one afternoon.

BILL: My father started the firm about sixty-five years ago, and my brother and I just automatically went into it from school. Then Dad was taken ill so we just took over. And then we formed a limited company. There's only about four employees, but we've got our regular clients. We've still got clients that Dad worked for when he started up. So they haven't got fed up with us yet!

We are registered house builders, so we do put up new properties. But we like doing restoration work. It's much more interesting. Lovely old houses round here. It's very nice working on some of those. Especially if you can just afford a little bit more time. The trouble is these days it's money, isn't it? You've got to do the job as quick as possible. It's a shame. If you could spend another day or two, the jobs would be that much better. But people just haven't got the money.

I never had an apprenticeship. I learnt practically every-thing off my dad, who was a carpenter. If you've got the ability, you can pick a lot of it up as you go along. I can turn my hand to quite a few things. Jack-of-all trades as they say. I'll plaster a ceiling, do the carpentry, brick fireplaces up. Electrical is fairly straightforward, but that is something I've never bothered with. My brother does the plumbing. So I think we do practically every trade except for electrical.

This used to be a gardener's cottage. We lived in a caravan in the garden for two years while we were doing it. I completely gutted the house and added a big peice on the back. But the diamond windows are the old cast iron windows. Usually they are lead. The old peg tiles are back on the roof, and all the roof timbers are all the old original ones. It was about two years before we moved in.

GLENDA: Pretty gruesome.

BILL: We moved in Easter time, and then it snowed hard and froze. The bedclothes used to get frozen. You got up in the morning and you couldn't move the bedclothes, they were frozen to the wall!

GLENDA: The clothes all turned black. I remember I lost my suede suit, and all things that I'd treasured!

BILL: We had the puppy in the caravan as well, so that was good fun.

GLENDA: It wasn't really.

BILL: We had to move in before this was finished because the caravan was getting Glenda down a bit.

GLENDA: I got rather claustrophobic in the end. I couldn't get to sleep. So we used to sleep in one of the boys' rooms, and trail across for breakfast in the caravan in our night attire, and the neighbours would call out, 'Morning Dixeys!' as we trooped over in the freezing cold.

BILL: Why I didn't get on so quick, I suppose, is the fact of doing the same thing all day. You don't feel like doing it when you come home!

GLENDA: Now we can use the house in connection with the Army. In summer sometimes we'll have a barbecue, and we had a sponsored sleep-out for the homeless. We had forty teenagers sleeping in the garden in cardboard boxes. They raised four hundred pounds, wasn't it?

BILL: And we've had events for children. Videos.

GLENDA: It helps our children. At the moment they seem quite happy to worship with us, but obviously it's got to be something they choose for themselves at some point.

BILL: They're both junior soldiers; but when they get to about sixteen, seventeen, if they want to become senior soldiers then they must re-commit their lives.

*    *    *    *

# Chapter Fourteen

## A  VERY  ENGLISH  INSTITUTION

The public house is a major British institution. Some men spend most of their non-working hours in pubs. Many go more briefly but regularly. And for the last few decades women have been going to pubs more, inceasingly without men and without the stigma of behaving improperly. So publicans are significant social figures. But though they vary in appearance and style the customer expects to be made welcome. This is not an assumption, however, that Nick Irwin's customers would take for granted. Yet he has his regulars. For some people Nick Irwin adds a spice to life.

Of middling build, unobtrusively dressed, and wearing glasses with slightly tinted lenses, his appearance gives little clue to his view of the world. For **Nick Irwin** is an old-fashioned buccaneer with an implacable hatred of officialdom. The mere sight of the enemy vessels of institutional order and state bureaucracy is cause for him to heave round with the grappling hooks ready. Even a bunch of geese won his support when threatened by a group of townspeople he considered unnecessarily bossy. He is also a Romantic. His description of the side street pub where the regulars played dominoes under the kindly eye of the landlady is pure idyll and his vision of what he would like his own pub to be is bathed in sentiment.

At one level Nick Irwin's values and attitudes seem like schoolboy nihilism and there are moments when he seems like a character straight out of the 'Beano'. But he is too intelligent to indulge in mere eccentricity. And though he bucked against the constraints of school and defied his teachers' efforts to harness his mind to the pursuit of formal study, his innate sharpness has caused him to mull over a number of intellectual issues. He is, in fact, a thinking man whose roguishness defends him against ideologues and over neat views of the world generally. So while he hates anything which smacks of the officious or the killjoy, he does not dismiss all exercise of authority. In the interests of realising the ideal pub he is quite prepared to impose a hard rule.

This, however, gives him a very different style from the bluff hail-fellow-well-met approach aspired to by many English publicans. The photograph we selected shows him with a slight glint in his eye. Though he can smile charmingly this is not a smiling picture. The set of his teeth looks a little dangerous, and a customer might feel interested but a little wary of this man.

# Nick Irwin

Publican, born 1951, Colchester, Essex.

*'It was a lovely pub, back street, full of locals.'*

We lived near the barracks in Colchester and the army camp fascinated us. We'd go through their dumps. Amazing stuff you used to find. Medals and buttons and bits of uniforms and stripes. And the odd bit of live ammunition. You built a fire in the woods and threw on these 303 bullets to see if they'd explode. They never did, though they always do in cowboy films. Probably very lucky they didn't! And we'd make dens in the ferns and trees. We used to go a long way from home, I suppose about three or four miles, to a place called Bounstead Brook. If you sat very quietly there you could see the water rats and the rabbits. And we used to go fishing for newts, and catch frogs. And time used to go so quickly, it'd be dark! Then we were too scared to walk back through the woods by ourselves, so we used to go via the road. Three or four times they called the Army out looking for us. One thing I really cannot understand is why it was always my fault. 'You're never to play with that Irwin again! Keep away from him.' Anyway, it was so lovely. The skylarks and the rooks... My interest could have stemmed from my grandfather.

He was absolutely marvellous. I loved him. Even though he drank Earl Grey tea and voted Tory! Loved him. He never treated me as a kid; he never treated me as anything but a person. That's what I liked. He always took time out to explain things to me and we used to argue sometimes.

He owned a corner of a field. 'Grandad's Field'. Don't ask me how he bought it! And on it he used to keep chickens, hundreds of the bloody smelly things. When my mother and I visited my grandmother, he used to come in, and every time he'd have a brown egg in his pocket. He used to take it out and say, 'Here boy, this is for you.' He had an old trader's bike. I used to sit in the basket and he'd take me down to his field. I always thoroughly enjoyed it. He had this weird machine for killing his hens. It was like a guillotine with no blade. He explained it to me. He said, 'If you're going to do that all day, you get a bit tired. This way you put them in, pull the handle; it breaks the neck and that's it.' I never could do it though. He also used to point out things in the country, like the golden pheasants, and the difference between a rook and a crow, which I can't remember now.

He used to take me to the Essex Show at Wivenhoe Park

where Essex University is now. I remember him taking me into the Pertwee stand, and he'd find a box for me to sit on, on top of the chair so I would be at the right level, and we'd have a slap-up meal. They once had some Jersey cows at the Milk Marketing Board stand and he called the girl, 'I'd like a glass of real, warm, Jersey milk for the boy. He's never tasted it, and he'll probably never ever taste it again.' He was so right! I never have tasted it again. It was bloody horrible! When I was fifteen I took a couple of friends to the Essex Show. They thought it was stupid. I couldn't believe it. It was something I wanted to share.

He worked for Colchester Borough Council as a dustman. He also had another little job, doing a bit of gardening for the nobs. He used to say 'Go up Nob Hill'. That's where he got his liking for the Earl Grey tea! He's one of the few relatives I ever got on...I held his hand before he died.

Academically my father used to push me and make sure I did my homework, make sure I wasn't out too late, didn't go to too many parties. He was the rod, the one you had to work extremely hard at to persuade you wanted to do something else. He was like all parents; they've got to live their lives better through you. I couldn't go to university, therefore you can. Why? I don't want all that stuff. How about, 'I didn't go on a Mediterranean cruise when I was sixteen but you can.' I'd much prefer that! They never say things like that, do they? Anyway, he was the one who kept me in check.

When I heard he had left us I hated him, for one day. Then I suddenly realized I could do exactly what I wanted because my father wasn't my father any more and I didn't have to do what he told me, because it was his choice to leave, not mine. What a relief! I could actually stay out late because I could work round my mother. And I did. My school work went from...I suppose I was four, five in the class, straight down to twenty-three, twenty-four. And I argued with everybody. I like arguing. I love arguing. It's terrific fun. Wind them up!

I enjoyed bunking off. I couldn't stand cricket but there was nothing else I could afford, so I used to go to watch cricket. And I enjoyed the sun, and there was a bit of romance, sitting there in the only school blazer in the entire cricket ground, wondering if anybody was going to spot you.

I'm hostile to certain parts of learning but not to learning as such, no. I love learning. I don't particularly like learning from books. New doesn't necessarily mean better. And there are certain subjects I wouldn't ever like to learn again. I still can't understand why I had to learn

algebra. I remember standing up and saying to Mr. Waxy Wainwright... he had this little waxed moustache like a 1940s spiv. I was so scared of him! He had a stick he used to smack on his desk. Anyway, I plucked up enough courage one day and said, 'Excuse me sir, can you tell me when in my life am I ever going to use algebra? Because I just cannot understand it, I cannot come to grips with it.' He said, 'Well you're the only one in twenty-six boys here who can't understand it. Is that right chaps?' They were all sitting bolt upright, 'Right sir, right sir!' But then he changed, because he said, 'Quite honestly, unless you're going on to something rather technical, I don't suppose you ever will use it.' Also I couldn't understand why our history books didn't mention the Second World War. The only books that interested me at school and in the libraries were those British Observer's books of birds and flowers and grasses and trees. Eventually I was asked to leave school. 'You're not suited to a grammar school, Irwin.'

I've done various things. I did a year in a mental hospital before I got so fed up with the staff I left. I would have stayed for the residents. I absolutely loved them. The most genuine people in the world. If they were in a bad mood they'd kick you or hit you. But if they were in a good mood they loved you and they put their arms around you and kissed you and breathed their halitosis breath. You'd wilt! I went to see the chief nursing officer and said,'Look, I'm sorry, I cannot take any more of this. We should not be offering these people just total institutionalism. I have got to go.' The nursing officer said, 'Oh, but why don't you go for promotion? When you become chief nursing officer you can change things.' 'And how long is that going to take?' 'Ten, fifteen years.' I said, 'What are you doing, now you're in a position where you can change things? You haven't done a bloody thing because you've become just as institutionalised. I'm not prepared to gamble that I'll still be as angry as I am now in fifteen years.' So I got out.

I found this job in Germany on the Rhine. They called me Leftie because I used to read 'The Guardian'. I only read it because every day a chap used to come in and watch the Rhine, and put his 'Guardian' in the bin, and I used to pick it up! One 'Guardian' would last you all day. Terrific. Lots to read. Then I came back to England, and drifted around. And before I went to Germany, before I actually became a nurse I'd got my lorry driving licence, HGV3. So I thought, 'Oh well, I'll just drive around for a little while.' And I loved it. It was fantastic. Good money!

I used to finish about lunchtime, and instead of taking the truck back to the warehouse I'd stop at this pub. He used to complain because the truck was so big that when I pulled up I used to cut all his light out and he had to turn the electricity on inside because nobody could see. Then one day he just said, 'Do you fancy running a pub?' I said, 'No, it's too much like hard work.' He said, 'I'll pay you what you're earning driving, plus I'll give you a flat, plus all your living.' I said, 'Can I start on Monday?' And that's how I got into pubs.

Nobody was allowed to smoke dope in my pub; nobody was allowed to commit any act of violence to myself or the staff, or the premises. If they did they were out. It was a lovely pub, a lot of people, a thousand a night. We did have fights, yes, we did have a lot of fights. But for a thousand people, all drinking beer and all under the age of twenty-eight, we did remarkably well. Nobody ever got knifed, nobody ever got a glass in their face, nobody got seriously injured. It was just fisticuffs.

I had a police force to help, hard building-type men, tattoos from fingers to ears, you know, who could look after themselves very, very easily. There were three brothers. The oldest one used to wet himself, the middle one used to eat glasses, pint glasses, he used eat them. The third one, they called 'Psycho'. He'd walk around all night with his willie out, saying to girls, 'Excuse me, would you like to shake hands with my best friend?' Luckily most of the girls knew him and they'd giggle or just tell him to piss off. But if I was hit and went down, they'd walk in.

It wasn't my kind of pub. But running it I used to enjoy. I've never been one to go to big brash pubs. I don't like jukeboxes. I used to go to a small pub, and when I moved there, I took the same rules with me. First, I am god within these four walls. If you want to sit with your feet on the chairs, great, do it in someone else's pub. If you want to spill your beer, do it in someone else's pub.

Then Greene King was going to close the Wagon and Horses. They didn't want me to have it, but I said, 'That's the best pub in Sudbury.' Because it was an old style pub, without any change. 'It should be kept open, and I am the man to do it.' It was the first pub I ever went to in Sudbury. I've no idea how I found it. I was with a friend who wanted a Bacardi and Coke with ice, and the old boy said, 'No ice, no Coke', he said, 'In fact, no Bacardi. We don't do cocktails here. Get out!' And I thought, what a marvellous man, I love him! He did no food, but on Fridays people could bring their own fish and chips in and he would supply the salt and vinegar. And they would all sit and watch 'Coronation Street', because he wasn't going to serve when 'Coronation Street' was on. And at any time, day or night, he'd say, 'That's it lads, I've taken enough money. We don't want any more people coming in disturbing our peace, do we?' And he'd lock the door. Twenty-seven years he went through. I'd like to be a publican for twenty-seven years.

I think women in pubs are a good thing. On a very base note it's much better to look at women than some of these gross men. I want women round my pub. And when I've got women in I expect the swearing... I don't say no F words, no C words no B words, but keep them down, though I will not have men duty bound not to drop an F or a C anywhere. And I don't like the way pubs are changing to attract women. I don't think any sensible woman needs to sit on a chintzy chair or a velvet-backed settle and have pretty little rose-coloured Laura Ashley curtains.  Any woman that's attracted to a pub like that I certainly wouldn't want to talk to.

Yes, of course children should be allowed in pubs.  But only if they leave the parents at home.  The more parents I see the less I think they should be allowed in pubs. They're so proud of little Johnny or little Janey, that they can't see how they could be annoying anybody just by running up and down screaming or throwing things around as they do at home.  Parents have no respect for other people's space. Awful Sixties thing to say isn't it. You're taking my space, man!  But they don't take into consideration, as they would if they were French, or Dutch, or German or... that there is a pecking order, and children come way, way down.  They should behave or go outside and play.  English children I'm afraid are not brought up like that any more. And I don't think it should be my job to walk around and tell children to stop running about.  They are very, very dangerous things to have running around in a pub with all that glasswear about. And I don't think it's my job to go to parents and say, 'Excuse me, but you do realize you and I are breaking the law, if I allow that toddler to drink your beer.' I've actually seen people giving their children shorts. They think it's fun. I think it's absolutely and diabolically stupid. So, I'd like to see more children in the pub, but I'd like to see the parents a lot more responsible.

My politics are socialist-ish, but I'm not totally left. Where have I picked them up?  Probably going to Essex University. I never went to university to learn; I went to university purely as a leisure centre but I used to meet some fantastic people and we used to talk away about Marx and Lenin. Honestly I had no idea what they were talking about. They were all spouting on. But when they got down to things that affect the people around me, I started getting really into political discussions with these people. You could even walk into lectures and actually take part, and no one knew who the hell you were.

I'm actually right-wing in some of my views; I'm not totally against the Tories, but my greater leaning is towards socialism.  I have to watch very carefully what I say, because I find myself at times seeing these young down-and-outs, and thinking, look, there's no need for this. You have to grow up; you can't expect society to support you. It's people like you who are affecting social-ism. Because of you, widows, single-parent families, people who need help, through no choice of their own, just through circumstances, are being checked on all the time, being snooped on, pushed around, being made to feel that they're a lower class of citizen.  And people like yourself are perfectly capable of holding down a job. If you want to be known as an anarchist and spray the circle and the big A up everywhere, I don't care... as long as you pay for it out of your own money.  Now that could be said as being right-wing. Also they were smoking dope in my pub once, and I had little words in their ear then. But I have to make sure it's not a personal thing, because I do quite under-stand young people wanting to be different.

I'm getting to the stage more and more of being active politically. None of my peers are as angry as me. They all say, 'Oh Nick, shut up, leave it out. You can't do anything about it.  You're too old for that now.' But I watch 'Today in Parliament' on television, and when the Tory Party leave themselves open for attack with a blatant lie, or just use one fact or one figure, I think, 'Come on, one of you must see this; get in there and attack! Make a bit of a fuss!'

There are many many more charities than there ever were being set up. Why? I remember when I was at the first big pub, one November, this old lady came in. She had a scarf on and two cardigans and a coat. Didn't fit her very well. She asked if I'd got any old newspapers? I said, 'yes, sure, what do you want them for?' She said, 'I want them to light the fire.' So I asked if she'd like me to bring them round. She said, 'Oh, it would be ever so nice.' I went round to this house. It was damp, it was cold. She didn't want the newspapers to light the fire, she was burning newspapers to keep herself warm. A friend of mine had a load of old wooden boxes. I smashed all those up, and took them back, and I got a sack of coal. I said, 'You are four or five doors away from the Social Security offices.  Have you been in there?' 'Oh, I don't know anything about that.'  I said, 'I'll tell you what I'll do, I'll nip across there, see what I can do.'

Do you know what they said to me? 'See Age Concern.' I said, 'No, I won't. I bloody refuse to. Get off your fat arse and get round there.  Be concerned.  It's your job as a servant of mine, a civil servant, to get out there and make sure that woman has some sort of heat.  Don't you dare tell me to go to a bloody charity,' I said, 'This is not Dickensian England.' 'Perhaps we can fix an appointment.' I said, 'It's damp, the carpet's mouldy. It's only five doors away. Come and see.' They're all looking up because I'm causing a scene. Oh, I was steaming. I wasn't shouting but my language was getting stronger and stronger. What I wanted was for them to say, 'Here's an interim payment.' I was so annoyed.

They called the police. And they took me to the police station. Then they just let me go. 'Just calm down, sir.' So I had to go to Age Concern. They sent someone round, and gave her some coal and some clothes and arranged for someone to go and help her clear up the house. She died just after Christmas. But that really got my goat. I still feel annoyed!

Although I didn't agree at the time with Mr. Beeching closing down the small railway lines, they've become really good for walking and every day I take the dogs out round Sudbury. It gets longer, because old fatty here's getting slow. What I really need is a bitch on heat permanently, about six inches in front of him. Then he'd move. But it's fascinating. Because we do the same circuit every day, you can see the changes. If you go across the fields today you can actually see how green everything is. Not the flowers, not the daffodils, not the snowdrops on the river bank, the actual greenery. It really is rich beautiful stuff, and you notice these things.

We've got a bunch of geese on the Meadows. They're the proudest bunch of geese. And they're toughies. They have a good old honk, honk. And they don't let anybody push them around. They'll certainly see off any dog. And now somebody's decided that the geese have got to be removed because they might bite children. Well if a child's stupid enough to go near a goose it deserves to be bitten if you ask me. But they've come up with some silly bye-law that geese aren't allowed to graze on common land. I think it's a shame to see them go.

Somebody asked me once how I'd describe my pub. I don't let any group of customers take over. Anybody and everybody can come in. And I don't like groups of just men coming in. I like to think it's a cross section. So I described it as being a place that you could bring your maiden aunt, your mother, your grandmother, your sister and your daughter, and all the men related to those, and feel at ease, I think most of my customers would actually stand in front of me and protect me, and I'd do the same for them. I like my customers - sometimes, and they like me - sometimes. You have to be a bit of jack-of-all-trades and a master of none. I know a little bit about everything, and I can talk to everybody about something. And if I really want to know something in depth I can always look it up in a book or ask one of my more knowledgeable customers. I've got one that actually went to Cambridge and Oxford. I'm pleased about that. He knows so much.

\*   \*   \*   \*   \*

# Chapter Fifteen

## REFRESHMENT FOR BODY AND SPIRIT

S ome people make no distinction between their work and play. Michael Hills the watchmaker in Chapter Three might go in such a category. For others work is either less stimulating or so exhausting that they need to refresh themselves between periods of it.

To refresh themselves people do all kinds of things. In a number of cultures bathing is an event comparable to going to the theatre in our culture. Recovering from tiredness can, paradoxically, involve hard physical activity. Derek Kisby, for example, played hockey for relaxation from his grocery business. Nor do we need to relax mentally to refresh ourselves. Watching a play may exercise both mind and feelings strongly. Often, indeed, plays which fail to tax us fail to revive us. Yet there are times when we want the mental equivalent of staying in bed late and we will listen to the Archers or watch a television soap just because they do not require effort.

We might describe the people in this chapter as purveyors of refreshment though the kinds of refreshment they are offering differ and the part they play in its production varies.

**Liz Cole** and Kathleen and **Ted Haywood** have all spent their working lives as teachers. But here we see them as members of the town's Amateur Dramatic Society. Their story is one of energy and innocence as they tell of how the Society, following the loss of its premises, had to find new ones. But the photographer adds to this simple story. The picture in the costume collection juxtaposes false heads with real ones to raise questions about the relation between the everyday world and the world of the imagination. It is a part of a photographer's skill to see and grasp such opportunities, no less in portraiture as in more purely documentary photography. The good photographer always looks for ways of composing a picture to give it balance and shape. It is an important skill but constantly prone to glibness. Here form emanates from meaning which is as it should ideally be.

We photographed **Caroline Graham** at home. Both her clothes and the bits and pieces on her desk and the window-sill emanate a sense of her personality. And when the camera freezes a moment of turn and engagement this helps the picture to retain a feeling of life. Caroline Graham's words, of course, add greatly to our interest in her image, for she is an articulate and engaging speaker.

The last pictures in this group show **Sue Longhurst** who is a secretary and pay-roll clerk at the local swimming pool. Though she has a more than average interest in sport, we were interested in her trim costume and the image it helped to create of the 'Neat-handed Phyllis' whose personality seems to be largely obliterated during office hours. At no point in the book does one need the spoken testimony more than here. In the first picture the energy and concentration of the little boy jumping into the pool, caught and expressed in his crab-like leap gives him a stronger presence than her. In the head and shoulders portrait Sue Longhurst seems a pleasant person. But it needs her words and the description of her homemaking to jerk the picture to life.

# Ted Haywood

Amateur Dramatic Society, Teacher, born 1918, South Shields, Tyne and Wear.

# Liz Cole

Amateur Dramatic Society, Teacher, born 1945, Sudbury.

*'We were so naive really, we just trotted in.'*

TED: The Dramatic Society was formed in 1921. It was, I suppose, like all dramatic societies in towns and villages, really just a bunch of friends amusing themselves. At the time we joined, in the early Sixties, there were usually two productions a year, the same old mob of people, amusing each other and the public. Certainly none of us had any pretentions at professionalism.

Kathleen and I had been teaching in Hartlepool and joined when we moved down here. In those days people used to come to Hartlepool and say, 'By God, this place was bombed during the war!' But it hadn't been. It had just fallen down. It was that sort of place. And we'd been there some eight years when the Director of Education appeared on television, saying how difficult it was to find teachers to go into the rural areas. So we wrote to Northumberland, and said, well, what have you got to offer us. And I liked West Suffolk, so we also wrote to them and said the same thing. West Suffolk sent me a list of vacancies and we were interviewed, offered jobs and undertook to buy this house. Then Northumberland sent us a list of vacancies. Had they been quicker off the mark... I wouldn't like to break my connections with the north-east. But I must admit it's a damn sight warmer down here!

LIZ: He's so southernised now, he says Newcarstle! I was born in Sudbury, my mother was born in Sudbury, and my grandfather was born in Sudbury. He was a local artist of some repute, and an architect. And my mother went to art school, and is very talented with embroidery. It's a bit diluted in me, but I teach art. I went to school in Sudbury, and my oldest friend has her career parallel with mine in the Dramatic Society.

We were back row mentality, and bottom of the class in most things. But we did shine in English literature. So it was very exciting when we actually became, when we were fourteen, henchmen, or walkers-on, in 'The Merchant of Venice'. We loved going on the stage and dressing up. But when our headmistress found out we were hauled out of class and had to stand with hanging heads while she said she wished that we spent as much time with our homework as we had with this play. The fact that it was Shakespeare and culture with a capital K obviously had passed her by. It was a mistake not to have used it, to make us less work shy. It was the only thing that interested us. And after speaking parts I got interested in backstage. You had an apprenticeship then, and you worked your way up. And it was strict. You were never late for a rehearsal!

When I began I was stage struck, and acting and hearing an audience laugh was like a glass of champagne going to your head, although I didn't drink then. Then I got interested in the craft of it, and it was a satisfaction to learn and do well at things. And then I discovered that the greatest satisfaction of all is to direct and let everybody else go on stage and have the stage fright and the nerves while you pull all the strings. So it was creative satisfaction.

Originally everything was in the Victoria Hall. It was a purpose-built theatre, 1889 I think. And I loved it. It was smelly, and the stairs were very steep. But as you went down you felt you were in a real theatre that had been going for hundreds of years. For a child it was very romantic. It was sad to see it go. We were invited back two or three years ago, to put on a mini melodrama, for some function they were doing. I went in and it was all beautifully floored, and everything was decorated. And it was horrible. It wasn't like a theatre at all.

I had a break when I went to college, and when I came back I moved into directing and stage management. We were the first all-women backstage for 'Beaux Stratagem'. I'm now a trustee. It sounds very prestigious, and I'm very impressed to have been asked to be a trustee. Occasionally I'll sit on a casting committee, or do makeup when I'm asked.

I wouldn't have had the confidence to go professional. But I do very much enjoy seeing the professional people now at the Quay, because we never had access to that. And every night we go to see a play, there's a different audience, from young people to middle-aged, middle class, to older people. It's wonderful. When we were at the Victoria Hall we had the same little row of ladies and the same felt hats every performance, and everything was geared to 'Will we offend them?' I think the Dramatic Society though does better audience-wise than other visiting companies if they're not well known, which is a shame. People like the Dramatic Society because they know they're probably going to get a full set, three acts, and lots of people. And one or two people still don't feel they're getting their money's worth without that. My father doesn't.

TED: As Liz said, the Dramatic Society used to perform in the Victoria Hall, which was owned by the local Conservative Club and we used to keep all our gear, our flats, and costumes, in some dilapidated stables at the rear of a pub. We talked from time to time about how nice it would be if we had our own workshop, where we could build sets and store our stuff. That was the height of our ambitions. The initiative to get our own premises came simply because the Conservative Club decided to convert the Victoria Hall into a functions room, ripped out the stage and all the lighting equipment and so we had nowhere to perform. We tried...where did we try?

LIZ: We tried the Upper School. The acoustics were deadly and it had no atmosphere at all. Still doesn't.

TED: The church was deadly.

LIZ: A double echo. Awful.

TED: Then we found the building that is now the Quay. It's been there two hundred years. It had been built as a granary but God knows all the various things it had been. It was used as a store for hay for Army horses in the First World War. It was the first power station in the town, run on a simple circuit. They took a cable from the power station, went from building to building and back to the power station, rather like Christmas tree lights. If somebody took the bulb out on Market Hill the whole ruddy town went out.

LIZ: When the society first walked down to see it with dusters and brooms it had been housing plant-hire. We opened the door and the walls were so thick! It was like being in a church, because the temperature was always cool.

TED: It was cold, not cool!

LIZ: It was covered in limewash, cobwebs; the upper floor had several generations of dead housemartins. We were so naive really. We just trotted in.

TED: The place reeked. And the roof leaked. And we had ideas that, over the years, we would, without anybody helping us, repair all this.

LIZ: We did for a long time. It was a big self-help thing. We mended the roof. And every weekend we would go and mend the ceiling and floors. But you couldn't keep your fingers from going totally numb. It really was bitterly cold. And we started to convert the top floor into a costume department. We'd begun to get quite a respect-able collection of costumes, but they'd all been kept in sacks and were damp and horrible. Then we actually cobbled together a working theatre out of cardboard and string. And we hired some portaloos. And we put on plays and people sat there with their three layers of clothing and brought their own cushions. The loyalty of the audience was amazing.

TED: Weekends, evenings, would find a squad of people

LIZ: Once I was upstairs in t my watch had stopped and I th go home. And as I was switc this policeman say, 'there's somebody moving about the building'. And they held me while they phoned and checked up who I was! It was twelve o'clock and I hadn't noticed. And they didn't even give me a lift home!

TED: As you said, we actually put plays on. We did 'Toad'. What else did we do?

LIZ: 'Under Milk Wood'.

TED: Good Lord yes. Then the authorities put their foot down.

LIZ: They had been turning a very kind blind eye I think, until the publicity we started to get meant they had to look at the conditions we were working under. And although the audience were willing to sit there and freeze and climb up into the portaloo, the fire regulations and hygiene regulations just didn't...

TED: So they gave us an ultimatum: either to get the building up to the basic standards required for a licence to perform, or shut shop. And we had a meeting, we always had meetings, to decide. We were faced with two alter-natives. We could shut down, sell the building and say, well, we tried. Or we could get the basic requirements. And this is what we did. How we ever raised the requisite money... we each covenanted about ten pounds a month.

LIZ: It was a lot of money in those days.

TED: And we got sufficient money to underwrite the job. So the theatre was converted, and ten years ago we opened with Max Wall doing the honours.

LIZ: If anybody had actually said to us when we made that decision, that what we were going for was a professionally run theatre, still owned and run by an amateur society, with all the legal problems and grant fighting, I think we'd have turned round and gone home. We were just a little society who wanted somewhere to put our plays on. I think we'd have been frightened to death if we'd have known what we were taking on.

\*    \*    \*    \*

# Caroline Graham
Writer, born 1931, Stockingford, Warwickshire.

*'I was so very, very grateful to the Open University.'*

I grew up not far from Coventry during the War. Planes would drop what was left on us as they went home. We didn't have an air raid shelter, so I used to put my siren suit and socks and shoes out when I went to bed and we used to run down to the brickyard, and shelter in the kilns with Thermos flasks and copies of 'Film Fun' and 'Dandy' and 'Beano', until the all-clear came. Sometimes you left a row of houses and in the morning there was one missing, like a tooth taken out. One day a flare dropped at the end of the entry where we lived, and my dad said, 'Fall down', and it went off like a great big firework, not very far from us. It was extremely exciting. I can't honestly remember being frightened at all.

My mother died when I was seven. I think I've never really recovered. I think if you lose a parent when you're very young, you miss them all your life. She died of pneumonia when she was thirty-two. I remember her being ill, and the arguments about bringing the doctor. I was a sickly child until I was seven and it was two and six for a doctor's visit, and we used to have two and six in a jam jar on the kitchen shelf. She kept saying, 'That money's for Jean.' Eventually on the Monday the doctor came. She died on Tuesday.

My father was so grief-stricken he couldn't cope with me, and I was passed around like a parcel to various people. I went to about seven schools before I was eleven. So I always felt an outsider. I discovered when I became middle-aged and got to know other writers, they all had this feeling, that they're outsiders. This surprised me. But that's the writer's condition. You constantly keep a beady eye on people, incidents, landscape. It's all raw material. Writers are quite ruthless and dispassionate. They take and use.

When I was about ten I came home and we had a series of aunties, or housekeepers who tried to look after me and my dad for a bit, and went. One took my mother's wedding dress and her white satin shoes when she left, that my father kept in tissue paper in a trunk. He cried for days. It was awful.

At eleven I sat the eleven-plus and failed. Then when I was thirteen I was at a council school, when the teacher read out that there was this opportunity to sit a scholarship,

and she said, 'Hands up all those interested.' A lot of her toadies in the front row put their hands up. And I put my hand up, and she said, 'What do you think you're doing Harris?' And I said, 'I'm putting my hand up, Miss.' And she said, 'Well put it down.' So I put it down, and she wrote the other girls' names down.

In the break, feeling very brave, I went to the head-mistress's office, and said, 'I want to put my name down for the scholarship.' So she asked, 'Why didn't you put it down when the thing came round?' I said, 'I forgot Miss.' So she said, 'Well you can't want to go very much if you forgot.' But she put my name down. And I won it. And it was never mentioned in class. That is what I mean by being an outsider.

So I went to the high school. That also was difficult because this was 1943 and there were only four scholar-ship girls in every year. The rest were paid for. My father went to a lot of trouble to find something for me to wear. I'll never ever forget it. They had green tunics and green and cream check blouses, and brown stockings and shoes. Somehow or other he got the money for the stockings and shoes. And then he altered a purple dress my mother had. He used to sew and darn beautifully. And the lady next door lent me a red cardigan. And I leave you to imagine the four hundred girls at assembly on the Monday morning, and one girl in purple and scarlet!

The headmistress, who was a wonderful woman, called me into her office, and produced a blazer and various things from a cupboard underneath the stairs. She put them in a bag and said, 'Now, my dear, you must go home and ask your mummy to sort them out.' I didn't say anything about not having a mother. Of course all the girls knew they were second-hand. There were quite a few remarks about this.

But we were very popular, the scholarship girls, at home-work time and were endlessly pestered to help with answers. And we were so longing to be liked and admired and belong and join, that we always helped, little toadies that we were! And we were always scorned again the next day. And next homework came round and we helped again. We never learned. Rather pathetic really. But that's how it was.

I had to leave when I was fifteen because there just wasn't any money, and I had to go and get a job. But I don't want to paint a one-sided picture. At the high school there were teachers who were exceptionally kind, who asked me to tea after school, and I had an English teacher who was immensely good with me.

And don't forget the working class, which I belonged to. It's difficult for middle class people to understand, who have been surrounded by books, but once I went to the high school my life was an absolute misery in the street where I lived. I used to be jeered at because of my uniform, and once my books were taken out of my bag and thrown into a stream. The grown-ups' attitude was, 'Get your nose out of a book and do something useful!' I know that's a cliche, but it was said again and again. And, 'What's a great girl like that still doing at school? My Aileen had been working for a year by the time she was fifteen and keeping me and her dad and helping out, and ...' You were made to feel like an effete layabout lolling about reading Shakespeare while other people were in the factory earning a crust.

I don't want to present myself as some sort of noble soul like Jude the Obscure struggling for education and every-one against me, though. The people in the road were earning six pounds a week in nylon factories. I had half - a-crown spending money and I was envious of them. They had make-up and went to dances; I had plaits and sat doing homework. So I didn't feel tremendously that I was being deprived of something. I did later when I was about thirty. Now again I don't because I've developed myself. Anthony Burgess was on the radio the other morning, and he said, 'Of course I had the tremendous advantage as a novelist of not going to university.' That cheered me up! But for a long time I had a lot of anger, and I felt cheated.

So, I went into Courtaulds mill on shift work. They used to come and knock on your bedroom window with a long hook on a pole. I know this sounds too Walter Greenwood for words, but it's true. You used to put your headscarf on and go out in the street, and there'd be women and girls everywhere, running down for the six o'clock shift. We used to work six till two or two till ten or ten till six. I did warping. Then I went into a nylon factory and did linking across the toes and down the heels.

All this time I was passionately interested in the theatre. The Midland Arts Theatre Company used to come three days to the Co-op Hall. I never missed that. And sometimes I used to bicycle to Coventry, and go to the theatre there, right up in the gods.

And then when I was seventeen I ran away to sea, and joined the Wrens, for adventure. I know it's hard to believe but I looked down the list of jobs that you could do in the Wrens, and one was writer. And I was so totally enchanted by this that I joined up almost on the strength of that. And of course all it meant was clerk. It wasn't a writer at all. And joining the Wrens wasn't a success,

because I'm the last person in the world to march in step and salute and do as I'm told. I was in trouble from day one. I used to sauce people, and I was never smart enough. In the end I ran away. As far as I know I'm still posted as a deserter. I was never any good at it.

Well, I got married and went to France. My husband was at SHAPE [Supreme Headquarters Allied Powers Europe] outside Paris. He just signed up for three or four years for something to do. We lived at Versailles, in an old crumbling apartment. It was wonderful. But even there I got into trouble because I met a marvellous historian and his wife. They asked us round, and we had a lovely time. Then Mike was had up at the corporal's mess, and I had a senior wife visiting me. They told us we shouldn't be fraternizing with officers. So of course I immediately did it again. I simply will not be ordered about. I'm just not forces material I'm afraid. Perhaps if I was in charge of everything I'd be all right!

Then I went to ballet school in France for three years, and I loved that. I was always a terrific film fan, and I wanted to be a dancer or a singer or something. I used to go once a week to dancing class in someone's kitchen. Her name was Doris Holloway. She had long red hair, and she used to sit on the copper, and we used to tap away on the quarry tiles. Every now and again we put shows on in the Scouts' hut. When I look back we were probably awful. But I had immortal longings in me!

When we came back from France I went to a drama school in London called The New Era Academy. It was a house on Camden Hill Square, and a bit of a hoot really. Then I got some work in the theatre. I had a very thick Birmingham accent which I had to lose before I got a job. Though you are a little limited, you ceratinly don't need to lose a regional accent now. But you did in the Fifties. You wouldn't have had a chance, believe me.

Films to me were a great escape, a wonderland with Joan Crawford and Bette Davis. Nothing to do with real life. Especially for a working class child Hollywood could be the Moon. Theatre was different. They're human beings. You could get up and walk up there. It's immediate in a way that films never are. My first experience was being taken to see 'Aladdin'. I must have been about six. Jill Manners in an orange shift and a peak-point hat! She sang, 'I'm going to lock my heart, throw away the key'. And that was it. I was totally and passionately involved. And I've never looked back. I absolutely love it. When the lights go down and the curtains go up, I still feel, 'ahhh!'

So I got my Equity card, and went off on tour with the

West of England Theatre Company. We did one-night-stands covering Somerset, Dorset and Devon. Then I went into rep at Ipswich and Belfast, and then I went to the Royal Court in Sloane Square. While I was there my husband was taken very ill, and of course I immediately gave up to be with him.

He was ill for two or three years, and I got a job at the gas office, clerking, to be with him. Then after he got better we broke up.

It was the Sixties, and I shared flats with different girls and we enjoyed ourselves. Then I fell in love, we had a child, and I stopped work, and did what I always said I wanted. I started to write. I came home with David to this flat in Hampstead and put him down in his cot, and thought, 'Well Caroline, you can no longer say you don't have the time.' Fortunately I was in reach of Morley College, which had excellent creative writing classes. While I was there I got taken on by an agent, and I started selling stuff to the BBC and places. Then when David was five, his father and I split up and sixteen years ago we came to live in Suffolk.

Down here there was no chance of working as I had been with the BBC. That was that. I thought 'Here I am, miles from anywhere with just a bicycle. I'm going to go barmy if I don't find something to do with my mind.' So I started with the Open University. I did six years with them, one year short of a degree. It was a marvellous experience. And I started writing radio plays. The first one was called 'High Spirits and No Cunning' and I sent it in and got it accepted. Now I'm on my seventh. So that was very jolly.

It's why I was so very very grateful to the Open University. I wrote a sort of daft Gothic fantasy. Then I did a couple of children's books for my son. He wanted a book with a BMX bike in it and there wasn't one. Then I wrote a thriller. And then I wrote my first whodunnit, which was very successful. It went into eight languages, and it won a prize. I was very chuffed. I've written a couple more now. And I wrote a few scripts for 'Crossroads'.

I was brought up C of E, but very strict. You had to go to Sunday School, and church in the evening. And it was a good whacking if you hadn't learnt your Bible. Parents think this is giving their children a good start in life. But I grew up loathing organised Christianity. Religion is a spring in the heart, and either you feel it or you don't.

One of the problems was that I was told that Jesus had taken my mother. And I believed for a long time that she was up there in the clouds with Jesus. Of course this set up great hatred in me. I mean, what would you feel if you were six, and someone had taken your mother away?

Then suddenly one evening I was sitting on the step crying and missing her, and I looked up at the sky. And I simply knew. I remember the minute to this day very very clearly. I must have been about eight. I suddenly knew that it wasn't true. So, the minute I had a chance I never went to church again. But you don't just shake it off. Being indoctrinated, it takes a long time to break away. It took me years.

But I was always interested in the spiritual life. The Sixties was of course the time for Buddhism. It was nothing esoteric or odd, and when I was in London I belonged to a Zen Buddhist class for six years. I missed it terribly when I came down here, and I didn't know what to do. The inner life for writers, that is their world. Then I came across a rather marvellous person. I was struck by her tremendous kindness and serenity, and she said she was a Quaker and they had a lunch every Thursday, and would I like to go, and I did. They had a half-hour meeting in silence before. Of course, the fact they met in silence was helpful for me, because Buddhists meditate in silence, though Quakerism and Buddhism are two totally different religions.

That was seven years ago. I've thought about the strangeness of a Quaker writing about violent things, and I must admit that it causes me concern. I've thought about stopping at one or two points. But whatever I do after my whodunnits, and I'm contracted to do another two, will not be emasculated because of my Quaker beliefs. I shall write truthfully about people. Your characters develop and grow and say what is right for them. And if I was ever asked to water down my work because of my beliefs, I would refuse.

I could live anywhere providing I could get to London for the galleries and the theatre, and friends. I love the Suffolk skies. It's a lovely county, and I've been very happy here. But I've lived in this house longer than I've ever lived anywhere. I love gardening. I've created this one. But I shall find another as this is too big now. The Quaker meeting I couldn't easily move away from. That means a lot to me. But that's people; that's not Suffolk.

But mostly when you are a writer you sit quietly all day. At least I do. I sit eight or nine hours at my desk. I'm probably, of course, only writing for two. The rest of the time you're just sitting, tearing your hair out, staring out of the window, or scratching your ears. Actually writing words down, you're not doing that for eight hours. If you were you'd write a book in a month, instead of a year.

# Sue Longhurst

Secretary, leisure pool, born 1961, Sudbury.

### 'Oh, what have I bought!'

My brother-in-law said would I help out here, as a personal favour to him. I'd just had my son and given up work to look after him so I said I didn't mind. I started coming down a couple of nights a week. Then my son started going to play school, and I was quite enjoying it and I felt I was a help because I knew about pay-roll, and it got so that I was working ten hours a week. Now my son's at school and I work nine till three. So I can take him to school and pick him up. It's great in the holidays. Like this week. He's off merrily playing in the pool with his friends, under supervision, so I'm free to work, but I know where he is. They're very good to me about my hours. If my son's ill and I can't get in, they're very flexible, like me coming in in the evening when my husband comes home, or I can take work home to do. I have a typewriter at home.

No, I don't think about a career here. There are opportunities because it's a nationwide company, but I'm not the sort of person that can drop everything at the stroke of a hat and move away. We had a vacancy at head office, which was to be in charge of a pay-roll, which I could do, but it would mean moving and it's not something that I'd consider at the moment. My son's just started school, and although I enjoy working my family comes first. There's certainly possibilities I would consider later on. I don't think I could travel a lot. I don't like driving, and I find you can be on the road for five hours. I really don't think I could stick that for long.

I think a lot of people in Sudbury wish that we could have had a conventional pool as well as a leisure pool for fun. But we get a lot of families which is good. I think it's given Sudbury a meeting point. And it's good to see so many people coming in from Chelmsford, from Colchester, from Ipswich.

We open at six-thirty in the mornings. Six-thirty to eight thirty we call 'Early Risers' - we get forty-five to fifty swimmers every morning before they go to work. A lot of them are commuters who come out of the pool, get dressed and catch their train to London. A lot find that early morning is a good time to come down and do their length swims, because when it is being used as a leisure pool, it's pretty busy and you can't actually swim properly in it.

Generally the pool's open till about eight o'clock. After that the bar area is open, and we have a late swim on a Thursday from nine till ten. Last night we had 'Adult Crazy Time'. We let the adults get all the inflatables out and the mats and things. It's surprising how many adults are big kids and just love to come for that hour. During the school holidays we do an hour of 'Children's Crazy Time', and they have the wave machine on full power, and the mats and balls in. We have a fifty-plus club and we have a bus-load come over from Colchester for that every week. We've also got the flume, which is, we can proudly boast, the highest in East Anglia at fifty-five metres!

Swimming's never been my great number one sport. I just learnt because you know, it's a good thing to do! My number one sport is netball. At school I was very sporty. I used to play County netball and County hockey, and do cross-country. After school I played in the Sudbury Ladies' League. I now run my own team, which is sponsored by the Kingfisher. I'm quite a dab hand at all sports. I just enjoy it.

I was actually born at 32, Plough Lane. It's one of the oldest parts of Sudbury, and it hasn't changed much since I was born. My dad died when I was three, and my mum was left to bring me and my sister up by herself with our brother who is nine years older than us. I lived there till I was six, and we then moved into Cross Street, just round the corner, down by the Spread-Eagle pub. And I stayed there until I got married ten years ago. Now my husband and I live in Plough Lane again, at number 26.

There didn't used to be hardly any traffic and I can remember us playing ball in the lane. And it's near the Meadows and when we were little, summer evenings, we used to go over and play rounders and things. I suppose that's where my sportiness started. I love the Meadows.

They are old cottages with quite a nice character, built in 1895. There's only one at the top of the lane now which has got an outside toilet still. Obviously when our cottage was built the toilet was at the bottom of the garden. A lot of the houses have been modernized, but you try to keep the old character. A lot of tourists walk down Plough Lane and comment on how quaint it all looks. You don't really appreciate it living there, so it's nice to hear it from someone else. I'm really interested in the history side of it, you know. I've read quite a few books on the subject, and I find it interesting to tell people what I know.

My husband works in the construction industry. He's a plumber by trade. When we went up to look at the cottage I took a look in horror, and said, 'Oh, I can't live here!' And he said, 'Yes we can, I can do a lot to this place'. But it just looked horrendous to me. There was seven layers of wallpaper on the walls. There were glass-panelled doors wallpapered over, and when you took it off all the glass underneath was broken. There was an old cupboard under the stairs which was absolutely full of old food. I can remember mouldy bags and thinking, 'Oh, what have I bought?'

We've spent ten years doing it. The family were a great help. We came back from our honeymoon to find the front room had been decorated as a surprise. We had a patio laid down and a lawn and my husband built a shed. We turned one bedroom into a bathroom and we've got a large living room and a dining room as well. About three years ago we decided that with my son growing up it was a bit small. Neither of us really wanted to give up the cottage. So we had a good long chat and we decided that we'd extend our mortgage, and we've built a kitchen extension. So I've now got a nice new fitted kitchen. And we're not really more than a stone's throw away from where the Meadows start. So that is very nice. Most people who visit say, 'Oh I would love to live here.'

Nowadays though the lane is thick with cars. I wouldn't trust my son to play out there now. He amuses himself in the back garden. Our next-door neighbour has got two boys, and we often just open the gates and they play with each other. I can remember going down to the Meadows when I was about seven or eight. But I was lucky, I did have an older brother who came with us. I'd certainly not let David go up there on his own now.

I took David to the 'The Little Mermaid', a Walt Disney production recently. He walked in, and just stared. Then he said 'My, what's that big TV?' He just sat there for the whole one and a half hours, mesmerised by the size of the screen. It was great. I mean he'll sit at home and watch his video, but this was the first time I'd taken him to the cinema. When he came out he said, 'Oh when can we go again Mum?' He was so chuffed with it.

After the initial shock of it, it's been quite fun doing the house. You can look in it now and say 'We did this'. And it's nice to remember what it looked like when we bought it. My husband fell in love with it instantly and said 'Yes, I can do this.' And he's done everything himself. I mean I've just gone round with a paintbrush or whatever. He's been really good. My pride and joy are my fuchsias. I have had quite a few successes with them. I enjoy that.

# Chapter Sixteen

## THE CAPRICIOUS FATES

**H**istorically, the stereotyping of the mentally handicapped in our culture, or, in more progressive terminology, people with learning difficulties, has at best been as some form of child. More often the public have seen the mentally handicapped as a species of sub-human, requiring custodians more than carers. While not for the most part neutering them like animals, until recently a blanket assumption has been that we should make sure such people have no sexual contacts.

Popular attitudes to the mentally handicapped continue to be coloured by the widespread human fear of the different. Mental handicap causes people to look, move, and speak differently. Their words and body language fail to offer us the clues we conventionally give each other when communicating our thoughts and feelings. This makes us feel insecure and so frightens. **Mary Barlow** and **Susan Cansell** describe how this affects the lives of those with mentally handicapped relatives.

Yet mental handicap is an integral part of the human condition. It is part of the life of any community. So one aim here is to try to show what we share with the mentally handicapped rather than to ponder over how they differ from us. This may help us to reveal them as individuals like ourselves. Martin Fryer and Jenny Clements help us to do this through their stories as carers of people with learning difficulties. But a central and essential part of this process was to listen to some handicapped people themselves. So Geoffrey Talbot and **Sally Yates** offer us their stories in their own voices.

**Geoffrey Talbot**, though bent and in a wheelchair, looks younger than his years. Despite his difficulties with learning he was able to support himself with odd jobs until his accident. His story reveals what used to be called a simple-hearted man.

Intelligent and articulate **Martin Fryer** provides a story which serves to help us to listen and respond to Sally Yates and Geoffrey Talbot. Like all the accounts here, it is also an outline of the course of his own life. So we see how a job entered from a desire for material betterment and to escape from drudgery comes to enrich and give meaning to his life in much broader terms. Martin Fryer was another person for whom work was largely his life.

We chose a pair of photographs of Martin Fryer to represent two equally important aspects of his approach to his work. A portrait of him in his office shows him in a ruminative mood, the proprietor of a new home for the mentally handicapped. In the other he joins some of his residents in front of the camera. The picture shows him as he leans forward to kiss and be kissed by one of his ladies. In freezing this moment of physical contact within the group the lens captures some of their camaraderie. It is a human moment.

In the case of the Yates sisters the visual and verbal complement and help to interpret each other in a particularly striking manner. Their story is one of unquenched vitality despite considerable hardship. These two sides of their lives are expressed visually in the two group portraits. Each portrait freezes a movement. This stimulates us to wonder what is going on and the kinds of accounts which suggest themselves add a poignancy to the sisters' stories which words alone could not provide. In the first the three women though in physical proximity, seem isolated from each other, their faces turning away in different directions, as each glances at something out of frame with a questioning or frowning look. We know that life has buffeted these sisters and in this picture we have a sense of people facing an uncertain world. In the second picture by contrast we see the three sisters leaning in towards each other in a tight, laughing knot. The close triangle of their heads suggests a warm family unit, one defence against a hard world.

Yet another kind of portrait is offered of Sally on her own, to add to her own simply told story. The pose is classic, as also the benign but serious look. This picture has to be read in the tradition of the 18th century painted portrait. By presenting Sally in a way which recalls how polite circles at that time liked to have themselves recorded for posterity the camera seeks to confer dignity and emphasize the similarities between Sally and ourselves.

# Geoffrey Talbot

Odd job man, Fairground worker, resident of The Dell, born 1927, Diss, Norfolk.

*'I've never hurt nobody in my life.'*

I went to school... Well, I used to go to school when I used to feel like it, but sometimes I more or less didn't used to go at all. I used to dodge it, hide up some place or the other. One night I broke in the school and I got everything out and laid it on the desks you see, and I started ringing the school bell, round about seven o'clock I did. And I don't know whether it was my mother or who the devil it was, told the teacher. She didn't hit me or anything. All she made me do was just put the things back where I'd got then from, you know. So I had to put the blinking things back again. I've been a funny person really, in my life.

Then when I left school I used to work on the farm, what they call horse-hoeing, leading the horse on the horse hoe. Used to horse-hoe sugar-beet. And I used to do casual work, thrashing and potato picking and all that, pea-picking and carrots.

I worked on the fair a long while. I worked on the dodgems. And sometimes I used to work on the waltzer. Used to travel all over the place. Sometimes used to come to Sudbury; sometimes they used to go like to Southend, or all round that way. I had to put these stalls up, these shooting ranges, these coconut shies and these swings. I used to take the money from them what used to go in the dodgems. And I used to entertain at the fair; used to box some of them what came, you see. And I used to give them a blinking good hiding. I'm afraid some of them used to get some nasty knocks.

I used to do work for a woman. I used to do like her gardening and clean the windows. And I worked at the pub too, washing and scrubbing the passages as you go in the pub.

The Christmas before last Christmas what's gone, I lost my brother, one of them. He was a good brother to me, he used to give me pounds. I only got one brother now. I generally go and see him every other week; he ain't too far off. But the one what I lost was more nearer than the one what I got now. But he used to smoke a heck of a lot and that was more or less his downfall. He used to light another cigarette off the one what he was smoking, because he was more or less what you would say, a chain smoker. He used to smoke too many in any case. And the doctor told him either he would have to give his cigarettes up or they would give him up. When I lost my brother it cut me up that did. I wouldn't do nothing. I didn't care whether I ate anything or whether I didn't, because he was my best brother. I mean he spent pounds on me. It cut me up and made me cry, I mean he was my flesh and blood.

I used to live with my mother and father, then my step-sister, and as a matter of fact I used to look after myself. But when I was living up Melford, one Sunday afternoon, I just happened to be picking up some bits like on the floor, so the place was a bit tidier and I more or less what you would say, overbalanced. And I laid on the side of my fridge you see, and I couldn't get up at all, because I broke a bone what they call the femur bone, the bone what makes you walk. And I had to crawl right out of my kitchen to the living-room, and heave myself on the couch. Then I had to have the operation. That's why I have to have this wheelchair.

Margaret Thatcher, she's nowt to do with the House of Parliament now is she? That man took her place, didn't he? Major. Some of them reckon he's all right, and some of them don't give him all that good a name, do they. I don't know whether you do or not. I mean it's none of my business. I don't poke and pry in other folks' affairs, you know. I'm honest; I keep a clear conscience and a clean face. And I've never hurt nobody in my life, you know, because I ain't got any cause to hurt people.

\*   \*   \*   \*

# Martin Fryer

Registered Mental Nurse, Proprietor of the residence for the mentally handicapped, born 1940, Shorditch, London.

*'The staff's heart was in the institution and not in looking out of it.'*

My forefathers worked in the rag industry in Shoreditch, making clothes. During the early part of the war they were bombed once or twice, so our family was evacuated when I was about four months old to this village outside Sudbury. Most people there earned their living from agriculture, and some people earned their living by their wits!

I think I can say that things in the country were fairly tough in those days. There was seven of us in a two-bedroom cottage, four boys in one room, and my mother and father and sister in another room. The toilet was a Norfolk longdrop up the garden, which occasionally you had to empty, and we used to go with buckets for water from a standpipe up the road.

The cottage had a large garden and we grew vegetables. Without that I think we would have had difficulty surviving. Our other main source of food was, of course, rabbits. We had lots of methods of catching rabbits. We went out with dogs and ran them down, we ferreted them, we shot them. And harvest time was a bounty because as they cut the fields the rabbits ran out in all directions, and we'd end up with twenty-five rabbits hanging up all ready to be eaten.

My mother struggled desperately with five children. My father was away working for DeHavilland's at Hatfield, I don't want to be disrespectful to my father, but he didn't provide most of the time. My earliest memories of my mother are of her going out into the fields, when the weather wasn't nice, in November and December, when the sugar-beet was being cut. She'd go to bed at ten and get up at three o'clock in the morning, before light, go out with her chopper and dig the sugar-beet up and cut the tops off, come back and get us all up ready for school, then she'd go back into the fields again and work until half-past three in the afternoon, collect us from school and then...well, it was just a hard life. She used to be paid very little. Later she got a job as the head cook at Jane Walker Hospital so her life improved. And we grew up and brought in a small income.

Let's talk about school. The education was desperately poor. Most of my time was spent in the school gardens. We spent very little time on education. If you could grow potatoes, that was your job. We learnt to drive tractors when we were about eight or nine. It was part of growing up. And at the thrashing our job as children was to kill the rats and mice as they came out of the stacks. We'd all surround the stack and there would be thousands of deaths! So my first job after leaving school at fourteen was on a farm. We had no education, and that was the only thing we knew.

I came to consider what I was going to do with my life one really cold morning when I was screwing the tops off turnips and my hands were all split open because there was about five degrees of frost. I thought, I've really got to do something with myself. I had a leaning towards helping other people, though I wasn't sure how I was going to do that. And you did need a basic education, which I didn't have. But I wanted to better my life. Then I saw a job as a nursing assistant in a nearby mental hospital advertised in one of the local newspapers. I applied and got it and packed up farmwork.

There was three thousand psychiatric patients in that hospital. They had their own bakers, carpenters, their own plumbers. It was a pyschiatric town. The hours, if I remember correctly, we started at seven o'clock in the morning and worked till quarter past nine at night, and if you was more than two minutes late you lost fifteen minutes of your pay.

In those days they were called lunatic asylums and people were called lunatics, imbeciles. 1959 the Mental Health Act did away with that and defined new terms. A new Mental Health Act about six years ago did away with the '59 terms. But the '59 Mental Health Act brought along all sorts of better things. And after I'd been there a year or two we also had a consultant come along, who had new ideas and things changed rapidly.

But to begin with I worked on Ward Two. Wards didn't have names. There was one hundred and eighty patients on the ward, all mentally ill. Forty-five were physically ill as well, and nine staff. Quite horrendous! In the morning, you'd have a razor and you'd be shaving, one after the other, until you'd shaved everybody on the ward. And each ward had what they called the Lions' Cage, exercise yards, with spikes that bent in so you couldn't crawl over the top. Our role was to see the patients got their exercise. Rain, snow, heat, anything, you would march round and round the yard exercising people. We also used to have padded cells, four or five in a line, for people suffering from various disorders like delirium tremens. And we used to do pad duty. We'd stand there early morning till late at night on pad duty. Couldn't be anything more boring.

The reason I moved into mental handicap was that I was asked to accompany a group of students to a mentally handicap hospital. The beds were so close you couldn't walk between them. I remember going to the children's ward, where I worked for many years later. There must have been forty-five, fifty children there from the age of two up to fourteen, all with different types of handicap. Totally indescribable. Some in little cots, others in full-size beds. I just could not believe that in the mid-Sixties, we could deliver care to children in this way; it was absolutely abysmal. And I thought no matter what happened I could never look after mentally handicapped people. It actually turned me up just walking round.

But what I'd seen nagged at me, and about a year after, I suddenly thought I'd like to go back. And I went over and talked to people there about re-training in mental handicap. And I moved, did my training and worked on all the wards. It was very, very hard work. We had jaundice, worms, a whole range of infectious diseases, measles, chickenpox, all at the same time on the children's ward. But I enjoyed the job.

I could give you examples of things that were unsavoury, but I don't think I want to. And there was staff who worked there who were much more institutionalised than the residents. What was needed obviously was change. In those days the feeling was that if you're profoundly mentally handicapped, you'll be an idiot all your life. You just had food stuffed in your mouth, and you were kept clean, and the drugs were whacked into you. And we still worked on the basis that we bathed everybody every night. So two people would be bathed in the bathroom, then two people would be drying them and two people would be putting their pyjamas on. No idea that we involve patients in their own life.

In 1971, I was offered a post as charge nurse in a much smaller hospital. It was very basic, and there was a lot that would be unacceptable today, but from the minute you walked in the door you could feel people were happy, and residents were free to wander around. I hope you feel that here. I would be pleased if you felt here what I felt the first day I walked in there.

There were also males and females there so at least you could have a dance. We also had a nursing officer and not only did I like the chap, he had enormously good ideas about individual care which caught my imagination. That's where I met my wife - we were trying to persuade people that there was a life for mentally handicapped patients outside of a hospital. We started by just taking them out for the day. The attitude of the staff! I remember one sister who, when you went to the ward and said, 'We'd like to get some of your residents out', would go round saying,

'You don't want to go out, do you?' The consequence was they all said, 'No Sister, I don't want to go out.'

Then in 1972 they sent me back to the previous hospital as acting Senior Nursing Officer, which is like being a matron. There was still no idea here that people other than institutional people should be involved in the care of the mentally handicapped, and I tried very hard to develop a family support service. But in the ten years I was there I never succeeded because the staff's heart was in the institution and not in looking out of it.

Then in 1982 there was a re-organisation of the Health Service, and a much more senior post became available and I ended up as Director of Nursing Services for the Mentally Handicapped for the West Suffolk Health Authority. I had an enormous staff, huge budgets, I became an administrator of a massive number of people. But I got more and more disillusioned and knew I didn't want to spend my life doing that kind of work till I retired.

I'd had in mind for many years to open a residential home of my own. The problem was money but my wife and I decided that we would sell our house and with the money develop the service. And we had a neighbour who was a builder, quite well off financially and willing to come into a partnership with us. He's still our partner today and very interested in people with learning difficulties. He's a very important person to us.

I always had a plan in my mind for small group homes, of six or eight people living together, with their own rooms, but shared dining-room and lounge, and their own kitchen so they could be involved in their own life. A little family of people living together who would help one another be a lot more independent than they'd been allowed to be, and with all the things that us as human beings should expect to have: privacy, dignity, the development of our skills, being involved in choice and decision-making, being responsible for what we do.

Looking back, and we're now five years into the project, I realize that the first group of people to come were not mentally handicapped, they were institutionally mentally handicapped. Some, especially the ladies, were admitted to mental handicap hospitals for all sorts of odd reasons. Simply having an illigitimate baby, or swearing at the squire... I mean I can actually name cases of that. Or stealing a packet of strawberries. One lady who is seventy-six years old spent sixty years in a mental handicap hospital, from five years old. I don't think there was such a thing as social workers in those days, and people were actually locked up, certified.

Then their whole life was taken away from them. They were not involved in cooking their own food. I know

people who thought the heated trolley cooked their food, they didn't know you had to peel potatoes, and they used to think the laundry basket did the washing. Because everything was done for them. There was an adult ward at the large hospital I was at where the beds were so close together you couldn't put in wardrobes. The consequence was that the nurses used to keep all the clothes in a locked cupboard up the corridor. People couldn't get up in the morning and decide what they were going to wear. The nurses used to make up a little bundles of clothes. They didn't belong to anybody; they were just the ward's. And they'd pop them under the pillow. That's what you wore.

I happen to think that some of the mental handicap hospitals are fine places and people in them are happy, no question about it, but because they don't know anything else, right.

First we had two units open at the Dell, and about seven staff. People came in, sat down and did nothing. They just sat there. They did what they were used to doing. They were also used to sharing bedrooms and two of the ladies in particular, missed each other. 1987, when I used to go up to Bungalow Two, and this is honest, I used to cook their tea for them. In 1989 they cooked my tea for me. I remember Chris and I sitting and wondering how we were going to cope.

We invented fading. If you're going to wash the dishes up,

somebody hands you the dirty plates, you wash the dishes, somebody dries up. And as they take over, you fade. With a person who for forty years hasn't functioned in a shopping environment for instance, you'd sit down and go through where you're going. I mean you can't get an ice cream in the Post Office can you? Then you go down to town and into the shops. You've got to understand that you've got to pay for things and if you don't pay you'll be stealing. And you've got to understand value for money.

A consultant psychiatrist said to me, 'How do you counter the argument, that what you are doing Mr. Fryer is shifting people out of a mental handicap hospital into a mini-institution?' And to some extent I can see that. My only answer is that they come here and have the privacy and dignity of their own room, and their own facilities. They go to town and do their shopping. They have choice, they make their own decisions, they're responsible for what they do. They do a whole range of things that you and I would expect to do as a natural part of life.

I started off saying that many of these people in my opinion weren't mentally handicapped, they were institutionally mentally handicapped. But I think if you are going to move somebody from a mentally handi-capped hospital where they've been many years, you've got to improve the quality of their life. If that's not going to improve, why do it? Doing it just to empty a place, I don't believe that's a good enough reason.

# Sally Yates

Born with Downs Syndrome, 1945, Chelmsford, Essex

*'I get paid.'*

I do job at coffee shop. Washing up, cups and plates. Cleaning the tops, putting things away. Cups and saucers, put them away. Spoons, forks and knives, put them away. And I get paid. And I go the Red Cross. I wash cups up. Put things away. Wash plates up, tins, dishes, the whole lot. And clean up as well. And I take the coats off. Help the ladies. I help them out of taxis. I do Dad's work for him. Help him out. Dust. Do all that.

And take the dog out. Bobby is his name. I take him out for walks. I've got photos of Bobby. Jumps up on me sometimes. Sit on my back. Give him a cuddle, a little kiss. He comes to me. He's friendly. He loves people. He likes children. People walking in the road, he loves them. Jumps on them sometimes. He makes a fuss of them.

Save my coffee shop money. I'm saving with the Post Office. I'm saving up to have my hair done, new clothes. I've got a lot of money I think. I count it all, how much I've got in there. Got a lot.

I go to the Adult Training Centre. Help Christine clean cupboards out. Wash clothes. And cook dinner myself. Chicken legs, carrots, peas, gravy. Stir it up. I go up town and do the shopping and that. I have dinner out sometimes, in pubs. Chicken nuggets, chips and peas, and a drink as well. Coke.

And I've been Germany. On a boat. I can say 'Danker'. I can say that. I've got photos. I'll bring them up and show them to you.

I do stitching. Made a jumper, waistcoat, and a skirt, a denim one.

And jumper, and trousers. Wore them out. Got holes in them! Now I do icing. For cakes and that. Lot of flowers I made. We do sell them.

Netball. It's my sport and I won something. It's my trophy. It's upstairs in my bedroom.

I went to Ipswich. Buttons, Cinderella. That woman got married or something. Got married with Buttons. And a man dressed up, a prince, all dressed up. He dressed her up or something. I enjoyed it.

Sally Yates' sisters -
# Mary Barlow
Home-help, born 1949, Chelmsford, Essex.

# Susan Cansell
Factory Supervisor, born 1951, Great Waldingfield, Suffolk.

*'...you find excuses not to bring friends home.'*

MARY:  We come from Chelmsford originally. That's where I was born, and Sally.  Grandad had all this junk, just like Steptoe & Son. You couldn't move for everything from newspaper to rags. Bales of stuff. They lived on the ground floor and had the bed in the front room. The kitchenette was chock-a-block; it was all stuff on the stairs; and the rooms upstairs were chock-a-block, brass beds, cutlery, jam pots, lead; anything and everthing. People would come to him with bits, and he'd buy bits. He never seemed to sell anything.

He was a colourful character Grandad was. He had a gammy leg, I don't know why that was the term, a 'gammy' leg.  After Gran died his house was pulled down to make way for the fire station so he was re-housed. And he had a heart attack when he was clearing his coals in his fireplace, and he fell into it, and there was a big fire. We had to go to the inquest. And I can remember having to help Dad clear up.  We got a couple of shovels. There was boxes of ashes everywhere, because he was still a hoarder. I chuck things out.

Do you want to hear about Mum's mum, the Romany granny?   She had seventeen children. Mum was the youngest. I never remember her not living with us.  She came when we were in the hut at Waldingfield and died in the downstairs front room up Acton, about eighteen months before Mum. They used to say, didn't they, people have got a death-rattle on them. I can remember Granny had that death-rattle for two days. It was awful. And I hated it because I wasn't allowed to sleep with her. Because Gran was my favourite. I always used to sleep with her.

Poor old gal! She was a character. She used to always be digging up roots or boiling something up, making us drink it. She'd do a lot of things with dandelions. Mum used to say, 'You'll poison my children with your remedies. You're not giving that to my children.' 'That'll do them good', she used to say. 'They won't get rheumatism if they drink that'. She knew something about it I think, because nothing ever hurt us. We always seemed healthy.

SUSAN:  I was born in Waldingfield on the aerodrome, in a Nissen hut. It's got on my birth certificate, '64 Technical site'. Because Dad worked for a fruit and vegetable firm, and they had a yard where the Nissen huts were. He used to go round doing the fields and the fruit, and take them to the shed to be packed up.   Anyway the doctor felt that we'd be better off in a house, so she got us a council house up Acton. And I remember moving because that was such a grand thing, to have stairs, and go up a storey.

Where we went, Sally went. We were brought up with that. We all had to be together. Mother always said, 'Keep together, and look after Sally'. There were some nasty people in the village who ridiculed you,  children Sally's own age, who had no understanding. You'd go out and one or two kids would name call. But when we'd been in the village a while, people came round and always had a good word for Sally. But Sally never went to school. She wasn't picked to go to primary school. She was quite old before she started any kind of primary education and we sort of looked after her.

Mother and Father used to go pea-picking. You didn't pay tax or anything You just all went en masse as a family and picked as much as you could.  Dad used to be the main jobber and weigh it all up. We just used to be working side by side with our mum.

The beginning of the season we went beet-hoeing. Mum and Dad used to hoe and we used to pick out the weedy bits, and throw them to one side.  From that, we did carrot-topping, Then we'd pick peas and blackcurrants, and all the soft fruits. Then we used to go apple-picking and pear-picking and plums, because Dad used to look after an orchard at Bures  and do all their pruning.  Very much a jack-of-all-trades, Dad.  He used to turn his hand to anything and everything.

I reckon we must have missed some school. Mind you, a lot was done when we were on school holidays, like lifting potatoes.

MARY:  It stopped when Dad had that stroke when he was thirty-two and couldn't drive any more. Then he had the ulcer. And then Mum died.

SUSAN: Mum was ill for a long while. We had to make do and fend for ourselves then.

MARY:  After Mum died I don't think Dad knew really what to do with us. We were there and he just got on with it. He managed the best he could. It didn't do us any harm though. We've all turned out responsible citizens.

SUSAN:  He did his best. We never went on holidays, but Father took us down to Dovercourt to the sea-side and to

*Mary, Sally and Susan*

*Mary, Sally and Susan*

see the boats go out at Harwich. We had fun, the four of us together.

MARY: I was eleven when Mum died. I was the eldest out of the four, apart from Sally. So we grew up and sort of looked after each other. But me when I left school I took the mother role. I didn't work. I stayed at home for about two years.

SUSAN: Then, as we got older, in the Sixties, that was the Mods and Rockers phase with me! The Mods' cafe was in North Street, where the Indian restaurant is now. That was the 'Bambi'. All the Mods' scooters would be out the front. And the 'Juvinian', which is now a florist shop, about two doors away, was a Rockers' coffee bar. But they were all very friendly. There was none of this beating up. We'd go in the 'Bambi'. We'd go in the 'Juvinian'. The 'Bambi' was open till about three and four in the morning, so I really enjoyed it there.

MARY: There was a time in my life when I felt, oh, if Sally was normal what would it be like? I wouldn't be burdened. And I thought selfish thoughts.

SUSAN: I think it was because we thought we were different because honestly I can't ever remember coming across anybody, apart from open days at the Centre for Sally, who was the same. I had worthwhile friends; they loved Sally and that was fine. The worst thing was boyfriends. I was always terrified of what boyfriends would think. For ages I wouldn't take anybody home. And then, I stayed with this one particular person, and he said, 'Why won't you take me home? Do you live in a mansion, or what?' And Mary invited him up one day when I was at work. And when I got home he sat there, drinking tea.

MARY: Her face!

SUSAN: It did break the ice, because he kept thinking I was a snob and I lived in a mansion. I thought, if only you knew! I just live in an ordinary house that could do with a bit of a face-lift!

MARY: You get to a certain age, perhaps in your teenage years, and then you start thinking... Like Susan said, I thought we was the only people, when I was a child, who had someone like Sally. And you find excuses not to bring friends home.

When all the family had left school and I went to work at CAV I was nineteen. I didn't want to talk about Sally. I was reluctant to make new friends because... And very unsure for a long time who to make friends with. I'd think, 'I don't think I'd like that person because, would they accept Sally?'

After I was married there was a girl over the back used to come and have coffee. She met Sally and she stopped coming. For a long time I didn't query it. Then I said, 'Oh, come over for a coffee, you haven't been over for weeks'. And she said, 'Oh, well I'd rather not. I'm not being funny but I had a bad experience with somebody like your sister. I'm very frightened of people like that now.' And she was a grown woman! From then on I just nod to her at a distance. I don't have her in. It's been like that all the time. You'll get people who don't accept.

I think I must have been nine or ten before I realised Sally was different. I used to say, 'Why isn't she coming to school?' Then as we got older, that guilt thing started. My son accepted it till he was about ten. Then the same thing. When Sally was about, he used to say, 'Oh, I don't want Robert to come tonight Mum'. And I knew straight away what it was. He said, 'Robert says she's different'. I said, 'Of course she's different, but she loves you, she's still your aunt'. And he says, 'Well he talks about it. He tells the others at school'. And I said, 'Well there's nothing to be ashamed of'. And he said, 'I know there's not Mum, but I don't want him up'. It was a problem for about a year. He used to say, 'Why does she have to come here?' And I said, 'Because she's my sister'. When he brought his girlfriend home luckily Sally was here that first Sunday and the ice was broken.

I felt really bad when Sally started her job because all those years we'd held her back. She should have had a job years ago. And I think she could have done it, with our guidance and help if we'd trusted her and given her the confidence. Partly because of our...shame, it was easier to keep her in cotton wool rather than have all the aggro of her growing up. We used to go down to Lowestoft for a week in a caravan. Sally would even get lost at seventeen, in the loos, in the shower room. And...we'd all be in a flap. Even then if we'd have just given her the trust, she might have learnt more. And I'm still feeling guilty.

SUSAN: The best thing really, as time has gone on, is that Sally has had more opportunity. This last couple of years instead of taking people out of the community they're putting people back in, which they should have done when we were small. She should have come to school with us. I think we would have had probably a better childhood. But we did have a lot of fun, the four of us together.

MARY: And we have fun now. I hear my friends - they've got brothers and sisters and they say, 'Oh, I ain't got time, I haven't seen them for years'. They don't have the family get-togethers. We have barbecues. And we had a Christmas dinner in April!

SUSAN: That was lovely, that was for Steven, because he'd been out in the Gulf. We said when he got back we'd have his Christmas dinner, because he had rations.

Now there's this big secret going on I'm not supposed to know about. You see, the last three years, there's been a fortieth birthday every year. Sally first, Mary, then me, and Bill - he's last.

Jobs? Two I got made redundant at. Then on to Sainsbury's! I left Sainsbury's after I got married and was having my son. When my daughter was a year and my son three, I got a part-time job at the local hospital, Walnuttree. I worked there ten years, cleaning. The worst job was cleaning corridors. You've got people coming in and out all the time, and you don't get job satisfaction at all. But mostly I liked it. Then all new things came in, and the wages went down so dramatically, I felt I had to leave, and I got a little job as a supervisor in a chemical factory. And the money's good, and that's important to me.

Our council house, we're buying it now, and we're trying to get it round to how we want it. But the two children ...at the moment they're running away with my money.

MARY: When I went to CAV I was on petrol injection. It was very boring, very tedious work. When I married and left to have my son, I vowed I'd never go back into a factory. And I never have. Thirteen years ago I started a couple of hours a day as a Home-help. As Mark's gotten older I've taken on more hours. And it's job satisfaction. I get something back from it.

I've got an old gentlemen I go into. He's ninety-three. He used to be a London clippie, and he's really good fun. His son says, 'Oh, you've given Dad a new lease of life.' But he draws from me and I draw from him. I've learnt a lot from him.

I just sort of run his life, everything from making his bed to telling me what he needs in his food cupboard and taking him a meal every day. And I pop back teatime and make sure he's OK. He's just up the back, so it's nice and handy. I've got a couple of people who are bedridden. I go and sort them out, get them breakfast, help them get ready for the day. Then I've got dinner calls. They can be very disabled or even senile dementia. It's just very interesting work. Now we're caring for them more, rather than just being Mrs. Mopps. I used to sit there at CAV and it was just getting money. And I thought, there must be something better than this. Working with people you get involved. You'll get some grumps, but mainly they are good.

I felt I missed out on my childhood. Dad was ill. Then Mum was ill and got very sick and died, and we had to grow up quick. Dad just ticked over, thinking, 'I've got these four young children, one of them's handicapped'. I don't know how he coped.

Missed a lot of schooling I did too. Whenever there's sickness it always falls on one. Then you lose school and get behind. So you lose interest and you've got the problems at home. So you get on with that. But it was a funny sort of upbringing really. It was different to what my friends had, and I used to envy some of them. I used to think, 'Oh why can't I be like that?' It was an experience anyway. Things are easier now. There's more money about.

SUSAN: I reckon people have had it harder, but I thought it was quite hard.

MARY: We survived.

SUSAN: Basically we're a family of hard workers. Mum and Dad worked hard, and I think it rubbed off on us.

MARY: I just think I'm very lucky for what we've got now. We're buying our council house too. And I feel good and comfortable about everything. And I've been married twenty years, so I feel settled.

\*    \*    \*    \*

# Chapter Seventeen

## DUST TO DUST

We know that death is part of the natural order of things, but this does not console us when it snatches away those we care for. Confronted by its irreversible finality we crave help and in response to this societies invent the rituals of funeral ceremonies. These offer us ways of handling the grief and terror which death inspires in us as they dignify death. And paradoxically this simultaneously acts as a protection against the fear that death's presence inculcates that life is trivial. What we call respect for the dead is also an affirmation of the importance of life.

But the rituals of death will not work their power if they do not run smoothly. So the undertaker's expertise is pivotal. Our attitude to the undertaker is ambivalent, however. For he acquires much of his skill by being a bystander on occasions when others are experiencing intense emotion. We do not expect the undertaker to share these emotions, but we would be angry if he lounged about or cracked jokes. So we expect the undertaker to put on an act; and then part of us is offended by its falsity.

Despite the undertaker's most careful preparations the most solemn moments of the funeral can, nevertheless, collapse into bathos, and the grave can become the setting for pure comedy. Because the undertaker is human. So the management of the rituals of death is as prone as every other human activity to accident and error.

Once the mourners have departed, of course, the undertaker's performance is complete, and he is free to reveal a personal self. Indeed, there is no reason why he should not spend the evening over a pint of Guinness in the local while entertaining the company with jolly stories of funereal mishaps. The demands of the undertaker's work create a huge chasm between the public and private persona.

The undertaker presents the portraitist with an impossible task. For, more than most of us, the undertaker is a Janus figure.

**Harold Warren** combines a sense of the seriousness of the ritual of burial with an irrepressible air of jollity. His conversation is also naturally anecdotal. He recalls his life in the form of a series of stories, like beads on a string, complete and finished in themselves, rather than in the form of a continuous flowing narrative. Correctly or not it is tempting to see this as a way of handling the juxtaposition of death with the routines of daily life. The episodic form of his story certainly leaves one with a sense that there are areas of experience Harold Warren is no stranger to but is leaving to one side.

His portrait makes no reference to the darker side of life. The lovely lady blooms perennially and the bold pattern of the wallpaper asserts itself for ever behind him as he faces the camera with a look of unclouded cheerfulness. If however his smile expresses nothing of what he knows about the evanescence of human life; it is infectious. The undertaker who smiles like this and loves dancing asserts an individuality while generating an unquenchable human spirit.

# Harold Warren

Undertaker, Joiner. born 1908, Sudbury.

*'...you've got to show a bit of respect.'*

My father used to go down to work at six o'clock in the morning, and didn't leave off till six o'clock at night; and Saturday was a half day, they left off at four in the afternoon. But they couldn't have spent all those hours really slogging at work, could they? Eh? They did the work better than they do today though, and they used to make beautiful stuff, and had jolly good wood.

He was apprenticed as a joiner and then stayed on at a big local building firm. They had ninety joiners and old Mr. Grimwood used to go up twice a week to their London office in his top hat and frock-coat! I remember it very well. Because, when I was a little boy, before I went to grammar school, a nice summer morning, I'd walk down there, pick up my father and walk home for breakfast. And often I'd be standing outside the gate and old Mr. Grimwood used to come out the office to catch the eight-thirteen train up to London, and I got to know the old boy very well.

Things were very poor then. My grandfather was a horse-man. The men came along at six o'clock to work, then they'd have a breakfast in the field. And I remember my grandfather telling me, there was one man, he always used to sit away from the rest of them, and he wondered why. And he walked across to him one day, and what do you think he was having? He got a swede out the field, cut up into little pieces like pineapple chunks. He'd got a big family, so he fed the children and he ate a swede for his breakfast. Now I don't know what the youngsters would think today about that! And at the North Street School when I went, summer time, lots of children used to come to school with no shoes or stockings.

Later I went on to the grammar school. One thing I remember there was we always had a cricket match against the local farmers. There was a captain by the name of Mr. Frank Nott from Wickham Hall. And he was most popular with the boys, because the boy who got the highest score he always gave five shillings to, and the boy that took the most wickets he too had five shillings, and the boy that got him out, another five shillings. And at the finish of the match, when there was a little speech-making, he always asked the headmaster if he would excuse the boys homework for that evening. And that made him most popular! When my father came back from the First World War he started his own business in the early 1920s, and after School Certificate I went to work with him, until the War came along. Then I was a foreman carpenter up on the Waldingfield aerodrome. And then when the War finished I went up to London on pre-fabs. But when I had the opportunity to leave I came home.

Things are more comfortable than they used to be, perhaps, but we used to go down to work in the morning, and even if you didn't want anything you went into Dixon, Scott's, the old hardware people. You'd think they were having a row or something, there were so many in there! It was the same every morning. Different tradesmen all in there telling what happened the night before. Nowadays, they haven't got time for anything, have they? They're racing about all over the place.

There was four or five undertakers in Sudbury; we used to help one another. Nobody owned a hearse. We used to get one from the undertaker at Halstead. They were all just little businessmen, you know, carpenters and decorators, doing odd jobs and undertaking. What else did I do? Oh, carpentry work and decorating, Anything that anybody wanted! Windows, doors, ladders, chicken houses. Made hundreds of chicken houses.

They used to use a wheelbier and you had the horses and cabs following behind. The landlord at the Great Eastern Hotel used to run these horses and cabs. They'd be in a coal cart in the morning, and in a cab in the afternoon!

When a farm worker would be getting about twenty-eight shillings a week, a funeral went from seven pounds fifty to perhaps twenty-one pounds. You made the coffin a little better for the gentry. Perhaps they'd want an oak one. Now they're just made of chipboard, aren't they? They used to be right heavy. But the price was partly because you had to even things out a little bit. If someone come and ask you to do a funeral you couldn't refuse them could you? And sometimes you got up against somebody and you didn't get any money! But some poor people if they hadn't got the money they pawned things. There used to be a pawn shop on the corner of Friars Street, opposite Hills the watchmakers.

Nearly everybody then wanted the corpse to rest in the house until the day of the funeral, and their friends and neighbours all came to see the body. That's gone completely. Nowadays, if anybody dies at home they want the body removed right away. They phone the undertaker up if it's three o'clock in the morning, and want the body moved. And relatives go round to the mortuary, and see the deceased in the coffin, if they wish.

I used to belong to the boat club. There was some proper lads in the boat club. Never anything done spitefully like there is today though. No breaking shop windows, and painting slogans on walls and all that sort of thing, doing damage to a car. I remember one morning everybody going to work was looking up at the Gainsborough statue on the Market Hill. There was a chamber pot on Gainsborough's head! That was the boat club boys.

Another time a motor bus proprietor at Boxford had these old buses with a big rack along the top we used to hire to put the boats on. Coming away from Norwich one night, one chap... I can't think whether he was in the Income Tax Office, or... Anyway there were these lamp standards with bars across the road, so the lights were in the centre of the street. He's on top of the bus tying the boats down and we stop under one of these standards, and he starts turning somersaults on this bar. Of course the traffic moves on and so does our bus! There he is, left high up in the air. But it was all good clean fun!

I've driven a car since 1937. I drive everywhere! Just down this road, there's an alleyway by the cemetery, which cuts through to Constitution Hill. I got a friend there and I went round to see him one evening. I got the car out, and drove down our road, along the Waldingfield Road, up Constitution Hill, and down his road to where he lived. When I got back, the wife said, 'What did you take the car out for? Why didn't you walk down?' I never thought to, you know.

The wife and I, we had good times together. She had an operation put a stop to her having children, but we went for holidays all over England, up the east coast as far as Scarborough, down to Dover, all the way along the south coast, and all the way up to Liverpool on the west coast. And we went out to dances, out to meals. She was a very good dancer, fox-trot, quick-step, waltzes, everything. We used to go all around the district in the days before discos. They dance now and they don't touch their partner, do they?

Her parents kept the Black Horse public house in East Street and when the wife's father died we went down and lived with her mother and kept that open for seven years. I used to take over in the bar in the evening very often. I was a man of all trades, that's right. Then this bungalow was built and we moved up here, which was a good move. It's friendly up here. All nice people, you know. We help one another.

A week before our golden wedding the wife had a bad heart and...her knees were swollen up huge. I took her over to Bury Hospital and they sent her down for an X-ray. We sat in the room waiting. I expect it was about as big as across there down to that wall. We sat in the corner over there and they called for her to go and have the X-ray and she walked through the door, and dropped down dead. Just like that. A week before our golden wedding.

I'm not a mournful man, no, but you can't laugh while you're on the job if you're an undertaker. You had to be very sedate while you were on it, though I know when you came away from the house it was just another job. Some undertakers are off as soon as the coffin is in the grave. No opening the car doors for the mourners. But you've got to show a bit of respect. And I've been at funerals and had tears come in my eyes, people that I've known well you know. I knew nearly everybody in Sudbury.

Oh, I could tell you some stories! There was an old lady came once when the corpse was laid out. He'd been a smoker and she had this little Oxo tin with a bit of his baccy in it, and she had this pipe. She put the baccy on one side of his head and the pipe on the other. Then she looked at him and she said,'You've been a good old boy. Go and get yourself a drink.' And she put a shilling in the coffin. And you couldn't laugh, you know.

Another time I remember the webbing round the coffin, for some reason it hadn't been threaded through the handles as it should have been, and as we were lowering the coffin it jumped, and it jumped quickly. You'd have thought, wouldn't you, it would have gone sideways, But it didn't. The end came up. There was nothing you could do. It just stood straight up in the grave! Oh, I could tell you lots of stories!

*   *   *   *

# PART FOUR

# Taking Stock:
# the collaborative camera

# Chapter Eighteen

## PHOTOGRAPHS AND WORDS: HOW MUCH WISER ARE WE?

**D**espite the presumption of veracity... the work photographers do is no generic exception to the usually shady commerce between art and truth. Even when photographs are most concerned with mirroring reality they are still haunted by tacit imperatives of taste and conscience.
Susan Sontag: On Photography.

In terms of possible future projects in this genre **Faces with Voices** has raised a number of issues about conduct. Some of the people we approached, particularly people who had spent considerable periods in modest jobs, initially found it difficult to understand why anybody would be interested in them. A number of them also found the idea of being involved in the project daunting at first. Self-deprecation was strong.

Once people committed themselves to participate, however, all tried to be helpful and small gestures of hospitality were legion - cups of tea, glasses of sherry, sandwiches, cakes, gifts of garden vegetables. Common enough courtesies among friendly people. But often more important to us than perhaps the givers realised. For the initial bewilderment and anxiety, albeit among only some of the people we met, raised questions about the concept of the project. In theory what we were doing made sense. And if we got it right the people who emerged from the book would be interesting both to look at and to listen to. Several of the people who appear in the book are writers in their own right. Others are or have been public figures. The position of these people was different. But the book would, courtesy of the tape recorder, give a considerable number of the people in it a public voice they would not otherwise have had or been encouraged to seek. For them the process of realising their voices in print was also part of the process of adding fresh meaning to their faces, and implicitly acknowledging their contribution to the community.

Yet it would have been easier had we asked only to talk to them or only to photograph them. For the two together are very intrusive. First we were asking people to talk about themselves and their lives, and then to submit themselves, not simply to the embarrassment of being photographed, but to the mercy of a camera which, accustomed to looking for ways of recording the world honestly, would have no truck with flattery. We were, in other words, asking them to make themselves very vulnerable. It left us feeling in need of reassurance that we were acting properly.

The famous have for a long time suffered all kinds of invasions of their privacy. One of the latest expressions of this is the current fashion in literary biographies for presenting personal details which, were the subject alive, would give them great pain and, even though they are now dead, might still be felt to damage their public image. Whatever the cost to truth we would not wish in any way to be parties to such an exercise.

Once we started, however, our anxieties about intruding lessened. As people warmed to what they were doing listening became compelling and engrossing. Lives seen by those living them as ordinary and commonplace started to reveal stories of courage and endurance, with the narrators themselves displaying capacities for self questioning, deep feeling, and a lively enjoyment. Varied but vital people began to emerge.

\*    \*    \*

So the time has come to review the project as a whole. The town was important but only as a backdrop. The aim was never to produce a neat vignette of a late twentieth century community. Had it been the book would be seriously flawed. The real subject of the book was the presentation of a set of portraits of unfamiliar faces so as to convey to the general public a full and meaningful sense of their richly varied individuality.

If we could do this in Sudbury, by implication, it could be done in fifty other comparable small towns in the country.

Success, therefore, in making the people here come across as rounded, full-blooded figures would constitute confirmation of the richness of everyday life across a whole band of communities.

The method employed for realising the book's aim was to present the series of specially commissioned photographic portraits alongside brief matching life stories offered in the spoken voice, and a small selection of old photographs. Out of the intermeshing of these different materials we hoped a feeling of each person's individuality would emerge.

In preparing the book there has only been space for very truncated stories. In addition, the absence of any protective cloak of anonymity meant we must ensure we did not embarrass anyone. Nevertheless, in selecting what to include, we trust we have avoided the insidious dishonesty of either sentimentality or nostalgia.

Knowing their stories undoubedly helped when photographing them and subsequently affected the selection of photographs to print. People's expressions in close-up and their surroundings in middle-distance shots gathered noticeably in significance. In other words, what constituted a good photograph could no longer be judged without reference to the accompanying voice. Form and content, as they should, became genuinely indivisible.

There has been talk recently of a crisis in documentary photography. It seemed to us that one thing this project has shown is that where humanism still blooms there remains an important role for this kind of photography. Indeed as a genre with a strong humanist impulse it still has great unexplored potential.

We will probably, of course, always have to accept that there are limits to what books like this can do. A real life subject always finally evades capture. Bound by fact such studies do not enjoy the freedom of the novel. So as history is always bedevilled by mystery, the centre of the living person remains finally an enigma. But if through the words and pictures presented here we have prised open the oyster a little and so helped to raise awareness of the value and quality of everyday life, we will be satisfied.

## JUNE FREEMAN

**June Freeman** is an intellectual gypsy. She began by reading English but for her Doctorate moved into Sociology. This developed an interest in the Sociology of culture which eventually led to another intellectual shift, this time into the visual arts. Since then she has curated a series of exhibitions on low status art forms which have been shown in art galleries throughout the country. She also writes about historical and contemporary craftwork and design but this is the first time she has undertaken a project about photography. What, however, ties all her activities together is an interest in people. They never fail to surprise and fascinate her.

## JANINE WIEDEL

**Janine Wiedel**, a native New Yorker, is a freelance photographer who has been living and working in England since the early Seventies.
Her photographs have been widely exhibited both in the U.K. and abroad, and include three one-person shows at The Photographer's Gallery, London. Her work is used by many newspapers, magazines and book publishers, and is also included in many major collections.
Working in the documentary tradition, her long term projects include: Eskimos of Baffin Island, Tinkers of Ireland, Women of Britain, The English Classroom, Industries of the West Midlands, and most recently, a study of the people of Dover for The Cross Channel Photographic Mission.

Previous Titles:
Classroom Observation, *Methuen, 1975*; Irish Tinkers, *Latimer Press, London, 1976*; Looking at Iran, *A&C Black, 1978*; Vulcan's Forge, *Archetype, 1979*; Dover, a Port in a Storm, *CCPM, 1991*